SECURITIZED CITIZENS

Canadian Muslims' Experiences of Race Relations and Identity Formation Post-9/11

Securitized Citizens examines how the post-9/11 era has shaped the lives of young Canadian Muslims. In this work – based on fifty in-depth interviews conducted with young adult Muslim Canadians in Vancouver and Toronto – Baljit Nagra addresses three important sociological questions. First, how are national belonging and exclusion experienced by young Muslim adults in post-9/11 Canada? Second, how do young Canadian Muslims reflect on and reconsider their cultural, religious, and national identities in light of the pervasive discourse about the Muslim "other"? Third, what do their experiences tell us about contemporary meanings of Canadian citizenship?

In documenting well-educated young Muslims' encounters with state surveillance practices and daily interactions with mainstream Canadian society in the years following 9/11, Nagra asks what these experiences show us about national belonging and racialized processes in our society. In a broader sense, the findings shed light on current issues and understandings with regard to citizenship, multiculturalism, race relations, and identity formation.

BALJIT NAGRA is an assistant professor in the Department of Criminology at the University of Ottawa.

BALJIT NAGRA

Securitized Citizens

Canadian Muslims' Experiences of Race Relations and Identity Formation Post-9/11

UNIVERSITY OF TORONTO PRESS
Toronto Buffalo London

ISBN 978-1-4426-3197-7 (cloth)   ISBN 978-1-4426-2866-3 (paper)

∞ Printed on acid-free, 100% post-consumer recycled paper with
vegetable-based inks.

Library and Archives Canada Cataloguing in Publication

Nagra, Baljit, 1980–, author
Securitized citizens : Canadian Muslims' experience of race relations and
identity formation post-9/11 / Baljit Nagra.

Includes bibliographical references and index.
ISBN 978-1-4426-3197-7 (cloth).   ISBN 978-1-4426-2866-3 (paper)

1. Muslims–Canada–Ethnic identity.   2. Muslims–Canada–Interviews.
3. Belonging (Social psychology)–Canada.   4. Citizenship–Canada.
5. Canada–Race relations.   I. Title.

FC106.M9N34 2017   305.6'970971   C2017-904417-6

University of Toronto Press acknowledges the financial assistance to its
publishing program of the Canada Council for the Arts and the Ontario
Arts Council, an agency of the Government of Ontario.

Canada Council   Conseil des Arts
for the Arts   du Canada

ONTARIO ARTS COUNCIL
CONSEIL DES ARTS DE L'ONTARIO
an Ontario government agency
un organisme du gouvernement de l'Ontario

Funded by the   Financé par le
Government   gouvernement
of Canada   du Canada

This book is dedicated to all those who have suffered at the hands of racism, and who have had the courage to speak of these painful experiences and mount strategies of resistance.

Contents

Acknowledgments

When I started the journey of writing this book, I did not realize how challenging and rewarding it would be. I need to thank numerous people for their support during the years I have spent working on this book. I have benefited from having the most amazing academic mentors that have helped shape me into the academic that I am today. These mentors include Dr. Ito Peng, Dr. Paula Maurrutto, Dr. Anna Korteweg, Dr. John Myles, Dr. Tania Das Gupta, and Dr. Patti Tamara Lenard. Their incredible mentorship and guidance enabled me to complete this passion project of mine. I would also like to thank the brilliant academics whose work has and continues to inspire me. These include but are not limited to Sherene Razack, Jasmin Zine, Sunera Thobani, Himani Bannerji, Stuart Hall, Nandita Sharma, Edward Said, Homi Bhabha, Ghassan Hage, Mary Waters, and Yen Le Espiritu. I also am thankful to the Social Sciences Humanities Research Council of Canada and the Faculty of Social Sciences at the University of Ottawa for funding that helped with the completion and publication of this book. This book would not have been possible without the guidance and support of Douglas Hildebrand, the editor from the University of Toronto Press. I am also thankful for the thoughtful and insightful suggestions of the anonymous peer reviewers. Their feedback allowed me to strengthen my analysis and better the book manuscript. I am also deeply indebted to Elizabeth Thompson who helped with the editing and proofreading of this manuscript. I also am grateful for the support of my colleagues at the Department of Criminology at the University of Ottawa.

I will always be deeply indebted to the many young Canadian Muslims I interviewed for my book. I would not have been able to write this book without their participation and willingness to share their experiences with me. The kindness and courage these young Canadian Muslims display in a world that is increasingly hostile to them is something that has inspired me and something that I will never forget. I particularly have to thank my friends Ether Al Adan and Sharifa Khan who helped me with the interviewee recruitment procedures for my study.

On a personal note, I would like to thank my parents (Sarabjit Nagra and Jaswinder Nagra). From my mother I have learned kindness, patience, dignity, and empathy. From my dad I have learned how to be brave and to be vocal about issues that are important to me. Thank you Mom and Dad for encouraging me to follow my dreams. I am also thankful for the support of my siblings (Ravi, Daljit, Kulveer), nieces and nephews (Khushi, Eshawn, Sohan, Preity, and Jiya), as well as my wonderful extended family members and many sweet friends for their unwavering support while I worked on this book. Finally, I would like to thank my late grandmother Swaran Kaur Gill, who was a great role model for me and who paved the way for my family to come to Canada. She is someone that I will always dearly love and miss.

SECURITIZED CITIZENS

Canadian Muslims' Experiences of Race
Relations and Identity Formation Post-9/11

1 Introduction

In 1903, W.E.B. Du Bois uttered a prophetic and now famous statement when he said that "the problem of the twentieth century is the problem of the color line." Approximately eighty years later and in another country, I understood what he meant. I was born in Victoria, British Columbia, the daughter of Sikh Indian immigrants, and I grew up there during the 1980s and 1990s. It is a city with a predominantly "white" British background (Schrier and Ip 1991), and as a racialized minority, I remember experiences of racism throughout my childhood. Once, when my family and I were walking through our neighbourhood, we were interrupted by a car full of young white men who hurled racial insults at us and yelled, "Get out of our country." Another time, a simple trip to the gas station with my father was disrupted by a stranger screaming at us to "leave Canada." My parents never explained why such incidents occurred. But I soon realized that we were not always thought of as belonging to Canada and that I might be reminded of this at any time. As a result, I questioned my Canadian citizenship. I was ashamed of my Indian identity, and I avoided wearing Indian clothes or speaking Punjabi in public to conceal my Indian identity as much as possible. As the years passed, these incidents of overt discrimination began to disappear and became more of an exception than a rule. While I still faced instances of subtle discrimination, it became less acceptable for people to hurl racial insults in public.

On 11 September 2001, the world changed. As I watched the Twin Towers collapse, I remember feeling that this was the beginning of a new era; in this book, I refer to this era as the post-9/11 era. In this time, terrorism has become a key concern for Western nations, and countries worldwide have introduced anti-terrorist legislation. Security and surveillance practices, especially at airports and borders, have increased substantially (Helly 2004; Razack 2005; Sharma 2006; Thobani 2007). The United States has invaded Iraq and Afghanistan, claiming that these countries fuel terrorism directly targeted at the West. At the centre of the changing world are members of Muslim communities who are increasingly projected as enemies to Western nations (Choudhry 2001; Macklin 2001; Helly 2004; Thobani 2007; Razack 2005).

Despite my personal experience of the "color line," I did not realize the full impact of the post-9/11 era on Muslim lives until I moved to Toronto in 2003. I made Muslim friends in Toronto and witnessed them facing discrimination. To my surprise, my Muslim friends told me stories of being asked to leave Canada, the stigmatization of their religion, and violent confrontations, leading me to question how prevalent this type of discrimination was among Muslim communities and what effect it was having on young Canadian Muslims. As a sociologist, I decided to explore the experiences of young adults who were both Muslim and Canadian. I began a long and interesting journey that has yielded rich and important insights into the experiences and feelings of young Canadian Muslims.

The resulting work, *Securitized Citizens: Canadian Muslims' Experiences of Race Relations and Identity Formation Post-9/11*, is a pioneering study that closely examines how second-generation and well-educated young Canadian Muslims living in Toronto and Vancouver have come to understand their experiences of living in Canada after 9/11. This book speaks to a certain time period – it captures the experiences and feelings of young Canadian Muslims in the three to seven years following 9/11 (2004–8). Through the use of personal narratives, it develops a critical analysis of the meanings that dominant groups and institutions tried to impose on this group of young people and how Muslims, in turn, contested these conceptions by constructing alternative meanings.

In my fifty in-depth interviews with Canadian Muslim men and women, I was able to address three important sociological issues: First, how was national belonging and exclusion experienced by young Muslim adults in post-9/11 Canada? Second, how did young Canadian Muslims reflect on and reconsider their cultural, religious, and national identities in light of the pervasive discourse about the Muslim other? Third, what do Canadian Muslims' experiences tell us about contemporary meanings of Canadian citizenship?

As a result of my interviews, I was able to document the experiences of well-educated young Muslims in their encounters with state surveillance practices and in their daily interactions with mainstream Canadian society in the years following 9/11. In this book, I ask what these experiences show us about national belonging in Canada and the racialized processes in our society. I show how second-generation and well-educated young Canadian Muslims from a variety of different cultural backgrounds negotiated, strategized, and expressed their identities as Muslims and Canadians at a time when their religious affiliations were politically charged issues, not only in Canada but globally. In a broader sense, my findings shed light on contemporary meanings of citizenship, national belonging, multiculturalism, race relations, and identity formation.

Briefly stated, many young Canadian Muslims had the sense of living in a hostile environment. They were harassed by both the state and members of the public. In their view, this harassment challenged their citizenship and suggested that they were seen as potential threats, not loyal Canadian citizens. Their safety and security were jeopardized: they were victimized in public spaces, they suffered a loss of religious freedom, and their economic security was compromised. They reported increased state surveillance directly targeting their Muslim identity, not only at airports and borders but also in their daily lives, suggesting to them that Canadian citizenship may not hold the same value for them as it does for others.

In addition, second-generation young Canadian Muslims were racialized and increasingly othered through stereotypical conceptions of their gender identities. While Muslim men were perceived as barbaric and dangerous, Muslim women were imagined to be passive and were oppressed by their communities. This racialization of gender identity had an impact on how Canadian Muslims were treated by other Canadians and on how they experienced surveillance. As a result of these dominant conceptions, young Canadian Muslims faced the dilemma of challenging these stereotypes in their everyday lives.

Not surprisingly, such experiences had an impact on second-generation Canadian Muslims' identity formation, both as Muslims and as Canadians. Perhaps paradoxically, to cope with the stigmatization of their religion and in a bid to reclaim Islam, many openly asserted their Muslim identities. To understand this social process, I have extended Alejandro Portes and Rubén G. Rumbaut's (2001) work on "reactive ethnicity" and theorized Muslim identity formation in a post-9/11 context, something not yet done in academic literature. Interestingly, I have found that while claiming their Muslim identity, most also retained their Canadian identity and refuted the notion that they were not Canadian. By using the symbolism of multiculturalism and by developing hybrid identities, interviewees tried to create alternative notions of what it means to be Canadian.

Muslims in the Canadian Context

Canada has a growing and diverse Muslim population. The earliest record of Muslim presence dates back to 1871, when the Canadian census recorded thirteen Muslim respondents (Yousif 1953). Since then, the number has increased tremendously, largely due to political and economic unrest in many Muslim countries (Abu-Laban 1983). The Canadian Muslim community, for the most part, is a product of two waves of immigration – one pre- and the other post–Second World War, with the latter wave being the larger of the two (Abu-Laban 1983). From 1911 to 1951, the overall growth rate of the Muslim population was slow, perhaps due to restrictive immigrant policies. At the midpoint of this period, in 1931, there were only 645 Muslim residents in Canada, most having a Syrian or Lebanese background (Abu-Laban 1983).

The largest influx of immigrants came to Canada after the Second World War, mostly during the 1960s. Five factors influenced the immigration of Muslims during this period: economic advantages, educational opportunities, political alienation from their ancestral lands, the pull of kin and friends already in the country, and the freedom of faith and expression guaranteed by Canadian law (Nimer 2002). The single most important characteristic of this postwar Muslim immigrant wave was diversity. While they shared a common religious designation, immigrants came from different parts of the world: the Middle East, India, Pakistan, Bangladesh, Turkey, Iran, Eastern Europe, East Africa, the Caribbean, and elsewhere (Abu-Laban 1983). These Muslim immigrants had equally heterogeneous educational and occupational backgrounds.

Traditionally, Canada has presented a host of challenges for Muslim immigrants. First, since Muslims differ from the traditional "Canadian" archetype on a number of variables, including language, culture, and religion, the process of adjusting to Canadian life has not been easy: they have had to learn a new language and become accustomed to new social practices (Nimer 2002). Second, Muslim immigrants have not necessarily encountered a welcoming host country. The later wave of immigrants arrived as part of a large influx of emigration from Asia (the source region for a significant number of Muslims), and many native-born Canadians feared this inflow would have a negative impact on Canada's white heritage. As a result, Muslim immigrants have often experienced a hostile reaction from other Canadians and have been vulnerable to discrimination (Abu-Laban 1983; Nimer 2002; Helly 2004).

Since the 1960s, the Muslim population has increased substantially in Canada, with many second-generation Muslims born and raised in the country (Nimer 2002). In 2001, Canada's Muslim population numbered 579,640, with 70 per cent residing in Vancouver, Toronto, and Montreal,[1] all of which are major cities (Statistics Canada 2001). In 2006, the Muslim population was estimated to be 783,700 (Statistics Canada 2006). Muslims now constitute the largest non-Christian religious group in Canada (Statistics Canada 2001), and demographers claim that Islam is the fastest growing religion in North America (Nimer 2002).

Though they share a common religious affiliation, original source country varies among Canadian Muslims, as noted. As a result, the Muslim population is diverse, representing many languages and religious traditions in Islam[2] (Nimer 2002). Members of the community are well-educated: Muslims hold the second highest level of education attainment out of all religious groups in Canada. Sixty per cent of Muslim adults have some post-secondary education, which is 10 per cent higher than the national average (Beyer 2005). However, their higher level of education does not correspond to higher income: there are more Muslims in the lower-income bracket (earning $30,000 or less) than any other religious group (Beyer 2005). This suggests that Muslims may be facing some form of economic marginalization in Canada.

Since the 11 September attacks in the U.S., Muslims in Western nations have been vulnerable to increased discrimination (Stein 2003; Fekete 2004; Helly 2004), resulting in the racialization of the Muslim religious identity (Byng 2008). Therefore, in the post-9/11 era, "Muslim" identity is vulnerable to the same social processes of systematic inequality, external labelling, and otherness that other racial groups are subject to.

As in many Western nations, however, anti-Muslim sentiment is not new in Canada, and post-9/11 thinking has merely sharpened the focus of attack. Academics note that since they first came to Canada, Muslim communities have been subjected to orientalist depictions (Helly 2004; Thobani 2007; Razack 2005). Edward Said (1979, 1981) argues that from the end of the eighteenth century to the present day, reactions to Islam and Muslims have been dominated by a radically simplified mode of thinking – by orientalism, that is, which is described in more detail later in this chapter. Through the lens of orientalism, anything viewed as being "oriental" is categorized as inferior, traditional, and backward. This depiction of Muslims has resulted in both first- and second-generation immigrants facing negative stereotypes about Islam and their communities in Canada. Even before 9/11, then, Canadian Muslim communities were observed in a negative light, presented as a threat to the nation and to the equality of men and women (Helly 2004). This negative perception was disseminated by the media: popular media in both Canada and the U.S. portrayed Muslims as violence-loving maniacs. Studies examining more than 100 television shows featuring Arab/Muslim characters from the years 1975 to 1976 and 1983 to 1984 have found the image of Muslims as violent to be pervasive (Bahdi 2003).

Anti-Muslim sentiment in Canada was heightened during the Gulf War in the 1990s. Muslim students encountered explicit discrimination in schools, malls, and other public places; Canadian Muslims reported being targeted by the Royal Canadian Mounted Police and by the Canadian Security Intelligence Services (CSIS). Many felt silenced, devalued, and misrepresented (Khalema and Wannas-Jones 2003).

Before 9/11, Muslim communities were also scrutinized for their religious practices. For example, in 1994, students wearing the hijab were expelled from schools in Quebec. This occurrence resulted in a national debate about Islam, fundamentalism, and women's rights. While the ban was overturned by the government, its underlying sentiments did not go away and have only intensified since 9/11 (Helly 2004).

As in the U.S. and the U.K., however, the political environment in Canada has undeniably changed since 9/11. Although the anti-Muslim sentiment was arguably bad enough before the 11 September terrorist attacks in the U.S., Muslims have faced increased scrutiny through new security measures and anti-terrorist legislation (Choudhry 2001; Macklin 2001; Helly 2004). Bill C-36, adopted on 7 December 2001, modified twenty-two existing laws with a view of increasing security (albeit at the cost of lost freedom for many). The affected laws included the Criminal Code, the protection of personal information, access to information, and the request for evidence (Helly 2004).

While various studies have documented Muslims' experiences living in the U.S. and the U.K. after 9/11 (Peek 2003, 2011; Gupta 2004; El-Halawany 2003; Kundnani 2002), there has been a lack of studies that critically examine Muslims' experiences in Canada. Although Canada has similarities to the U.S. and the U.K., there are important differences in its integration of ethnic and religious groups. Specifically, Canada is often seen as the world leader in multiculturalism, and it was the first nation to adopt a multicultural policy (Wood and Gilbert 2005; Bannerji 2000). Multiculturalism is state-initiated in Canada and includes legislation and official policies linked to their appropriate administrative bodies. By contrast, the U.S. has a long-standing assimilationist or "melting pot" culture, which promotes the Americanization of cultures (Alba and Nee 2003). Although the U.K. does not follow the American pattern, it has not legalized multiculturalism (Bannerji 2000). Since Canada is perceived as being more inclusive of minority groups than other Western nations, examining its changes post-9/11 and its treatment of Muslim communities may shed light on the 11 September event's global impact.

Canada's Foundation as a Racial State

In order to understand Muslims' experience in Canada, it is important to review the history of minority groups before and after the introduction of multiculturalism in Canada. Although the Canadian state, through its multicultural policies, presents itself on the global stage as an egalitarian society, academics argue that its treatment of Muslim communities post-9/11 reveals its foundation as a racial state (Thobani 2007; Razack 2005). Michael Omi and Howard Winant (1994) believe modern nation states should be understood as racial states, as they were founded on deeply racialized processes which involved internal unification and the differentiation of peripheral others. In a similar vein, Floya Anthias and Nira Yuval-Davis (1992) note that race and racism serve as a structuring principle for national processes in terms of defining both the boundaries of the nation and the constituents of national identity. As a result, Benedict Anderson (1991) cautions that nation states should be viewed as "imagined communities," not actual realities. To this, Gillian Creese (2007) adds that nation building projects rely on "imagined communities" of belonging, which operate through discourses of race that tend to homogenize and erase differences internal to the nation and separate citizens from both internally and externally located racial others.

Many scholars have argued that, as in most other Western nations, race has played a central role in how the Canadian nation state has historically been imagined (Thobani 2007; Razack 2005; B. Anderson 1991). The 1867 nationalist project tried to meld Canada's different regional identities into a nation with a distinct culture and identity.

At the heart of this imagined "Canadian community" was the notion that Canada was a white man's country (Dua 2000). Not surprisingly, then, Canada's national identity was historically defined as "white," despite the ongoing vitality of First Nations communities and the presence of early immigrants from both Asia and Africa (Creese 2007). This imagined white nation was tied to the discourse that certain races were not suited for citizenship, thereby justifying their mistreatment and subordination (Creese 2007; Dua 2000). In the Canadian context, the adherence to such a discourse can be seen through the country's long history of indigenous colonization, white settlement policies, and racialized immigration policies for the settlement of people of colour (Dua, Razack, and Warner 2005).

Because nation states are "imagined communities," Benedict Anderson (1991) elaborates, they tend to be plagued with anxieties. Similarly, Homi Bhabha (2004) notes that the success of colonization and the resulting nation states are secretly marked by a radical anxiety about its aims, its claims, and its achievements. Ghassan Hage (1998) adds that because nation states are "fantasies," nationalists are always attempting to control and objectify the other. In the Canadian context, this can be clearly seen in the overt racial management of the Aboriginal population under the Indian Act until the mid-twentieth century (Thobani 2007). In the foundational movement of Canadian nationhood, the British and French were cast as the true subjects of the colony, and Aboriginal people were portrayed as enemy outsiders, thereby justifying their enslavement, torture, and murder (Thobani 2007). The expulsion of First Nation communities from the new Canadian nation was a cornerstone of the Canadian nationalist project (Dua 2000).

Nation building through controlling the other has, in fact, always been a part of Canada's political and social culture, and its victims have not been restricted to one ethnic group, or religion (Boyko 2000). One notable example of such control is demonstrated in early Chinese immigration to Canada from 1850 to 1920. During this period, Canada was transitioning from a capitalist economy dominated by the fur trade and fisheries to one based on agriculture and industrial production (Dua 2000). The construction of railways to transport labour and to consolidate a national market was crucial to this transformation. Since the Canadian government was unable to attract British and European immigrants to do the work, the railway construction allowed a limited number of immigrants to come from China (Dua 2000; K.J. Anderson 1991). Right from the start, however, these Chinese immigrants were perceived as a threat to the process of nation building. Since they did not fit into the narrative of Canada as a white nation, Chinese immigrants were viewed as temporary workers only, rather than potential citizens of Canada, and they were separated from the dominant white society (Dua 2000; K.J. Anderson 1991). Thus, they were refused voting rights, denied naturalization, legally prohibited from owning certain kinds of property, forced to work and live in poverty-stricken ethnic enclaves, and forbidden to sponsor spouses and children (Dua 2000; K.J. Anderson 1991). Later waves of incoming Asian immigrant workers continued to be subject to strict regulations by the government, which included a $100 head tax on early Chinese immigrants (Thobani 2007).

The experiences of early Chinese immigrants to Canada provide merely one example of the exclusions and injustices that were part of Canada's nationalist project. Others include the "continuous journey" regulation that forced the Komagata Maru to be turned away from Vancouver Harbour in 1914, the internment of Japanese Canadians during the Second World War, the slavery of African Canadians, the discriminatory Canadian immigration laws that imposed admission restrictions based on race and ethnicity until the 1960s, and many more (Aiken 2007). All these examples point to the great lengths the Canadian state went to in excluding racial others from the Canadian political landscape in a bid to cement Canada's image as a white nation.

During the late 1960s and the 1970s, Canadian society was transformed. Key policy changes included the elimination of overtly racial classifications in immigration policies, increased access to Canadian citizenship for previously excluded groups, and the adoption of state multiculturalism (Thobani 2007). Beginning in the 1960s, new regulations sought a more objective system of immigrant acceptance (Aiken 2007). The introduction of the point systems in 1967 and the new Immigration Act in 1976 marked a significant shift from the "white" Canadian immigrant policy to values of universalism and equality (Aiken 2007). As a result, Asia replaced Europe as a major source of immigration to Canada (Aiken 2007).

The drastic makeover of Canadian immigration was directly related to the dynamics of global capitalism. Due to high taxation and lack of access to lucrative professions and trades, Canada had become less attractive to European immigrants. Therefore, the Canadian state had to allow for more immigration from other places, such as Asia, if it wished to capitalize on the economic contributions of immigrants (Thobani 2007). In the 1980s, thousands of immigrants and refugees from nontraditional sources in Africa, Asia, and South America were admitted to Canada (Aiken 2007). Despite their contributions to Canadian society, however, many (non-white) immigrant groups were imagined as a burden on taxpaying Canadians and a drain on social and economic resources. Although they held formal citizenship, many were treated as second-class citizens (Thobani 2007). As before, those who did not fit into the white community found themselves on the periphery.

The implementation of new immigration policies coincided with the development of multiculturalism in Canada in the 1970s. Multiculturalism created a new discourse of nationhood, with pluralism and cultural tolerance at its centre (Mackey 1999). According to this discourse, Canada was portrayed as innocent of racism (Mackey 1999). Multiculturalism enabled the state to represent itself as having accomplished the transformation from an overtly racist settler state to a liberal-democratic one. It also allowed the state to silence the protests of immigrant groups demanding more rights (Thobani 2007).

While perceived as positive (and something about which Canadians frequently boast), multiculturalism has been criticized by academics. Sunera Thobani (2007) argues that multiculturalism maintains members of immigrant groups as cultural strangers to the national body while hiding the country's colonial and racist past. Himani Bannerji (2000) emphasizes that multiculturalism is problematic because it replaces the focus on racism and power relations with a focus on cultural diversity. She believes that the emerging multicultural ethnicities are often the constructs of colonial, orientalist, and racist discourses. In a similar vein, Patricia Wood and Liette Gilbert (2005) argue that a focus on cultural diversity hides racism, discrimination, and marginalization.

According to many academics, the mistreatment of Muslim communities in the post-9/11 era brings to the forefront Canada's foundation as a racial state, something hidden by multiculturalism. Sherene Razack (2005) argues that the marginalization of Muslim communities has intensified the boundaries and borders that mark who belongs and who does not belong in Canada. Thobani (2007) states that the linking of immigration and Muslim communities with hatred and fear after 9/11 reproduces past encounters in the present moment; the reappearance of racialized peoples again makes possible the production of a white identity. In her view, the image of the crazed non-Christian savage in the earlier era of Western expansion (attributed to earlier marginalized groups) has re-emerged with a vengeance on the global stage. While earlier immigrants and refugees were imagined primarily as a drain on social and economic resources, the Muslim population has been constructed as a serious threat to the survival of the West (Thobani 2007). According to Thobani, this othering of Muslims is crucial to the sense of nationality among Canadians in the post-9/11 era.

The perceived terrorist threat from Muslim communities has allowed another round of public demands for increased restrictions on immigration and citizenship. Anti-terrorism measures implemented in Canada, in particular, are profoundly reshaping the meaning of Canadian nationality and citizenship. Thobani (2007) mentions that before the events of 9/11, the London subway bombings, and the global effects of the U.S.-led "War on Terror," Canadians might have considered the processes of outright exclusion from citizenship, such as those experienced by Japanese Canadians, as isolated – a shameful moment in the nation's past. However, it is clear that these processes can be applied to Muslims or any other non-preferred group, resulting in the suspension of their citizenship rights and in their presentation as a threat to a nation in crisis (Thobani 2007).

Most certainly, Canada's close proximity to the U.S. has played a role in undermining the citizenship of Canadian Muslims. At the end of the Cold War, the U.S. remerged as the world's only superpower, confident in its hegemony. The 9/11 attacks destroyed this image by demonstrating to the world that the U.S. was not invincible (Thobani 2007). In trying to reassert its power and to redefine its global reach, the U.S. claimed the right to override the citizenship of Muslims in other nation states, including Canada (Thobani 2007; Helly 2004), demanding that Canada follow its anti-terrorist framework and security procedures.

Rather than questioning demands from the U.S., the Canadian government responded by trying to harmonize with U.S. policies, enforcing the "no-fly list," for example, and signing the Smart Border Declaration, negotiated between Canada and the U.S. to increase security and ease the flow of goods and people at the Canada–U.S. border (Dua, Razack, and Warner 2005). Canada has also participated in the war in Afghanistan and implemented its own terrorist legislation (Dua, Razack, and Warner 2005). Canada's adherence to U.S. policies is tied to its dependency on trade with the U.S. (Dua, Razack, and Warner 2005; Thobani 2004). Since Canada signed the Free Trade Agreement with the U.S. in 1988, the vast majority of its exports (88 per cent) go there (Arat-Koc 2005). Thus, the closing of the Canada–U.S. border immediately following 9/11 and the potential future tightening of the U.S. border was a cause of concern for the Canadian government and for Canadian business leaders (Arat-Koc 2005).

Thobani (2007) argues that by following the U.S., the Canadian nation state supports the expansion of the American empire by helping to hunt down and destroy the Muslim enemy as and where defined by the U.S. By failing to protect Muslim communities from the backlash immediately following 9/11, Scott Poynting and Barbara Perry (2007) feel that the Canadian state has legitimatized the mistreatment of Muslim communities and the discourse surrounding the Muslim other. For instance, Poynting and Perry (2007) note that while the Canadian government took immediate action to introduce anti-terrorist legislation, no public calls for peace were made, and no measures were introduced to reform hate crime legislation, both of which could have helped Muslim communities.

While academics have extensively written about how Canadian Muslims have been excluded from Canadian citizenship and cast as a threat to the nation, what remains unanswered is how Canadian Muslims personally experienced this exclusion and how they responded to it. In what follows, I explore, through the use of in-depth interviews, how being viewed as an enemy within the nation shaped the experiences and feelings of second-generation and well-educated young Muslims in Canada in the three to seven years following 9/11 (2004–8). Were these Canadian Muslims fearful for their safety and security? What forms of discrimination did they face? What impact did this discrimination have on their lives? Did they feel targeted by state surveillance practices? How did gender play a role in their experiences? How did young Muslims react to such discrimination? Did they resist? And how did they negotiate their identities as Canadians, as members of different cultural groups, and as Muslims in this climate?

Important Theoretical Insights and Concepts

The influential work of Homi Bhabha (2004) has yielded the valuable insight that rather than seeing colonialism as something in the past, we should view its histories and cultures as constantly intruding on the present. Similarly, other academics emphasize that colonization is an ongoing project sustained by interlocking systems of oppression (Razack, Smith and Thobani 2010). Therefore, in order to begin understanding race relations in the post-9/11 context, we need to begin with the racial discourses of colonialism.

Beginning in the late fifteenth century, European nations – particularly Spain, Portugal, England, France, and the Netherlands – sent explorers, exploiters, missionaries, and settlers across the world, most of which was previously unknown to them (Cornell and Hartmann 2007). Entire continents entered European consciousness for the first time, consisting of populations that differed both physically and culturally from Europeans (Cornell and Hartmann 2007). Colonizers perceived the indigenous populations they encountered as being primitive, savage, and barbarian.

Race as a political ideology emerged at this historical moment. European colonizers promoted an ideological division of the world whereby Europeans were considered physically, culturally, and morally superior to racially distinct others. A racial discourse separating humans into different hierarchical categories was developed, and race was presumed to be premised upon biological characteristics (Aiken 2007). Physical characteristics were used to categorize people as others and were thought to determine a person's race (Miles 1989). While "blackness" or "brownness" became associated with evil, ugliness, and filth, "whiteness" became affiliated with everything that was pure, clean, virtuous, and beautiful (Aiken 2007).

Power relations played a key role in the emergence of this racial discourse. Stephen E. Cornell and Douglas Hartmann (2007) claim that the ability to designate race and to set one culture against the other is in itself an assertion of power. It was not a simple desire to explore the world that motivated Europe's captains and missionaries but rather a massive quest for wealth, political clout, and power. Colonizers justified their activities, in part, by citing race: human groups, they said, are inherently different from each other, and those differences constitute natural physical and moral hierarchies (Cornell and Hartmann 2007). This helped to legitimatize the idea that people from other nations were a resource to be exploited by European explorers. In her examination of colonialism in South Africa, Hannah Arendt (1951) agrees with this interpretation. She notes that colonialism used racism as a political ideology to promote the expansion of its economic power and to justify the exploitation and displacement of indigenous populations. Because Europeans found nothing in their own behaviour that could justify their superiority, they used the idea of race to distinguish between themselves and the "savages" who lacked human culture and human characteristics (Arendt 1951).

Racism was popular among colonizers not only because it legitimized exploitation but also because it confirmed their sense of superiority and provided them with a new community to belong to by virtue of their skin colour (Arendt 1951). Robert Miles (1989) adds that when one uses real or alleged biological characteristics to define the other, one defines oneself by the same criterion. For example, when European explorers defined Africans as "black," they were defining themselves as the opposite: "The African's 'blackness' therefore reflected the European's whiteness. These opposites were therefore bound together each giving meaning to the other in a totality of significance" (Miles 1989, 75).

Simply stated, at the heart of this colonial racial (that is, racist) discourse was the assignment of different levels of moral worth based primarily on physical characteristics. Europeans were considered more intelligent and at a higher stage of evolution than inferior races. Even though science disproved it, this racial discourse persists, continuing to frame imperialist regimes, capitalism, neocolonialism, globalization, and nationalist projects (Cornell and Hartmann 2007).

However, Vijay Agnew (2007) reminds us that race is fluid, and the values and meanings attached to race can change with time and place. For example, while the cultural practices of colonized groups were always deemed inferior, biology was at the forefront of colonial racial discourses. Now, however, the use of culture has become paramount in racial discourses. Samuel P. Huntington's (1993) famous essay titled "The Clash of Civilizations?" is an example of such cultural discourses. Huntington explains historical events as a result of innate cultural differences and argues that in the post–Cold War era, the most important ideological distinctions are not political or economic; rather, they are cultural, and they drive most of the dangerous conflicts in the world. Homi Bhabha (2004) is critical of this approach, arguing that this polarization of cultures is simplistic and dangerous, because it ignores the continuing process of history and implies we cannot reconcile differences.

George M. Fredickson (2002) calls cultural racism the racism of the new millennium. According to him, culture serves as the basis of a racial ideology that discriminates against and prosecutes others, just as biology did in earlier times:

> Culture can be reified and essentalized to the point where it becomes the functional equivalent of race and that most of the minorities throughout the world that are victimized by discrimination or violence appear to be differentiated from their oppressor more by authentic cultural or religious difference than by race in the genetic sense. (Fredickson 2002, 145)

Cultural racism, then, is another way of talking about groups that were previously alleged to be biologically inferior and involves the use of cultural racializations to exclude them or to retain them in inferior positions (Mackey 1999). Cultural racism as a new form of racism shifts attention away from crude ideas of biological inferiority and superiority to a language of race that excludes by using seemingly non-racist liberal criteria such as culture, religion, civic engagement, national culture, and identity (Jiwani 2012; Mackey 1999). Such racism is articulated by defining the mainstream as "culturally appropriate" and normal, and racialized groups as culturally incompatible and too different to comply or to integrate (Agnew 2007). It also uses coded language that links "social cohesion" with national identity and preferred culture (Agnew 2007).

Although cultural racism does not appear to exclude and marginalize populations on the basis of biological heritage, an element of biology still exists. Simply stated, those who belong to inferior cultures are often not white (Agnew 2007). For Paul Gilroy (1990), cultural racism is simply racism that avoids being recognized as such, because it links race with nationhood, patriotism, and nationalism. According to Gilroy (1990), cultural racism constructs and defends a national culture, homogenous in its whiteness, that is perpetually vulnerable to attack from enemies from within and without. Cultural racism assumes a situation in which the nation and the citizen are in binary relation to aliens, foreigners, or immigrants who are collectively defined as the other (Agnew 2007). These others are then blamed for all the social and economic ills that plague the nation and are perceived as a threat, thereby justifying their marginalization in society. Nation building is therefore reborn through the "expulsion" of the other, who is considered culturally inferior.

The use of cultural racism is not new in Western nations. Said (1979) has long argued that the West has historically strengthened itself by labelling cultures from the East, including the Islamic religion, as inferior: "From at least the end of the eighteenth century until our own present day, modern Occidental reactions to Islam have been dominated by a radically simplified thinking that may still be called Orientalist" (Said 1981, 4). The basis of orientalist thought is a polarized geography dividing the world into two unequal parts: the larger "different" one called the Orient and the smaller one ("our" world) called the Occident or the West (Said 1981, 4). The distinction between these parts is key: anything Eastern (oriental) is categorized as inferior, traditional, and backward. Interestingly, even though the Orient has uniformly been considered as inferior, it has always been endowed with greater size and greater potential for power than the West (Said 1997).

The emergence of orientalism can be traced to the British and French cultural enterprise project. From the beginning of the nineteenth century until the end of the Second World War, France and Britain dominated the Orient (Said 1979, 1981). According to Said, it was during this time that orientalism turned into a dominant political vision. In the course of the nineteenth century, an assortment of theories justifying political domination turned up, which persisted into the twentieth century. Orientalism provided a rationalization for European colonialism by constructing the East as extremely different and inferior and therefore in need of Western intervention or rescue. According to Said, colonial rulers felt they could not rule properly without some of the knowledge of the Orient, which they tried to gain by translating various works from native languages into their own. Hence, the views and perceptions about the Orient that emerged into being were basically the result of the British and French presence and their interpretations of what they saw (Said 1979, 1981). This orientalist knowledge made management easier and more profitable, as it allowed the British and French to secure cultural domination over the lands of the Orient. It also served to prevent conflict among imperial powers. Said (1997) recalls that the colonial possessions of France and Britain were adjacent, frequently overlapped, and were often fought over. But it was near the Middle East, where Islam was supposed to define cultural and racial characteristics, that the British and French encountered each other – and the Orient:

> When you have a got a faithful ally who is bent on meddling in a country in which you are deeply interested – you have three courses open to you. You may renounce – or monopolize – or share. Renouncing would have been to place the French close to India. Monopolizing would have very near the risk of war. So they resolved to share. (Said 1979, 10)

What the British and French shared, however, was not only land but also an intellectual power – what Said has termed orientalism. In a sense, orientalism became an archive of information, commonly and unanimously held, and a unifying set of values. These ideas explained the behaviour of the Orientals. They supplied oriental people with a mentality and a genealogy. Most importantly, they allowed Europeans to deal with and even to see oriental people as a phenomenon possessing regular and generalized characteristics (Said 1979).

Therefore, the Orient was not just the place of Europe's greatest, richest, and oldest colonies. Rather, it represented, for the West, a deep and recurring image of the other. Orientalism was an invented body of theory and practice. As a discourse, it allowed the systematic discipline by which European culture was able to manage and even produce the Orient politically, sociologically, militarily, ideologically, scientifically, and imaginatively during the post–Enlightenment period (Said 1979, 1981). Orientalism allowed for a Western style of domination, restructuring, and authority (Said 1979). The land of the Orient was orientialized, not only because it was discovered to be oriental but because it could be made into that by Europeans.

Orientalism embodied the idea of European identity as superior in comparison to all non-European people and cultures (Said 1979, 1981). It produced an uneven exchange with regards to various kinds of power: political power (i.e., colonial power), intellectual power (i.e., linguistic power), cultural power (texts, values), and moral power (what we understand and they do not).

A central component to orientalism, then, was a European sense of entitlement to represent the Orientals in the West all by themselves. In doing so, the Europeans shaped the Orient in a way that was most useful to them. Orientalists created a stage strictly for European viewers, and the Orient was presented from a Western perspective. Everything the Orientals said and did was judged through Western eyes, irrespective of its context. This resulted in generalization – whatever orientalists saw was associated with the oriental culture, no matter if it was the behaviour of an individual rather than of a whole culture. In turn, Europeans defined themselves by defining oriental people. For example, when descriptors such as lazy, irrational, uncivilized, and crude were imposed as qualities of these people, Europeans automatically became active, rational, civilized, and sophisticated in comparison (Said 1979).

In his influential book titled *Covering Islam* (1997), Said states that orientalism has played a central role in how the West has historically approached Islam with incomprehension, hostility, and fear. There are, of course, many religious, psychological, and political reasons for this. Many reasons derive from a Western fear of Islam as a challenge to Christianity. European Christian scholars believed that Islam was heresy and that Mohammed was an impostor – a false Christ. The military power of Islam grew enormously as well. Persia, Syria, Egypt, Turkey, and North Africa fell to Muslim armies, and in the eighth and ninth centuries, Spain, Sicily, and parts of France were conquered as well. By the thirteenth and fourteenth centuries, Islam had reached as far as East India, Indonesia, and China. Europe responded to this assault by fearing Islam (Said 1997).

At the end of the Second World War, the United States took a position of dominance and hegemony once held by the British and the French in the Islamic world. In doing so, the U.S. continued to approach Islam from an orientalist framework and continued to produce gross generalizations about Islam (Said 1981). This exchange between Islam and the West, especially the United States, was profoundly one-sided, whereby anything negative done by the "West" was hidden, and everything negative done by Muslims was highlighted and associated with their presumed flawed nature. According to Said (1981), as far as the U.S. was concerned, Muslims were either oil suppliers or potential terrorists. There have been a series of crude and essentialized representations of the Islamic world, resembling French and British orientalist depictions, which are presented in a way that make it seem deserving of Western military aggression. For Said (1981), the fact that these distortions continued to occur at all was a function of power. This hostility towards Islam was tied to the fact what while other cultural groupings appeared to have accepted the United States as a world power, it was only from the Islamic nations that signs of determined resistance remained strong.

According to Said (1997), malicious generalizations about Islam have become, in the West, the last acceptable form of denigration of a foreign culture; what is said about the Muslim mind, character of religion, or culture as a whole cannot be said in mainstream discussions about Africans, Jews, or Asians. Despite popular belief, Islam actually defines a relatively small proportion of what actually takes place in the Islamic world, which includes dozens of countries, billions of people, diverse societies, multiple traditions and languages, and, of course, an infinite number of different experiences (Said 1981). Therefore, it is simply false to trace all this back to something called Islam, despite orientalists in the United States, Britain, and Israel insisting that Islam regulates Islamic societies from top to bottom. In the Western world, there seems to be an agreement that even though little is known about the Islamic world, there is not much there to approve of (Said 1981). Arguments about the complex factors of religious passions, struggles for just causes, human weaknesses, political factors, and the history of men and women in diverse societies cannot be made when Islam and parts of the Muslim world are dealt with by Western media, policy makers, and experts. Instead, Islam seems to "engulf all aspects of these diverse societies, reducing them all to a special malevolent and unthinking essence" (Said 1997, 7). As a result, whatever Muslims say about their sense of justice, their history of oppression, and their vision of their societies seems irrelevant.

The negative and simplistic representations of Islam are far-reaching in the West, where Islam is considered anti-human, anti-democratic, anti-Semitic, or anti-rational. It is assumed that Muslims react this way not only because they are genetically disposed to do so but also because they are irrationally fighting against secularism (Said 1997). Said (1997) emphasizes that such demonization and dehumanization of an entire culture functions to convert Muslims into the objects of punitive attention.

Although Said wrote about Islam before 9/11, his comments shed useful light on how Islam is perceived. Since 9/11, orientalist depictions of Islam have intensified. Now the gross oversimplifications and negative representations of Islam are increasingly used to create fears of terrorism in Western nations and to justify new security regimes, which permit both covert and overt racism against Muslims globally (Agnew 2007; Jiwani 2012). Far from attempting to understand the complexity of Islam, the West represents it as the end of civilization. Muslims are considered to be dangerous others who are not only culturally inferior but also a threat to Western civilizations. As a consequence, Muslim identity becomes not only a religious identity but a racialized one as well:

> The category of Muslim has been constituted ... not only as a religious and political but also as a racialized category. Such rhetoric re-invokes the figure of the crazed savage imagined in the earlier counter between Europe and its Other. The "War on Terror" has dragged this figure from the collective psyche of the nation to where it had been relegated in the mid twentieth century. (Thobani 2007, 235)

In this way, the discussion takes a giant leap from inferior cultures to the clash of civilizations. In the civilization framework, nations such as Canada, the U.S., the U.K., and France (as well as other EU nations) represent the liberal, modern, democratic, and egalitarian Western civilization (Arat-Koc 2005). Meanwhile, the Muslim civilization is considered barbaric, tribal, and outside the realm of Western civilization (Arat-Koc 2005; Razack 2004). Sherene Razack (2004) says this framework is informed by the notion "that 'we' know about democracy and 'they' do not; 'we' have values of integrity, honesty, and compassion that 'they' do not; that 'we' are a law-abiding, orderly, and modest people while 'they' are not" (14).

In this framework, those outside Western civilization are a threat to Western principles of democracy, making actions proposed by Western governments to seek protection from uncivilized others both necessary and justified (Razack 2004, 2005).

Post-9/11 Canadian identity has been redefined as a part of Western civilization through this discourse of civilization differences (Arat-Koc 2005; Dua, Razack, and Warner 2005). This revamped definition has a number of important implications. First, it has strengthened the transnational alliances between Canada and other Western states as they come together to defend their "universal" and cultural values against those of the Muslim world (Razack, Smith, and Thobani 2010). In the Canadian context, this has led to a sense of oneness with the U.S. as a white settler nation and imperial power (Arat-Koc 2005).

Second, appeals to liberal universal principles, such as rationality and equal rights, have helped legitimatize the dominance of white Canadian culture. Canadian identity is re-whitened, and non-white people are marginalized. Not surprisingly, white Western subjects do not see themselves as "white" or as racial subjects; rather, they see their customs, beliefs, and practices as universal and normative. Whites are not seen as a belonging to a certain "race"; they are rather viewed as the "human" race (Mackey 1999). Similarly, Razack and colleagues write that "the resurgent discourse of civilizationality and cultural superior 'west' has shifted the language of race from that of 'cultural' difference and 'tolerance' that has reigned since the 1970s multicultural era to one in which culture and civilization are increasingly conflated with whiteness" (Razack, Smith, and Thobani 2010, 7).

Third, the redefinition of Canadian identity has reintroduced old colonial discourses in the present. By deeming the practices of the Muslim world inferior, Canada (and Western civilizations in general) claims cultural superiority. As in colonial times, we see a simple, ideological division of the world, with the West being superior to the rest. However, while this divide was previously justified by references to biology and inferior cultures, it is now legitimized by citing the clash of civilizations. What has not changed is this grand division of the world is still closely tied to power relations. The discourse of civilization and cultural differences helps justify the West's invasion of Middle-Eastern countries such as Iraq and Afghanistan and their ongoing quest for oil and imperialistic power. It also helps legitimize social and economic disparities between white citizens and racial others in Western nations (Thobani 2007; Razack 2004).

In this book, I explore how through a language of culture, religion, and civilization, post-9/11 racial discourses create "legitimate/desirable" and "illegitimate/undesirable" members of the nation, reproducing past colonial practices and nation building projects. My work also brings to the forefront the centrality of racial discourses in everyday life and the profound impact they have on the national, religious, and cultural identities of Muslims living in Western nations.

Gender plays a crucial role in the way racial discourses are rearticulated in the post-9/11 era. Razack (2004) notes that empire building has always been a gendered project. The rhetoric of colonialism used the oppression of women to morally justify undermining and eradicating the cultures of colonized people. For example, child marriage and dowry practices were used by the British to validate their colonization of South Asia (Abu-Lughod 2002; Meetoo and Mirza 2007). As Saba Mahmood (2005) states, "Colonialism rationalized itself on the basis of the 'inferiority' of non-Western cultures, most manifest in their patriarchal customs and practices from which indigenous women had to be rescued through the agency of colonial rule" (189–90).

Historically, Muslim women were not always regarded as being oppressed, but with colonization, their representation became confined to the status of victim (Jiwani 2010). For colonizers, Leila Ahmed (1992) argues, gender segregation and women's veils were physical evidence of oppression; they claimed it was a moral duty to liberate women from "backward" cultures. Saving brown women from brown men also provided an important reason to keep brown men in line through violent practices (Razack 2004). Sadly, by failing to accept and incorporate different histories and cultures, Western feminism helped perpetuate colonial and racist discourses whereby Islam and other Eastern religions were viewed as innately oppressive of women (Abu-Lughod 2002). The language of Western feminism not only morally justified the assault on colonized societies; it also validated the idea that to improve the status of women, it was necessary for colonized Muslim societies to give up their cultural practices and adopt Western ways of living (Ahmed 1992).

Razack (2004, 2005) argues that since 9/11, feminism has re-emerged as a tool to support imperialistic endeavours, calling on Western secular tradition to protect women's rights. Former U.S. First Lady Laura Bush openly claimed in multiple interviews that the fight against terrorism was also a fight for women's rights. The fact that, before 9/11, the U.S. government ignored the pleas of both Afghan women and some American feminists to help women in Afghanistan was overlooked by many (Haddad 2007). The notion that Muslim women need "saving" has fuelled the "War on Terror" and was used as a justification for the U.S.-led invasions of Iraq and Afghanistan. This notion has also permitted the surveillance and the undermining of Muslim communities in North America (Razack 2004; Haddad 2007; Abu-Lughod 2002).

Razack (2004) contends that three main characters played roles in the global "War on Terror": the imperilled Muslim woman, the barbaric Muslim man, and the white European man, whose task is to annihilate Muslim men. Therefore, what fuels the "War on Terror" narrative is not only the perceived oppression of Muslim women but also the assumed barbaric nature of Muslim men. Similarly, Claire Alexander (2004) argues that Muslim masculinities are being racialized as deviant, dangerous, and socially and culturally dysfunctional. She adds that the construction of racialized Muslim masculinities draws upon the legacy of racialized pathologies, which in the past were largely reserved for black identities. Black identities, she says, have historically been inscribed with a hypervisible black masculinity that is perceived as subordinate to hegemonic ideals. In a similar vein, Raewyn Connell (1995) notes that black masculinity has been constructed as sexual and a social threat in dominant white cultures. This gender ideology has been used to justify the rigorous policing of and political racism directed towards black communities in a variety of Western nations, including the United States, South Africa, and France (Connell 1995). Alexander (2004) argues that a similar phenomenon is now occurring with Muslim men. Muslim masculinity is increasingly linked with the apparent growth of religious fundamentalism. As a result, Muslim men are now perceived as outside of and acting against the hegemonic norms of masculinity. In Alexander's view, this gender ideology is used to justify the regulation and social control of Muslim communities.

Overall, gender is crucial to the placement of Muslims outside Western civilization. Through the civilization framework, Muslims are confined to a premodern world that has not yet progressed into the age of gender equality. As in colonial times, gender reveals the difference between those who are modern and civilized and those who are not (Razack 2004). Gender defines the West as a place of values, with a superior culture and a unique commitment to women rights (Razack 2004).

This gender ideology perpetuates beliefs about Western superiority and reproduces colonial discourses in the present day. As the comments of my interviewees made clear to me, as will be shown, gender has affected the experiences of young Canadian Muslims in the post-9/11 era. They are racialized and othered through increasingly stereotypical conceptions about their gender identities.

A key concern of this book is how young Muslims experience national belonging and exclusion in Canada. Citizenship is a marker of belonging within the community of the nation and is manifested though processes of inclusion and exclusion (McDonald 2007); it is intrinsically connected with nationalism and racism, as citizenship boundaries are often drawn along racial lines (B. Anderson 1991; Thobani 2007; Razack 2004).

Citizenship, however, is often perceived as a static ideal, a juridical relationship between a person and a nation state. This form of citizenship, also known as legal citizenship, "is the formal status of membership in a state, or nationality as it is understood in international law" (Macklin 2007, 334). Legal citizenship in liberal democratic states is supposed to provide individuals with a continuum of legal rights and protections (Stasiulis and Bakan 1997).

Although minority groups have legal citizenship in liberal democratic nations, they may still be treated as second-class citizens (Young 1998; Sassen 2004; Ong 2004; Nakano Glenn 2002). Saskia Sassen (2004) notes that legal citizenship does not always bring equal citizenship; groups that have been historically marginalized because of race, ethnicity, and religion may continue to face exclusions despite being granted legal citizenship. Similarly, James Holston (1998) argues that formal citizenship is no longer an integral factor in securing substantive citizenship – access to a variety of civil, political, and social rights.

In order to understand the complexity in citizenship, Daiva Stasiulis and Abigail B. Bakan (1997) conceptualize citizenship as negotiated: because it is negotiated, it is "subject to change, it is acted upon collectively, or among individuals existing within social, political, and economic relations of collective conflict, which are shaped by gendered, race, class, and internationally based hierarchies" (113). Stasiulis and Bakan see citizenship as dynamic, continuously transformed, as "relationships are negotiated and re-negotiated in variable national and international conflicts" (118).[3] In what follows, I use these insights to explore how the post-9/11 era is redefining young Muslims' sense of citizenship in Canada.

To understand the contradiction of formal citizenship status and the lived experience of national belonging, it is important to review the imperialistic roots of citizenship. Citizenship has historically functioned as a divisive practice that separates citizens from different states and that also differentiates citizens from non-citizens, who occupy an inferior status within the nation state. While citizenship is often seen as progressive and leading to better social conditions, Barry Hindess (2004) locates its emergence within European imperialism: wherever there have been citizens, the territories they have belonged to have always included non-citizens. He cites the slaves of the early Roman Empire as an example.

Furthermore, Hindess (2004) writes that "the role of citizenship in the supra-national regime reflects the achievements of European imperialism in bringing the greater part of the world territories directly or indirectly within the remit of the European states system" (309). He elaborates that the origins of present day citizenship can be traced to a desire to create a common Western civilization and, moreover, that the notion of citizenship was based on an elitist view. Much of humanity was thought not to be ready for citizenship, and they might never be ready. Hindess (2004) conveys that Western political thought put forward an elitist view of the citizen, which saw it embodying qualities that were uncommon and, at the same time, natural and universal. He elaborates that the view that some were incapable of becoming citizens played an important role in the European Enlightenment. Even with today's globalization of citizenship, the effects of this elitist view remain, and can be seen in how some societies and groups are envisioned as less advanced/civilized and less capable of governing themselves.

These insights can be applied to the Canadian context. In *Exalted Subjects* (2007), Sunera Thobani discusses the emergence of the Canadian national subject. Drawing on Foucault's discussion of the historical fabrication of modern subjects through the deployment of particular political technologies, Thobani explores how European colonizers who once were subjects of other states established themselves as Canadians (8). She argues that the formation of the Canadian national subject was made possible through the process of exaltation – a political process that defined the national as belonging to a higher order of humanity. In the case of Canada, the historical exaltation of the national subject "ennobled this subject's humanity and sanctioned the elevation of its rights over and above that of the Aboriginal and the non-white 'immigrant'" (9). It is through this political process, Thobani contends, that white Canadians were exalted as national subjects while indigenous people and non-white immigrants were constituted as the other.

Exaltation, then, provided the basis for the master Canadian narrative: that the Canadian national subject was "stable, conscious, unified and an enduring figure, whose actions are shaped by reason" (Thobani 2007, 9). This narrative further held that Canadian nationals were law-abiding, responsible, compassionate, and caring citizens who needed protection from criminal, chaotic, and uncivilized, dangerous others. Thobani (2007) contends that the Canadian national subject was envisioned as embodying the qualities, values, and virtues of the nation, entitling it to benefits, privileges, and rights provided by the state.

This exaltation of the Canadian national subject was vital to nation state formation, Thobani (2007) asserts. First, it worked to hide the colonial violence that led to the creation of the state and the political, racial, ethnic, gender, and class dominations that characterized nation formation in Canada. The rights and entitlements that came from being Canadian were understood as being rooted in intrinsic worthiness of national subjects rather than ongoing colonial violence and racial injustices. Second, it is through exaltation that the Canadian national subject felt an allegiance to the Canadian state and developed a national Canadian identity. Exaltation provided a means for European colonizers to locate their own subjectivities within the realm of the Canadian nationality. Thobani argues that the practice of exalting valorized characteristics onto a political identity of the nation enabled "its individual subjects to constitute their own subjectivity as the embodiment and actualization of such characteristics" and thus facilitated the subjects' experiences of belonging to the community through the recognition and cultivation of such shared nationality (9).

Moreover, exaltation made the internal differences among Canadian nationals that arose from gender, class, region, and so on less visible, further cementing a shared Canadian national identity. As a result, exaltation functioned to deny the common humanity shared by national subjects, Aboriginals, and non-white immigrants. It instead paved the way for a common identity encompassing shared values and interests among national subjects, which was vital for the formation of the nation state: "The nation then begins to acquire an awareness of itself as an entity and gains international recognition – as the aggregate of its members and reflection of their particular qualities in the corresponding state system" (Thobani 2007, 19), allowing it to also distinguish itself from other nation states.

It goes without saying that the other played an essential role in the emergence of the Canadian nation state. A shared Canadian nationality was accomplished by exaggerating the differences between nationals and others and ignoring their commonalities (Thobani 2007). In fact, the other, who was devoid of the qualities and values of the nation, helped give meaning to being Canadian (Thobani 2007). Thobani (2007) asserts that the worthiness bestowed upon national subjects through the process of exaltation allowed for the ranking of Canadians, Aboriginals, and non-white immigrants in terms of their legalistic and sociocultural status. The national subject was institutionally and systematically defined in relation to the other. National subjects were perceived as being ontologically different from outsiders and intrinsically more deserving of greater rights, freedoms, and entitlements.

The establishment of formal Canadian citizenship, Thobani (2007) argues, was intrinsically tied the process of exaltation, and it also paved the way for nation state formation. Gearing away from liberal understandings of citizenship, which conceive of citizenship rights (from civil to political and social) as a historical mark towards progress and a mechanism to counter the economic inequalities, Thobani brings attention to the racialized nature of the rights-based regime of citizenship (69). She argues that while Canadian citizenship is often understood as an emancipator measure, it was in fact based on the institution of white supremacy:

> Citizenship emerged as integral to the very processes that transformed insiders (Aboriginal people) into aliens in their own territories, while simultaneously transforming outsiders (colonizers, settlers, migrants) into exalted insiders (Canadian citizens). The category citizen, born from the genocidal violence of colonization, exists in a dialectal relation with its Other, the Indian for whom the emergence of this citizenship was deadly not emancipatory. (Thobani 2007, 74)

By introducing the individual rights of domicile and land ownership to national subjects and simultaneously cementing the category "Indian" through the lack of rights, the institution of citizenship was key to the processes of nation building and economic development in Canada (Thobani 2007). The status of "citizen" then worked to further exalt the national subject, as that subject could now envision itself as being an equal among its fellow citizens while upholding the facade of equality, despite its emergence through colonial violence (Thobani 2007).

For over a century after Confederation, the Canadian state solidified white identity with legal citizenship (Thobani 2007, 75). Citizenship then was instituted in a triangulated formation:

> The aboriginal marked for physical and cultural extinction, deserving of citizenship only upon abdication of indigeneity; the "preferred race" settler and future national, exalted as worthy of citizenship and membership in the nation; and the non-preferred race immigrant, marked as stranger and sojourner, an unwelcome intruder whose lack of Christian faith, inherent deviant tendencies and unchecked fecundity all threatened the nations survival. (Thobani 2007, 75)

These foundational horizons worked to institutionalize "whiteness as embodiment of legitimate and responsible citizenship" (Thobani 2007, 75). While Canadian citizenship organized the membership of the national subject by giving them formal legal status and, in doing so, enhancing their exalted status as modern subjects, it simultaneously cemented indigenous people and "non-white" immigrants as racial subjects.

This racist foundation has had profound implications for access to Canadian citizenship, which exist to the present day (Thobani 2007). While non-preferred races were granted access to legal citizenship after the 1960s, this did not translate into equal access to rights and granted privileges. For one thing, Thobani (2007) argues, the granting of legal citizenship to Aboriginal communities was motivated by the goal of encouraging private ownership of land by Aboriginal people as individuals, thereby destroying their collective ownership of lands and making those lands available to "real" Canadians. Thobani writes that "access to citizenship rites was thus extended to Aboriginal people upon their reunification of Indian status" (82) and as a way to silence claims for Aboriginal sovereignty. Moreover, citizenship rights for those not born in Canada were regulated through restrictive immigration and sponsorship regulations. This is not to mention that the unequal status of people of colour is continually maintained through the ideological category of immigrants, a label subscribed even to second- or third-generation Canadians (Thobani 2007).

In sum, Thobani (2007) asserts that Canadian citizenship was founded with the clear intention to produce racial divisions and to help create the myth of a homogeneous nation state in light of actual heterogeneity. Hence, legal citizenship functioned as a mechanism for defining national identity. While legal Canadian citizenship may now be accessible to "racial" minorities, this does not erase the very racialized foundations of its inception and the political process in which the national Canadian subject emerged. This helps to explain why some Canadian citizens are able to claim nationality while others are unable to do so, despite holding legal Canadian citizenship. For this reason, Thobani argues, citizenship and nationality should be seen not as one entity but as coexisting in an overlapping manner.

In a similar fashion, my research illustrates that race continues to underpin Canadian national identity and that, as a result, young Canadian Muslims who hold legal Canadian citizenship do not have full access to national belonging. The racialized foundations of Canadian citizenship are apparent in Muslims' experiences of being repeatedly denied claims to national belonging, despite holding legal Canadian citizenship. The exalted (white) national subject remains a central figure in Canadian society and has, in fact, been revived through a language of race, religion, security, and gender, whereby Canadian national identity now claims superiority over Muslim others. As a result, religion, mixed in with issues surrounding security, culture, and gender, becomes racialized and functions as a structuring principle in defining national identity. This formulation works not only to revive the exalted national subject but also to create a transnational Western subject who now shares a transnational Western identity with subjects from other Western states.

In the following chapters, I bring to light the contemporary meanings of citizenship by examining young Canadians Muslims' lived experiences of national belonging and exclusion. To fully understand the contradiction between official citizenship status and national belonging, one has to examine the everyday experiences of racialized minorities. In order to do this, I turn to the different conceptions of citizenship and national belonging developed by Evelyn Nakano Glenn (2002) and Ghassan Hage (1998) in their work.

Drawing on the concept of substantive citizenship, Evelyn Nakano Glenn (2002) shows how citizenship is given meaning at the local level in everyday interactions. She argues that substantive citizenship has two main components: The first is the ability to exercise one's formal rights. The second involves how citizenship rights are recognized and enforced by national, state, and local government agents, as well as by members of the public. This encompasses an understanding of how citizenship is localized, which is important because the boundaries and rights that define citizenship are often interpreted and enforced (or not enforced) by individual actors operating at the local level:

> In some cases the actors are state, county, or municipal officials, for exam-ple a welfare department social worker ruling on the eligibility of a black single mother for benefits ... It is these kinds of localized, often face to face practices that determine whether people have or don't have substantive as opposed to purely formal rights of citizens. (Nakano Glenn 2002, 7)

Nakano Glenn (2002) argues that the actions of individuals are con-nected to the larger societal structure: when individual actors define and redefine citizenship boundaries, they draw on social norms and values. In the following chapters, this concept of localized citizenship is valuable in understanding how interactions with the dominant national community and state agents at the local level affect the national belong-ing of young Muslims in Canada. Chapters 2 and 3 illustrate how local-ized experiences of hate crimes, verbal assaults, insensitive questioning of religious practices, employment discrimination, racial profiling, and intrusive state surveillance result in the loss of national belonging for young Canadian Muslims and reveal how the figure of the white national subject, described by Thobani (2007), remains a central figure in Canadian society.

Nakano Glenn's (2002) contention that citizenship has a number of meanings helps to explain my interviewees' experiences of lived citi-zenship. While citizenship is a matter of belonging, there are different facets of belonging, and not all facets are available to all groups. The first facet is *standing*, or being recognized as an adult capable of exercising choice and assuming responsibility. The second is *nationality*, or being identified as a part of a people who constitute a nation. The last is *alle-giance*, or being viewed as a loyal member of the community (Nakano Glenn 2002). Do young Muslims feel they have access to nationality, allegiance, and standing in Canada? This question is explored in the following chapters.

To strengthen my analysis of how young Canadian Muslims experi-ence national belonging, I also rely on important insights from Ghas-san Hage (1998). Like other academics, Hage makes an important distinction between official citizenship or the formal recognition of one's national status, and *practical national belonging* – "one's everyday acceptance or non-acceptance as a subject of belonging by the domi-nant national community" (49–55). In Hage's view, looking at official citizenship alone does not allow us to see how certain persons, on the basis of their class, gender, ethnicity, and race, are made to feel more or less accepted than others. He conveys the idea that citizenship is not effective in measuring national belonging, because it does not allow us to learn about the degree of acceptance that is accorded to Canadian citizens by the dominant national community. While the concept of citizenship implies that one is either a citizen or not, national belonging as a concept has a cumulative logic. Hage writes that "although legal citizenship guarantees certain rights and privileges, it is in fact only a pass into the game of achieving an embodied and performed citizenship that is recognized as legitimate by the dominant national community" (55).

Therefore, Hage (1998) argues for a sociological conception of national belonging, which refers to how people experience and deploy their claims to national belonging in everyday life. He conceives practical national belonging as a form of symbolic *national capital* that can be accumulated within the nation. Symbolic national capital includes

> the sum of accumulated nationally sanctioned and valued social and physical cultural styles and dispositions (national culture) adopted by individuals and groups, as well as valued characteristics (national types and national character) within a national field: looks, accent, demeanour, taste, nationally valued social and cultural preferences and behaviour. (Hage 1998, 53)

The aim of accumulating national capital is precisely to convert oneself into national belonging – to be seen as legitimate by the dominant group. Hage (1998) states that there is a tendency for a person to be seen as a national subject based on the amount of national capital he or she has accumulated. Thus, a person born to the dominant group who has accumulated national capital in the form of linguistic, physical, and cultural dispositions will be perceived as a national subject; on the other hand, someone who has managed to acquire the dominant national accent and certain national practices but lacks the physical characteristics and disposition of the dominant national type will not be perceived as such. Therefore, no matter how much national capital a Third World-looking immigrant accumulates, the fact that he/she acquired it, rather than being born into it, will never grant the same level of belonging as that possessed by the national aristocracy. In other words, there is a difference between those who acquire national capital and those who are born with it (Hage 1998).

In sum, regardless of how much national capital racial others possess, they will not be considered as equal to white Canadian national subjects. Aspiring nationals may claim to belong to the nation, with the expectation of feeling at home. However, this is a form of *passive belonging* and differs from *governmental belonging* – the mode of national belonging to which the dominant group often subscribes (Hage 1998, 46). Governmental belonging encompasses the belief that one has rights over the nation, as, for example, the right to contribute to its management and to decide who should belong and not belong. Hage (1998) argues that those who are in the dominant group often claim governmental belonging in their everyday interactions with others.

In the following chapters, I use these insights to inform my analysis of how race relations play out in the everyday lives of young Canadian Muslims. Because Canadian national identity now claims superiority over Muslim others through a language of religion, security, and gender, this has impacted how claims to national belonging are made. Governmental belonging by white Canadian national subjects is now expressed through efforts to make Canada safe from Muslim "terrorists" and to protect Canadians from "inferior," patriarchal cultural practices.

Because their Muslim identities are now imagined as a security risk, and because they are seen as belonging to backward, oppressive, and anti-Western cultures, the way young Canadian Muslims try to gain *national capital* has been impacted as well. I have found that they attempt to acquire national capital by presenting themselves as "safe" citizens. This takes various forms, depending on the context. In their everyday lives, Canadian Muslims are mindful of their behaviours, and they make efforts to represent their religion positively. When encountering state surveillance at airports and borders, acquiring national capital involves concealing their Muslim identity (e.g., women remove the hijab and men shave their beards) and adopting a more Western look.

Because their gender identities have been racialized, acquiring national capital also takes gendered forms for Canadian Muslims. Women try to demonstrate that they are educated and independent individuals; men project themselves as liberal, egalitarian, and peaceful. In other words, young Canadian Muslims strive to acquire national capital by attempting to construct alternative meanings of what it means to be Muslim men and women, outside of what has been imposed on them by mainstream society.

Table 1.1. Age distribution of the interviewees

Number of interviewees	Age
5	18–19
8	20–21
13	22–23
11	24–25
7	26–27
3	28–29
3	30–31

Description of the Research

I employed a qualitative research methodology for my study. Initially, I conducted a focus group interview with ten young Canadian Muslims, aged eighteen to twenty-three. The focus group interview served as a venue to begin exploring the experiences of young Muslim Canadians and to identify what key themes would be explored in subsequent individual interviews. I then derived the data for this book from fifty in-depth interviews with twenty-four Muslim men and twenty-six Muslim women between the ages of eighteen and thirty-one. More information about the age of interviewees is provided in Table 1.1, and a detailed description of each interview is provided in the appendix. In-depth interviews are useful for studying the perspectives and opinions of marginalized groups as they allow for the dissemination of their stories (Esterberg 2002). The interviews took place between 2004 and 2008, thereby allowing me to learn about the experiences of Muslims in the three to seven years following 9/11. Hence, the interviews speak to a particular time period. Notably, they capture my interviewees' experiences, perceptions, and feelings in the immediate aftermath of 9/11.

Permission was obtained from the University of Toronto Research Ethics Board to perform this research. The interviewees are guaranteed anonymity and have been given pseudonyms. The interviews were tape-recorded, transcribed, and coded thematically. They were analysed with the NVIVO qualitative analysis software program, which allows ideas and themes to be linked.

The interviewees chosen for this study had to identify themselves as Muslim. With the exception of one informant who had converted to Islam, all were born into Muslim families. Potential interviewees were informed that this study would explore young Canadian Muslims'

Table 1.2. Number of years living in Canada for interviewees not born in Canada

Number of interviewees	Years living in Canada
16	10–24
7	5–9
7	1–4

Note: Twenty out of the fifty interviewees were born in Canada.

experiences of living in Canada after 9/11. There may be an inherent bias in the sample due to self-selection, as individuals often choose to participate in research projects in which they strongly believe. Although the sample may include individuals who feel strongly about Muslim issues, especially those pertaining to 9/11, this allows me to study those Muslims who have been most impacted by the post-9/11 era.

The focus of this study is on second-generation (born or raised in Canada) and well-educated young Canadian Muslims. Eighty-two per cent (41 of 50) of the interviewees are Canadian citizens; 40 per cent of these interviewees were born in Canada, while 60 per cent are naturalized citizens. Thirty interviewees (30 of 50) were born in other countries, but the majority came to Canada either as young children or in their early teens. A breakdown of the length of time interviewees have lived in Canada is provided in Table 1.2. Overall, 80 per cent of my interviewees (40 of 50) were either born in Canada or came to Canada at a young age (under the age of fourteen). Although I did interview a few young Canadian Muslims (10 of 50) who were not born or raised in Canada for purposes of comparison, my main analytical focus was on the experiences of second-generation Canadian Muslims. I was particularly interested in learning how this group of young Canadian Muslims, who grew up thinking of Canada as their home, experienced national belonging and exclusion in the immediate aftermath of 9/11. I wanted to know how discourse on the Muslim other impacted how they made sense of their religious, cultural, and national identities. Of course, the experiences of Canadian Muslims who were not raised in Canada or who recently immigrated to Canada are equally relevant to a study of the processes of racialization, nation state formation, and identity formation. Such experiences should be addressed in future research.

Interviews were conducted in Vancouver and Toronto. These sites were chosen because 70 per cent of the Muslim population in Canada

Table 1.3. Education status of interviewees

	Undergraduate degree	Graduate/professional degree
In the workforce	8	2
In university	24 (in progress)	16 (in progress)

lives in metropolitan areas (Statistics Canada 2001). Further, by includ-ing interviews from both Vancouver and Toronto, the study documents the experiences of Muslims in Eastern and Western Canada.

During young adulthood, people explore a range of choices and begin to make commitments to interpersonal relationships, work and career, and ideology (Mannheim 1952). It makes theoretical sense to focus on Muslims in their young adulthood because they are in an important stage of identity formation and may have been more impacted by the post-9/11 era. The interviewees are all well-educated: at the time of the study, they had all completed a post-secondary degree or were in the pursuit of one. A more detailed overview of how many were still attending university and how many were in the workforce at the time of the study is provided in Table 1.3. This study focuses on well-educated Muslims, because the vast majority of young Muslims in Canada have some post-secondary education: 76 per cent of Muslim men and 67 per cent of Muslim women between the ages of twenty-one and thirty who immigrated to Canada after 1970 have some post-secondary education; as well, 81.5 per cent of Canadian-born Muslim men and 81 per cent of Canadian-born Muslim women who are between twenty-one and thirty years of age have some post-secondary education (Beyer 2005).

The sample reflects the diversity of Islam. The interviewees come from different national origins: India, Pakistan, Fiji, the West Indies, Libya, Bangladesh, Egypt, Saudi Arabia, and East Africa. A more detailed overview of their national origins appears in Table 1.4. By choosing this diverse sample, my goal is not to homogenize the expe-riences of young Muslims. I recognize that these young adults come from cultural groups with different histories and political backgrounds. However, it is theoretically important to look at Muslims from a vari-ety of different cultural backgrounds because of the way Muslim iden-tity has been racialized as the dangerous other in the post-9/11 era. Religious affiliations are often used to construct racialized identities of "imagined communities" (B. Anderson 1991b). Since 9/11, there has

Table 1.4. National origin distribution of interviewees

Number of interviewees	National origin
8	Egypt
3	Saudi Arabia
13	Pakistan
5	India
9	India/East Africa*
3	Bangladesh
1	Tanzania
1	Morocco
1	Iran
1	Syria
1	South Africa
1	West Indies
1	Jamaica
1	Fiji
1	Pakistan/Germany

Note: "National origin" refers either to the birthplace of the interviewees' parents or, if the interviewees were born abroad, to the respondents' own birthplaces.
*Although these interviewees or their parents were born in East Africa, their ancestral origins can be traced to India.

been a racialization of Islamic personhood based on their perceived religious difference (Chon and Arzt 2005). In this context, once someone has been identified as Muslim, he/she is likely to be discriminated against, despite his/her cultural background or skin colour (Chon and Arzt 2005). Therefore, it is important to look at the commonalities between Muslims from diverse backgrounds if we are to understand the ways being Muslim has become a racialized identity marker.

The interviewees belong to a variety of Muslim traditions, such as Ismaili, Shia, and Sunni, and they speak various languages. Even though many do not wear religious symbols, twelve of the women wear the hijab. With the exception of one interviewee, who is half German and half Pakistani, all are visibly non-white. Diversity in the sample is important; it ensures that findings are less likely to focus on experiences specific to a certain Muslim religious tradition or a particular ethnic or linguistic group.

Dorothy Smith (1987) argues that if we want to study what is happening to a group of people, it is imperative to begin from the actualities of their lives. Furthermore, Frances Henry and Carol Tator (2006) convey that while the dismissal of the lived experiences of racial minorities through claims that they represent "perceptions" and "subjective experiences" is pervasive practice in academia and in public discourses, these experiences are in fact "a body of systematic evidence of individual and systematic racism directed against people of colour" (122). Therefore, I use personal narratives as anecdotal evidence of real forces in society, not merely subjective experiences or isolated individual experiences. I particularly realized the importance of doing so during my interview with Fardeen, a twenty-six-year-old man who immigrated to Canada from Egypt in 2003. When I asked him whether he felt Muslims were subject to extra checking at airports and borders, he took offense at my use of the word "felt." He replied, "It isn't that I feel that Muslims are extra searched. The fact is they are subject to extra surveillance." With this, I realized the importance of connecting personal experiences to broader social relations, and I attempt to do so in the following chapters.

Research Challenges and Limitations

Academics have come to understand that researchers hold multiple positions when conducting research: they are both insiders and outsiders (Naples 2003). This was the case for this study. I was an outsider because I am not Muslim. Although I did not explicitly tell my interviewees that I come from a Sikh family, I did tell them if they enquired. I found that many could tell that I was not Muslim because of my very traditional Sikh first name. When I began this project, I was not sure whether I should be doing research on a community to which I did not belong. Could I adequately understand the experiences of young Canadian Muslims? Nor was I sure how receptive young Muslims would be.

In the end, my position as a non-Muslim played a positive role in some respects. My interviewees provided many details about their religion and their communities, as they recognized I was not Muslim and would not know such things. This information provided depth to my research. Furthermore, because I was not part of the Muslim community, interviewees may have felt greater freedom to talk about their religion without fear of reprisal.

When conducting this research, I also discovered I was an insider to a certain degree. Some interviewees indicated that because I was a racialized minority from a South Asian background, they felt that I could understand their experiences. They were comfortable discussing issues related to racism. Because I was in the same age group as the interviewees, the vast majority felt a sense of kinship. We shared some common reference points, allowing me to build a rapport with them and enabling them to share personal information with me.

However, my position as a non-Muslim was also a big challenge in my research. The biggest obstacle I faced was gaining the trust of Muslim organizations and recruiting interviewees. Many calls, emails, and flyers for the study placed in Muslim mosques, local Muslim youth groups, and Muslim student organizations were left unanswered. Some people whom I initially contacted declined to be interviewed or refused to pass on the study information to others, as they were not sure of my intentions and/or were afraid to speak up in a climate where they felt they were already being "watched" and "seen with suspicion" by others. In fact, a few people I contacted mentioned being tricked into speaking with CSIS officials claiming to be researchers. Others said they were reluctant to speak with anyone they did not know, because they had been misquoted and misled by the media in the past. After being refused by mosques, Muslim youth groups, and some Muslim university student organizations, I finally relied on a few personal networks to secure meetings with executive members of the University of Toronto and Simon Fraser University Muslim student organizations. After lengthy conversations, in which I explained the intentions and purpose of the study, I developed key contacts within these two organizations. These contacts then helped me find potential interviewees by sending out emails to student group listservs.

At the end of each interview, I relied on snowball sampling and asked the interviewees if they knew of anyone else I could interview. This allowed me to interview young Muslims that were not a part of these students' organizations. However, I restricted the number of referrals from each interviewee to avoid oversampling from a specific group. By using a snowball sample method, I was able to interview some individuals who had gone to other universities and who were already in the workforce.

The problems I faced in recruiting interviewees highlight the challenges of doing research within a group to which you do not belong. It also shows the difficulty of doing research on racialized and marginalized populations. Muslim university students and university graduates may have felt more comfortable coming forward to speak about their experiences because their education put them into a more privileged position. They may have been more aware of their rights and less afraid of reprisal for speaking out about their experiences than those from less privileged backgrounds. This signifies how processes of marginalization and stigmatization may make it more difficult for researchers to gain access to those most affected by racism. For example, as a result of this barrier, I was unable to learn about the experiences of young Muslims who may have dropped out of high school due to racism, those unable to afford a university education, those in precarious work, and those who were unemployed. The inability to gain access to these groups through Muslim mosques or local Muslim youth groups is a limitation of my study. My interviewees are no doubt from privileged backgrounds due to their university educations. Consequently, this study does not speak to the experiences of young Muslims from less privileged backgrounds and, hence, is not able to address how social class could impact life in Canada post-9/11. This is an important topic for future research.

Despite these limitations, my interviews with these well-educated, second-generation Canadian Muslims are a useful point of entry in beginning to understand how young Canadians Muslims' lives have been impacted by the post-9/11 era. My interviewees' experiences of national belonging and exclusion raise questions and important concerns about multiculturalism, racialization, state surveillance and security, nation state formation, and citizenship.

Overall, this study does not claim to represent all young Muslims in Canada. Since this is not a randomly chosen sample, it cannot be generalized to the wider population with any degree of statistical confidence. Rather, it is designed to take an in-depth look at the experiences of this sample of young, well-educated, urban, second-generation Canadian Muslims, and what they can tell us about citizenship, national belonging, multiculturalism, and identity formation post-9/11. Since my goal is not to evaluate the honesty and accuracy of their responses, I take interviewees' accounts at face value. That said, I do look for contradictions in their stories and for examples of what they say to avoid any inaccuracies.

There are also further limitations to this study. As mentioned earlier, since the focus is on young, well-educated Muslims, the sample primarily consists of individuals from middle-class backgrounds. Furthermore, this study does not speak to how experiences of discrimination differ between younger and older Muslims. A cross-generational study is required to examine this issue. Furthermore, since the key focus of this study is on second-generation Muslim Canadians (those born or raised in Canada), it does not look at the experiences of recent immigrants, nor does it consider those who have received post-secondary education abroad. The ways that experiences of immigration to Canada (e.g., devaluation of foreign credentials, deskilling of immigrants, challenges in acquiring permanent residence status and Canadian citizenship) may intersect with the demonization of Islam for Muslim Canadians is an important research question for future research. Finally, the study does not address the experiences of second-generation Canadian Muslims living in different parts of Canada, such as Quebec, Atlantic Canada, or the Prairie provinces. How Canadian Muslims experiences of national belonging and exclusion are affected by living in rural parts of the country or by living in a French-speaking province like Quebec, which has a unique history of bilingualism, are questions that cannot be answered by this study.

Overview

A key focus of this book is the meanings that dominant groups and institutions tried to impose on young Canadian Muslims, and I devote chapters 2 and 3 to this issue. As noted, this is the first empirically based study to provide an in-depth exploration of young Canadian Muslims' experiences in the immediate aftermath of 9/11. To this end, chapter 2 provides a general overview of the wide range of experiences young Canadian Muslims had with other Canadians following 9/11. In their day-to-day living, Muslims were made to feel like outcasts in Canadian society. The widespread perception that they were a threat to the nation and outside the purview of Western civilization turned Canada into a dangerous place for them. Muslims experienced a loss of safety and security, and public places, especially public transit, became racialized spaces. They felt their religious freedom was threatened by the lack of respect shown towards their religious traditions, and they faced workplace discrimination, which threatened their economic security. Finally, young Canadian Muslims felt they were othered through stereotypical conceptions about their gender identities, with men perceived as dangerous and violent and women as submissive and oppressed.

Chapter 2 also reveals the multiple strategies young Canadian Muslims have employed in resisting the preconceptions imposed upon them. First, in an effort to stop harassment, interviewees reported discrimination to the police and other institutions, efforts that were often unsuccessful. Second, they strived to be on their best behaviour in order to dispel negative stereotypes. Third, they contested stereotypical conceptions of their gender identities by asserting themselves as educated, strong, and peaceful. By doing the opposite of what is expected of them by society, they attempted to construct alternative meanings about what it means to be Muslim women and men. This was hard work: in trying to resist the labels that society had imposed, they paid a high emotional price. Although this shows the individual agency and resistance of the interviewees, it also illustrates the burden of contesting imposed societal meanings in the post-9/11 era.

Chapter 3 reveals how the creation of the Muslim other helped justify a state of exception, which involved the suspension of law in the name of security. I find that Canadian Muslims experienced this through increased surveillance, both nationally and internationally, at airports and borders, and in their daily lives. Their experiences of racialization and gendered surveillance precluded their equal access to substantive citizenship and marked them as unworthy of both legal and human rights. This chapter is relevant for both policy makers and academics, as these issues have been overlooked in academic literature. My interviewees recalled the targeting of their Muslim identities by invasive questioning and intrusive practices at airports and borders. They perceived these state practices as attacking their Muslim identity and challenging their citizenship. Although they have legal citizenship, their experiences suggest a lack of access to substantive citizenship. They experienced surveillance through complex processes of racialization and believed their gender identity played a role. They also reported experiences of surveillance in their daily lives; this resulted in a climate of fear and further questioning of their substantive citizenship in Canada. Chapter 3 concludes by showing the ways young Canadian Muslims attempted to deal with state surveillance at airports and borders. They refused to fly, challenged security personnel, became politically active, and concealed their Muslim identities. Sadly, many felt compelled to comply with the surveillance, even though they believed such practices undermined their citizenship as Canadians.

Overall, chapters 2 and 3 document that young Canadian Muslims believed they were often seen as an enemy to the Canadian nation. Their Muslim identities were perceived as dangerous, and they were not recognized as being Canadian. In the remaining chapters, I extend my analysis by focusing on how young Canadian Muslims negotiated their identities as Muslims, as members of different cultural groups, and as Canadians in the aftermath of 9/11.

Chapter 4 explores how Muslims make sense of their Muslim identity in post-9/11 Canada. To reclaim their Muslim identity, resist the abuse of Islam, and cope with discrimination, many affirmed their Muslim identity. To understand this social process, I theorize about Muslim identity formation in the post-9/11 era, something not yet found in academic literature. To do so, I extend Alejandro Portes and Rubén G. Rumbaut's (2001) theory of "reactive ethnicity" and construct the term "reactive identity formation."

Chapter 5 fills another surprising gap in the academic literature by examining how the post-9/11 era framed young Muslims' attachment to their cultural identities (i.e., their connections to the national origins of their parents). The vast majority of interviewees did not indicate having a close connection to their cultural identities in this period, and multiple factors played a role. The fact that their Muslim identities, as opposed to their cultural identities, were highlighted by society is one such factor. Living in a diasporic community and the push for revivalist Islam (a return to the "basic" principles of Islam) were other factors that explained why interviewees spoke of a weak attachment to their cultural identities. Moreover, a collective Muslim identity that crosses cultural boundaries and helps to resist the demonization of Islam was emerging among young Canadian Muslims.

Chapter 6 represents the last piece of the puzzle by considering how young Muslims negotiated their identities as Canadians in the post-9/11 era. Although they were not recognized as Canadians by others and have had their Canadian identities challenged, most interviewees retained their Canadian identities, and a few even reported strengthening it. My interviewees' attachment to their Canadian identities post-9/11 is complex, however. First, the prevalence of the discourse of democratic racism helps to explain my interviewees' attachment to their Canadian identities. In addition, many defined a Canadian identity through multiculturalism, and hence, they perceived the discrimination directed at them as anti-Canadian. They used the symbolism of multiculturalism to hold onto their Canadian identities and to redefine what a Canadian identity is supposed to look like. Finally, by maintaining dual Muslim/Canadian identities through hybridity, they presented alternative notions of what it means to be Canadian.

2 The Loss of National Belonging: Daily Experiences of Young Canadian Muslims Post-9/11

Introduction

Sometime in 2007, Nashida, a twenty-three-year-old, hijab-wearing woman born in Canada to a Pakistani family, went to a restaurant bar for her friend's birthday. An evening that was supposed to be a celebratory one soon turned ugly. The following happened at the restaurant:

> I noticed this white guy was staring at me, and I was getting very scared. He walked towards me and started yelling, "Why in the hell is this Muslim woman here? Is she going to bomb this place? Get out of our country." And I started crying right there and I left. We are told that we live in a good multicultural country where everyone is able to do what they wish, and how we are supposed to have freedom. Well, it wasn't the case.

After Nashida conveyed this story to me, I wondered how someone could have so much anger towards a virtual stranger just because she was Muslim. Why did this white man think he had the right to label this woman as a terrorist or feel entitled to demand that she leave Canada? Was this a random incident, or did other Muslims face similar discrimination? Did Canadian Muslims face other types of discrimination as well? And, most importantly, what do such incidents tell us about Canada? Using my interview data, I explore these questions in this chapter.

I devote this chapter to a broad overview of the different types of experiences my interviewees have had living in Canada post-9/11. Although all are constituted by types and levels of harassment, I roughly classify their experiences into the following divisions: a loss of safety and security; a shift from racial to (racialized) religious discrimination; a racialization of public spaces; threatened religious freedom; a jeopardized sense of economic security; and a racialization of gender identities. The final commonality is an interesting one: to counter these types and levels of harassment, they adopted multiple strategies of resistance.

By documenting the different types of discrimination young Canadian Muslims faced post-9/11, I not only give a voice to their lived experiences; I also address what these experiences tell us about the processes of national belonging and exclusion in Canada. As discussed in chapter 1, holding formal Canadian citizenship does not necessarily mean one belongs to the imagined community of Canadians (Creese 2007). Instead, belonging is negotiated in specific material sites such as neighbourhoods, workplaces, schools, shops, and street corners (Creese 2007). In this chapter, I show how, post-9/11, young Muslims' sense of national belonging was undermined in their everyday living by their social, political, and economical marginalization. I will also show how young Canadian Muslims tried to acquire national capital in order to be seen as legitimate Canadian citizens and to curb the discrimination they encountered.

Exploring young Canadian Muslims' experiences of national belonging and exclusion gives me the opportunity to reflect on how multiculturalism functions in ordinary living. Benedict Anderson (1991) says that nations are distinguished from each other by the stories they tell about themselves. Since the 1970s, Canada has been telling the world it is a multicultural country that respects cultural diversity and facilitates the peaceful coexistence of multiple ethnicities and religions (Wood and Gilbert 2005). Although Canada now presents itself with this multicultural identity, as discussed in chapter 1, Canadian identity has historically been based on whiteness (Thobani 2007; Boyko 2000; Bannerji 2000). For example, academics such as Sunera Thobani (2007) and Sherene Razack (2005) argue that the Canadian state was founded by ejecting Aboriginal people. They add that Canada strengthened its racial status as a homogenous and dominant white majority through its marginalization of early immigrant groups such as the Chinese and Japanese (Thobani 2007; Razack 2005).

During the 1960s and the 1970s, the Canadian state made a radical shift and adopted multiculturalism as a state policy, representing itself as a liberal democratic nation that had moved far beyond its racial beginnings. But is this peaceful coexistence a reality, or in Benedict

Anderson's words, just a story Canada tells about itself? Has Canada really moved away from being a white settler nation to one that equally values all citizens regardless of race, religion, and ethnicity? Or is multiculturalism a facade? These questions guide the analysis in this chapter.

Canadian Multiculturalism and Its Critiques

Before I begin my analysis, it is important to review the history of multiculturalism in Canada and the criticisms that have plagued it. In 1971, a policy of multiculturalism was introduced into the House of Commons by Prime Minister Pierre Elliott Trudeau (Reitz and Breton 1994). But the development of multiculturalism in Canada was tied to multiple forces, not just to the efforts of Trudeau. For one thing, it was directly connected to the establishment of the Royal Commission on Bilingualism and Biculturalism in 1963. The commission's goal was to make recommendations on how to ensure the development of Canada as a nation included an equal partnership of the two charter groups: the British and the French (Breton 1986; Reitz and Breton 1994). However, this goal led to concern among other ethnic groups, particularly the Ukrainian community, that such a partnership would undermine their cultures and their contributions to Canadian society. Protests from these groups led to a shift from biculturalism to multiculturalism. Fearful of alienating non-British and non-French Canadians, Pierre Trudeau opted for multiculturalism (Reitz and Breton 1994).

The multiculturalism policy was also created in response to the concerns of the growing number of ethnic minorities in Canada (Breton 1986; Reitz and Breton 1994). It followed Canada's new immigration policy, which was put forward in the 1960s and prohibited discrimination on the basis of race, national origin, religion, or culture (Esses and Gardner 1996). Another argument suggests that multiculturalism was developed as a policy so that Canada could be regarded as a unique country with its own national identity (Esses and Gardner 1996), especially given the growing concern that an increasing American presence would result in a loss of identity for Canadians (Breton 1986). Significantly, the development of multiculturalism in Canada was tied more to political motivations than to a genuine concern for equality.

The 1971 multicultural policy focused on Canada's demographic diversity and the symbolic celebration of different cultures as a part of Canadian heritage (Kobayashi 1993), but it was criticized for not creating structural equality for minority groups. To appease these critics, the government enshrined multiculturalism in the Canadian Charter of Rights and Freedoms in 1982. The subsequent 1988 Multiculturalism Act included both the recognition of cultural diversity and the legislative promise to promote equality, political participation, and institutional reform (Kobayashi 1993). The tenets of multiculturalism were embedded in other policies as well, such as the 1986 Employment Equity Act (Perry 2010).

Multiculturalism has undergone many transformations, but the proposed central mission remains the same: nation building by creating a more inclusive society (Kymlicka 1995; Banting and Kymlicka 2010). It claims to provide social justice, fair and equitable treatment, tolerance, cultural diversity, and a common national identity (Perry 2010). Canadian multiculturalism is frequently understood in terms of three different yet related notions: a specific government policy of pluralism, a social reality of a culturally and demographically diverse society, and a political ideology advocating cultural pluralism (Kallen 1982; Wood and Gilbert 2005).

In addition, Augie Fleras (2009) argues that multiculturalism functions through an ideology and as a set of practices. As an ideology, multiculturalism creates an image of how Canadians should live and interact within a pluralistic society. This includes valuing diversity and being tolerant, respectful, and non-discriminatory of others. As a set of practices, Canadian multiculturalism is supposed to embody fairness and equity, whether by individuals, groups, or institutions (Fleras 2009). However, a gap is often left between what multiculturalism promises and what it actually delivers. Many academics have commented on this contradiction.

Himani Bannerji (2000), for example, notes that the foundation of multiculturalism is problematic because "the core community is synthesized into a national 'we,' and it decides on the terms of multiculturalism and the degree to which multicultural others should be tolerated or accommodated" (42). To Bannerji, the "we" of multiculturalism is merely a colonial European identity slightly reworked into a Canadian identity. This Canadian identity still excludes non-white immigrants and the Aboriginal population.

Similarly, Eva Mackey (1999) argues that multiculturalism supports nation-building projects that sustain white Canadian culture at the core. Although in Canada there is no common culture for all classes, regions, or cultural groups, the idea of creating a common core culture continues to be integral to the project of nation building in Canada. This has not changed with multiculturalism. For example, national culture is still viewed as a whole and integrated way of life, with all Canadians sharing universal values, laws, education, and institutions (Mackey 1999).

As Mackey (1999) sees it, nation building in Canada constructs its white dominance through culturally unmarked and supposedly universal notions of rationality, progress, and equality; multiculturalism plays an important role in this process because it allows for the control and management of differences. In other words, difference is allowed via multiculturalism but in carefully limited ways. Dominant groups accept limited amounts of heterogeneity as long as the core cultural hegemony of the dominant society is maintained. Mackey says that multi-cultures are not a problem as long as these cultures are loyal to the Western project of nation building and are properly managed. Therefore, the unified white project remains dominant, simply because multiculturalism allows for limited difference. Mackey adds that multi-cultures are by definition subordinate, and the core (white) culture is by definition dominant. Those among the latter see themselves as "real" and authentic Canadians who tolerate and even celebrate the "colour" and the "flavour" of multicultural others.

In a similar vein, Ghassan Hage (1998) argues that both white racists and white multiculturalists see themselves as nationalists, and they see the nation as a space structured around a white culture. Through this lens, Aboriginal and non-white "ethnic" people are merely national objects to be moved or removed according to the national will. To this, Sedef Arat-Koc (2005) adds that multiculturalism defines "tolerance" as the central way to deal with cultural differences. However, inherent in the notion of tolerance is a sense of who is in charge and who defines the boundaries of a community or nation. Tolerance, therefore, involves a fundamental inequality of power between those who tolerate and those who are tolerated (Arat-Koc 2005).

Multiculturalism has also come under fire for hiding the historical displacement of First Nations communities and the mistreatment of early-racialized minority groups. Critical race scholars such as Bannerji (2000), Razack (2004), and Thobani (2007) argue that multiculturalism conveniently ignores acts of colonial violence, slavery, genocide, land theft, residential schools, and racist immigration policies. They stress that multicultural policies celebrate the white tolerance of racialized others by erasing the colonial ways of white settlement. Simply stated, many academics say multiculturalism obfuscates power relations – both past and present.

Multiculturalism has been charged with conceptualizing ethnic identity as fixed rather than fluid and situationally impacted by social and political factors. Bannerji (2000) believes that multiculturalism fails to take into account how cultural identities are often politically and socially constructed. There is nothing natural or primordial about the cultural identities that multiculturalism claims to respect, she says. Further, the officially recognized multicultural ethnicities are often the constructs of colonial, orientalist, and racist discourses (Bannerji 2000). In a similar vein, Nira Yuval-Davis (1997) argues that multiculturalism defines ethnic communities as homogenous groups who speak with a unified cultural or racial voice – in reality, this is not true. She also emphasizes that voices of ethnic groups are constructed as distinct from the majority culture; consequently, the more authentic a group is perceived to be, the more recognition it receives. Yuval-Davis believes this encourages ethnic retention and causes immigrants to organize along ethnic group lines bearing little resemblance to their homeland.

Some say multiculturalism shifts the focus from social justice and racism to ethnic identity and cultural diversity (Bannerji 2000). For example, Bannerji (2000) writes, "The concept of diversity simultaneously allows for an emptying out of actual social relations and suggests a concreteness of cultural description, and through this process obscures any understanding of difference as a construction of power" (36). Christian Joppke (2004) notes that multiculturalism fails to deal with the socio-economic problems that immigrants face, including unemployment and economic marginalization. These and other academics believe that because multiculturalism factors social justice into the recognition of cultural diversity, deeper structural relations of power, such as racism, sexism, or heterosexism are tossed aside (Bannerji 2000; Joppke 2004). As a result, Bannerji (2000) states that minorities in Canada organize along the lines of ethnic communities, not as communities based on class, gender, and racialization, which would be more powerful. In this sense, multiculturalism does not benefit non-white immigrants; it encourages minorities to focus on diversity issues and not on more important issues such as racism. Seyla Benhabib (2003) goes so far as to suggest replacing multiculturalism with policies and programs that encourage group solidarity across colour, ethnic, and racial lines.

Some academics (e.g., Razack 2005; Thobani 2007) argue that the mistreatment of Muslim communities since 9/11 reveals Canada's foundation as a racial state, something hidden by multiculturalism. In Thobani's (2007) view, public demands for increased restrictions on immigration and citizenship post-9/11 have reshaped the meaning of Canadian nationality and citizenship. Many say that Canadian Muslims have been cast outside the realm of Canadian citizenship, thereby highlighting the problems of Canadian multiculturalism (Razack 2005; Thobani 2007; Joppke 2004).

In what follows, I use Canadian Muslims' experiences to consider how multiculturalism plays out in real life. Does multiculturalism protect young Canadian Muslims from discrimination in the post-9/11 era, or has it failed them? Are their religious and cultural identities respected? Do they have equal access to important social institutions, such as the labour market? Is the value of their Canadian citizenship equal to that of white Canadians? These questions are explored in the following sections.

Early Experiences in Canada

Many of the young Canadian Muslims in this study grew up feeling like outsiders in Canada. The majority of my interviewees (68 per cent) experienced discrimination while growing up; only a minority did not. Maria, a hijab-wearing twenty-four-year-old woman, born in Canada to a Tanzanian immigrant family, is one of the latter:

> I grew up in Waterloo, and our neighbourhood was so nice, and all the kids were friends, and we didn't fight about colour. My father is a business-man, and his circle of friends is very diverse. They are all businessmen, so we used to go out fishing together and never felt any discrimination from anybody.

However, Maria is in the minority, as most do not paint such a rosy picture but instead stress a hostile environment.

Feeling like an outsider goes back to when the interviewees' parents arrived in Canada and is often based on skin colour, as Sakeena, a twenty-seven-year-old woman born in Canada to a Pakistani family, says:

> I often hear stories about when my parents first came to Canada in the 1980s. For instance, my mom would be in a store looking for clothes to buy, and the saleslady would just walk away. I think my parents have

gone through a lot when I think about it ... Especially because my parents used to live in a very small town that primarily was Caucasian; there weren't a lot of coloured people there. And they struggled a lot to form a solid business there, and to be taken seriously, and to get customers, and all those kinds of things. And I'm sure a lot of it had to do with discrimination, because they were as well qualified as anybody, or more, but it comes down to the colour of your skin, I think.

Sakeena's parents came to Canada from Pakistan in the 1980s. At that time, Canada had recently changed its immigration policies and allowed thousands of racialized immigrants and refugees from non-traditional sources such as Africa, Asia, and South America into the country (Aiken 2007). The vast majority of immigrants were from precisely those groups that had been historically discriminated against on the basis of national or ethnic origin. Although they were allowed into the country, however, they were not necessarily made to feel welcome. Sharryn Aiken (2007) points out that while immigrants from Europe are welcomed into Canada, immigrants from Asia and Africa are met with fear and hostility, particularly in regards to their ability to assimilate into Canadian society, as Sakeena's comments make clear.

Not surprisingly, then, the interviewees faced experiences of exclusion while growing up in Canada. A twenty-two-year-old man named Zaahir, who immigrated to Canada from Saudi Arabia when he was four, recalls the following:

I faced a little bit [of discrimination], but I don't think it was because I was Muslim. It was because of my skin colour. I remember being in middle school and people would call me racist terms, so I would get angry. At the time, I understood it is part of school life, that kids tease other kids. But now I see that it was racism.

Zaahir grew up in Vancouver during the late 1980s and the early 1990s. Even though multicultural policies had been around for many years by then, children like Zaahir were still facing discrimination rather than experiencing inclusion in Canadian society.

While some interviewees feel they were discriminated against because of their skin colour and ethnic heritage, others feel discrimination is tied to their identities as immigrants. Saud, a twenty-two-year-old man born in Canada to a Pakistani immigrant family, and Yazeed, a twenty-one-year-old man who immigrated to Canada from Sudan when he was twelve, mention the following:

> SAUD: We have always faced discrimination. We lived in North Burnaby, and we went to North Elementary, and we were not the mainstream. We were like the only Pakistanis at the school. So we always felt discriminated against. It was more to do with us being Pakistani. So there would be childish things, like making fun of the accents. We integrated during grade seven and started picking up a Canadian accent, but before that we faced the usual discrimination. I think it mostly had to do with looking different; it had very little to do with religion and faith. It was more Indo-Canadian discrimination than Muslim discrimination.
>
> YAZEED: I faced racism on multiple levels. I had it from friends. I mean, I used to call them friends. I came here at the age of ten. Grade five was perhaps the hardest one. Being a new immigrant, the new kid in, I did speak English, I knew how to speak English, I just had an accent, I think I still do. So I was treated differently from the other students.

Saud's and Yazeed's experiences raise important issues about belonging in Canada. Academics concur that new immigrants are often seen as outsiders (Thobani 2007; Bannerji 2000; Razack 2004). Since they do not initially fit into mainstream Canadian society, they are sidelined and mistreated, as Saud's and Yazeed's experiences clearly show. Such experiences put intense pressure on immigrants to assimilate – and most do so.

Skin colour, however, plays an important role in who gets labelled as an immigrant and who does not. Gillian Creese (2007) points out that it is often people of colour who are labelled as immigrants and then discriminated against. While most Canadians claim an immigrant heritage, some are defined by that status while others are not. More particularly, the immigrant status of those from Europe is often erased, and the immigrant identity of people of colour is highlighted. This is apparent in the differential treatment of Saud and Yazeed.

English plays an important role in the imposition of an immigrant identity. Creese (2007) points out that one legacy of colonialism is a world where English is recognized as the language of knowledge and which privileges those who speak it fluently, especially in North American, British, or European accents. She elaborates that the right to be seen as linguistically competent involves "the right to speak" and "the right to be heard." Therefore, struggles over language competency are not so much an issue of miscommunication as they are negotiations over power and social location; misrecognition often seems intentional (Creese and Kambere 2003, 56). As Saud and Yazeed tell us, one's immigrant status can be reaffirmed through one's accent and then used to differentiate people of colour.

The majority of the interviewees who faced discrimination while growing up in Canada feel that discrimination was connected to their skin colour and immigrant identities, suggesting also that these were the primary identities imposed on them by society. However, seven interviewees indicated that discrimination was directed at their Muslim identity. For instance, Dawoud, a twenty-five-year-old man who came to Canada from Saudia Arabia when he was less than one year old, says,

> When I look back, I see incidents where maybe I was bullied in the cafeteria or someone said something derogatory about Muslims or Islam. This happened before 9/11. At the time, I never really took it as that. At the time it was always personal – it was, well, it was never that someone said something about Islam. And I think part of the reason was, throughout my high school years, I did not really associate very strongly with Islam. So if anyone said something about Islam, it didn't offend me.

When Dawoud reflects on the discrimination, he now connects it to being Muslim. He did not recognize this before, partly because he did not strongly self-identify as a Muslim, and partly because his Muslim identity was not highlighted by society before 9/11.

It is important to point out that Dawoud is one of two men in my study to say they were discriminated against as Muslims before 9/11. The remaining five interviewees who report facing discrimination as Muslims before 9/11 are women; four wear the hijab. Amineh, a hijab-wearing twenty-three-year-old woman born in Canada to a Libyan immigrant family says,

> Well, during my elementary school time I was in a Muslim school, so I never was harassed, but when I moved to public school, I was harassed big time. I used to have this one guy [ask] me, "Do you keep bombs under your scarf?" and then one time he pulled it off ... Everybody else treated me like I was a kind of weirdo, and nobody really wanted to be my friend in the beginning ... um, I never got accepted into the popular school in high school. You know that you are not treated the same. I also got

discriminated against by my counsellor because I came from the Muslim school, and he was like, the standard of education is not that good in a Muslims school. He was like, "Your grades are too good. I don't think that you are going to do so well here," and as a matter of fact I did even better, and I was better than all of the other students.

As Amineh's comments suggest, the discrimination she faced may have been endorsed by school officials, directly impacting her sense of freedom to practise her religion and thus affecting her sense of belonging in Canadian society.

Overall, my interviewees point to a general lack of respect towards Islam in Canada. Evidently, there was some resentment of Islam and the wearing of the hijab in Canada even before 9/11. Here, Edward Said's insights into orientalism (discussed extensively in chapter 1) prove especially useful. According to Said (1981), orientalism has played a central role in the way Islam has been seen by the West: Islam has historically symbolized terror and devastation and been seen as producing hordes of barbarians. Today, orientalist depictions of Muslims continue to prevail in the popular media and affect the ways non-Muslims view Islam and those who practice and identify with it (Said 1981). The resulting hostility is revealed in my interviewees' experiences of being bullied for their religious identity even before 9/11.

Overall, the interviewees' experiences of growing up in Canada lay bare the racial foundations of the nation. Although Canada introduced multiculturalism in 1971 and later made changes to its immigration policies, these acts did not translate into an environment where cultural and religious diversity was respected. Canada remained a bordered space that only partially admitted racialized immigrants. Although Muslim immigrants from countries such as Pakistan and Saudi Arabia were allowed to immigrate to Canada, they were excluded from the imagined community of the nation and subject to discrimination and harassment, which was heightened by ongoing orientalist perceptions of Islam. This is not surprising given that immigrants from places like Asia and the Middle East have been historically been labelled as the "other," a construction that played a vital role in the emergence of the Canadian nation state (Thobani 2007). As the other, these "immigrants" were seen as being devoid of the Canadian nation's qualities and values (Thobani 2007) and, as a result, were not welcomed by the dominant national community.

The hostility towards Islam has intensified post-9/11, and attention has drastically shifted to the Muslim identity as the new racial other. The sense of danger is not new, as the nation of citizens in Canada has always imagined itself vulnerable to strangers (Zine 2012). Homi Bhabha (2004) points out that the success of colonization is secretly marked by a radical anxiety; as a nation state formed through colonization, Canada is no different. Mackey (1999) argues that from colonial times to the present, Canadian national identity has been seen as a crisis-ridden, fragile, insecure, and weak entity, which needs protection against constant attacks from racial others. Jasmin Zine (2012) says that in the post-9/11 context, the Muslim has come to represent the central figure that haunts the nation and threatens an already weak national Canadian identity, leaving Muslim Canadians in an extremely vulnerable position. Atiya, a thirty-year-old woman born in Canada to an Indian-Fijian immigrant family, would agree with this; she notes, "Before, the [discrimination] was mostly to do with my skin colour and not to do with my religion. Now, it [has] definitely more to do with my faith than with my skin colour. The times have now changed."

Atiya is not alone. Denise Helly (2004) found a sixteen-fold increase in hate crimes experienced by Muslim individuals or in Muslim places between September 2001 and September 2002. The Toronto Police Service Hate Crime Unit reported fifty-seven hostile acts committed against Muslims in 2001, representing a substantial increase from 2000, when only one hostile act against a Muslim was reported (Helly 2004). In 2006, when seventeen young Canadian Muslims men were arrested for allegedly plotting a terrorist attack, the Canadian Islamic Congress feared the possibility of a backlash. Their fears were not unfounded – within a day of the arrests, a major Toronto mosque was vandalized (Poynting and Perry 2007).

How prevalent is this type of discrimination among my interviewees? Thirty out of the fifty interviewees (60 per cent) indicate that they have experienced discrimination related to being Muslim since 9/11. Forty-one interviewees (82 per cent) have families or friends who have faced such discrimination in the same period. Knowing that your friends and family have been discriminated against is upsetting, so the high percentage is important. Therefore, I include the related experiences of friends and family in my analysis. While the remaining nine interviewees do not know of direct experiences of discrimination, they remain very concerned about the treatment of Muslim communities in

Canada. In fact, only one interviewee of the fifty has no concerns about Muslims facing discrimination in the post-9/11 era.

Sadly, Muslim interactions with other Canadians often result in the degradation of their sense of citizenship as Canadians. According to Evelyn Nakano Glenn (2002), it is important to treat citizenship as localized, because the boundaries defining citizenship are often interpreted and enforced by individuals operating at the local level. Similarly, Hage (1998) highlights the important role of everyday acceptance or non-acceptance by the dominant national community on the practical national belonging one feels as a national subject. The following sections show how in their normal daily interactions with other Canadians, young Muslims feel less safe, experience the racialization of public spaces, are stigmatized because of their religious practices, lose their economic security, and suffer the racialization of their gender identities, all of which raise important questions about national belonging in Canada. The remainder of this chapter also illustrates that exalted white national subjects remain key figures in Canadian society, who now express *governmental belonging* in their efforts to protect Canada from "terrorists" and "inferior" cultural practices.

Loss of Safety and Security

Irrespective of where they were on 11 September, almost all respondents say their first reaction was shock and disbelief. Amineh relays the following:

> It was just so mind boggling that I did not even think anything. I could not even think anything. I was just in disbelief. And then I thought a lot about what Muslims would say, and the second thing was like, dear God, I hope it was not Muslims that did this. It can't be Muslims that did this, you know. That Muslims can't do something like this. Then you just go wonder what is going to happen next. There is just a feeling of dread.

The interviewees mourned those who died and expressed anger towards the perpetrators who had given Islam a bad name. Not only were they upset about the loss of life, like the rest of the population, but they were faced with the troubling notion that Muslims either would be blamed for this or were actually responsible. Zora, a twenty-two-year-old naturalized Canadian citizen with a Bangladeshi background, mentions:

I think many Muslims were praying that Muslims were not responsible. It was a double fear and a double sadness for us. We were afraid that terrorists could come in and harm us. However, we were also afraid that because they have been identified as being Muslim, we are going to suffer a backlash because of that.

These sentiments illustrate what Anne Aly and Lelia Green (2010) call the majority and minority dynamics around fear. In their study of Muslim Australians and non-Muslim Australians post-9/11, they found that while both groups express fears about a possible terrorist attack, Muslims are also concerned about a backlash against themselves, their families, and their communities. As a result, Aly and Green note a social climate of pervasive fear among Muslim communities in Australia. Since 9/11, Muslims experience fear much differently than the rest of the population.

Canadian Muslims had a similar experience, and, unfortunately, the Canadian government failed to protect Muslim communities from the backlash that followed 9/11. Scott Poynting and Barbara Perry (2007) write, "No public calls for peace and understanding were forthcoming; no strengthening reforms to hate crime legislation were ever considered (in contrast to the rabid action on the anti-terrorist legislation) and nor were increased police or prosecution vigilance on the public agenda" (162). This lack of protection had serious consequences for my interviewees.

Immediately following 9/11, stories began to circulate about Muslims facing physical harassment. Aalia, a hijab-wearing twenty-one-year-old woman who immigrated from Egypt when she was thirteen, became concerned for her personal safety after hearing stories about Muslim mosques being vandalized:

I was not really afraid for Muslims' security in the beginning, but then I heard of an incident where some people, who were in their last years of high school, five or six people, ... they took a rock and crashed the door of our mosque in Peterborough, and after that I was concerned that people do not realize that it was individuals that did that, and that it was not the religion that was the problem. So after that I was concerned because obviously there were some people that thought every Muslim ... was to blame. So that was when I was worried.

A number of interviewees mentioned the vandalization of mosques. Such violence is a clear attack on their religion, and it frightened them.

Many became fearful of frequenting public places and made changes to their daily routines. Atiya recalls:

Yes, I was afraid, especially going out with my dad and with my mom because they distinctly look Muslim. My dad wears a little goatee beard, and my mom wears the scarf, and at that point I was not wearing a scarf, so we were afraid of going places together. We had kind of resolved that if we had to go pick up something, we would go with either my brother or my father, so at least one of the men would be there. So we were definitely scared ... and we would get weird looks, you know, when me and my mom would walk into a store.

Things taken for granted by other Canadians, such as going to the mall or to a grocery store, became difficult. Fardeen, a twenty-six-year-old man who came to Canada as an international student from Egypt when he was twenty-three, says that some Muslim women wearing the hijab refrained from using the subway in Toronto right after 9/11 because they were afraid someone would push them in front of the subway train.

Overall, I found more Muslim women than men feared for their safety. Muslim women who wear the hijab are easily identified as Muslim. However, Muslim women who do not wear the hijab were also fearful, leading me to question whether Muslim women feel less physically able to defend themselves against potential hate crimes than Muslim men.

Nevertheless, safety was a concern for some Muslim men, and Fardeen mentions that a Muslim friend from Toronto moved in with his neighbour, who was not Muslim, for a few weeks after 9/11 because he was afraid that "someone would attack him in his home." As this story shows, some Canadians offered support to the Muslim communities. Aaeesha, a twenty-four-year-old woman who immigrated to Canada from Pakistan when she was five, says, "Because we're from a small community, a lot of people would call my dad at work and stuff to make sure he was okay." However, despite such support, I found that many were afraid to frequent public places in the immediate aftermath of 9/11.

As a result of this fear, the interviewees debated whether to conceal their Muslim identity in public. Falak, a twenty-one-year-old woman who immigrated to Canada when she was sixteen and who has an Indian-East African background, did so to ensure her safety immediately following 9/11:

I had started hearing things that had happened in England, like a Sikh man was attacked because people felt that he was a Muslim, so I was very scared, um, but I did not want anyone to think that just because I am a Muslim that I agreed with what had happened. I tried to stay away from situations or conversations about it, and if anyone asked me about my religion, I would tell them the sect that I am. I would not say that I was a Muslim. I would tell them that I am Ismali, but not that I am a Muslim. I refrained from it because I basically did not want people to get mad at me basically.

While Falak hid her Muslim identity, others refused to do so. In fact, most interviewees affirmed their Muslim identity in the post-9/11 era, an issue explored in chapter 4.

They did make changes to how they practised their religion in public, however, as described by a thirty-year-old man, Barkat, who was born in South Africa and came to Canada as a young child:

I used to feel very comfortable praying in public. After 9/11, I didn't feel very comfortable praying in public. Whereas before I used to just pray in the street anywhere … now I don't really, not because I'm afraid, it's just Muslims are out there a little more, and there is a little bit more negative press. And so it just circles in the back of my head. And I know that we're in Canada, and Canada's a pretty safe place, but it always just plays there, like, you know, "Dude, you better hurry up. Get in here, and get out of here."

Clearly, some Canadian Muslims felt they had lost the freedom to practise their religion in public. In fact, how to practise their religion immediately following 9/11 concerned the community at large. A major celebration for Ismaili Muslims[1] was postponed for a year after 9/11 in both Toronto and Vancouver because of the fear of retaliation. Aamir, a twenty-three-year-old man who was born in Canada to an East African-Indian family, says:

We have pictures of Aga Khan [religious leader] and it's quite common that people keep them in their cars or keep beads called "tasbeez" that would clearly identify them as Muslims. And there were announcements in our mosque to take those down, and that it would be better not to be so visible because someone might damage the car or something. Yeah, so just for safety measures.

Although some interviewees said they were encouraged to deflect attention away from themselves by removing items that would iden- tify them as Muslims, they refused to do so, because they did not want to turn their backs on their beliefs and religion. Indeed, Aamir was shocked that his community leaders made such recommendations.

In sum, being perceived as a threat and having their Muslim identity vili- fied was difficult for my interviewees. They lived in a climate of fear, afraid of public places, fearful of displaying their Muslim identity, and unsure of how to handle the situation. While some felt compelled to conceal their Muslim identity, many refused (see chapter 4 for an explanation of why young Muslims refused to abandon their religion, despite safety concerns). By and large, their sense of safety and security were jeopardized in the immediate aftermath of 9/11, and their everyday lives were impacted.

These experiences raise important concerns about belonging in Cana- dian society. The vast majority of the interviewees were either born or raised in Canada. Canada is the only home they have ever known. However, in the immediate aftermath of 9/11, these interviewees did not feel safe in their own country. The fact that Muslim Canadians lost their sense of safety so easily says something about the lack of power racialized minority groups in Canada hold compared to other, white, Canadians. It also reveals how white Canadians were in a powerful location to intimidate Canadian Muslims and to jeopardize their sense of safety. Tim Wise (2008) asserts that an important element of white privilege is not being blamed for the negative actions of others from the same group. For example, the Oklahoma City bombing in 1995 in the U.S. was seen as a result of the actions of Timothy McVeigh and Terry Nichols; blame was not extended to other white Americans. Muslims do not have access to this element of white privilege and they were all held accountable for 9/11. In a similar vein, Thobani (2007) writes:

> National subjects who fail to live up to the exalted qualities are treated as aberrations, their failings are individual and isolated ones. The failings of outsiders are however, as seen as reflective of the inadequacies of their community of their culture and indeed of their race. Conversely their suc- cess is treated as individual and isolated exceptions. (6)

When Public Space Becomes Racialized Space

White Canadians, as the dominant national group, hold great power in Canadian society, and this can be seen in their control of public space. In principle, being able to utilize public places without harassment is the right of all citizens. However, academics have long argued that public spaces are not safe for all citizens and that racism is always a spatial project (Dua, Razack, and Warner 2005; Razack 2002). Enakshi Dua and associates (2005) say that we are constantly led to believe that Europeans built the nation, while the existence of First Nations communities is ignored. David Goldberg (2002) points out that colonizers claim the land of the colonized as their own thorough a process of violent eviction, justified by the notion that the land was empty or populated by those that had to be saved and civilized (129). In this national mythology, white people came here first, developed the land, and are therefore entitled to the land (Razack 2002). Aboriginal people are presumed to be dead or assimilated. European settlers thus have become the original inhabitants and deem themselves the owners of the land (Razack 2002).

This historical legacy of white entitlement to land in North America has direct consequences on how race relations play out in our public spaces. Razack (2002) reminds us that public space is a social product shaped by unequal social relations and calls for a critical understanding about how spaces are racialized. Similarly, Patricia K. Wood and Liette Gilbert (2005) say that "public space is a space of presence, recognition, participation, and citizenship – it is the means by which difference is negotiated, affirmed or contested" (686). The victimization and othering of Muslims in public places suggests these spaces have increasingly become racialized in the post-9/11 era. Aneesha, a twenty-year-old hijab-wearing woman who immigrated from Pakistan when she was less than one year old, and Yazeed (mentioned earlier) describe harassment in the public sphere:

> ANEESHA: Post-9/11, I was called a terrorist. I was walking home from school and a car with a bunch of white guys drove by and they screamed out, "Terrorist! What are you going to bomb next?" Another time, I was told on the bus going home, "Oh, you're making our soldiers die in Afghanistan." So there was a blame being put.
>
> YAZEED: Two years ago, right by my house, a white guy came up to one of my friends on the sidewalk and started swearing at him. He said, "You f___ing Muslim." My friend, he is a big guy, built up. He's pretty intimidating, but I think that guy hit him with a bike chain ... My friend was very angry.

Thobani (2007) argues that in the post-9/11 public discourse, collaboration between "real" citizens and law enforcement agencies is presented as vital to the elimination of terrorism. As a result, the new burden of citizenship includes a constant hyper-vigilance towards potential terrorists. The promotion of this new hypervigilance may help explain why some Canadians feel they have the right to verbally abuse Muslims and accuse them of terrorism. Wielding this hypervigilance, they impose the identity of "dangerous Muslim" on all Muslims, including my interviewees, seeing them as something to be controlled. Razack (2002) cautions that we need to pay attention to how racialized minority groups come to know themselves in public space, as well as what is produced within that space in terms of relational practices.

What I see in this public space is the exalted national subject expressing governmental belonging under the guise of hypervigilance. Hage (1998) refers to governmental belonging as the mode of national belonging that encompasses the belief that one has a right over the nation, expressed in the right to contribute to its management and to decide who should and should not belong. My interviewees' experiences illustrate that in the post-9/11 era, governmental belonging is expressed through the hypervigilance of trying to make Canada safe from terrorism, pointing to how claims of national belonging are being made through a language of security.

In a specific application of hypervigilance and governmental belonging, public transportation has become extremely dangerous for young Muslims. The interviewees tell many stories of discrimination on buses, Toronto subway trains, and the Vancouver sky train. They have been pushed, sworn at, and spat upon, and they have heard negative comments and had things thrown at them. Nashida, a twenty-three-year-old woman born in Canada to a Pakistani immigrant family, and Abdual, a thirty-year-old man who came to Canada in 2007 as an international student from Egypt, say the following:

NASHIDA: One of my sisters-in-law experienced something on the subway. She was coming back from her university, and she is a very tall person, and she wears the scarf. And as she was getting off, she noticed this white man staring at her and saying things – like muttering things. She was getting really scared, and she tried to call her brother, but [there is] no signal in the subway. So eventually when she got off the subway, the man got up and pushed her. She actually fell down. And no one helped her.

ABDUAL: One time we were in the subway station, one morning in the weekend. My wife and I were doing something in the summer with our kids, and there was this white guy. He came and started to curse and swear to us very loudly. He was standing behind us and saying, "Go away Bin Laden. Go back to your country – leave this country."

Zeba, a hijab-wearing twenty-two-year-old woman born in Canada and with an Indian background, is extremely self-conscious about how others see her on the subway. She says that she never opens her bag to take anything out, not even her cell phone to check the time, because she does not want to scare anyone or draw attention to herself. Amineh, a hijab-wearing twenty-three-year-old woman born in Canada to a Libyan family, stopped taking the sky train in Vancouver and started driving to school after she started "getting harassed a lot." But what about Muslims who cannot afford a car?

This raises the issue of how social class can play a role in who is safe from harassment and who is not. In her study of Arab communities in the U.S., Nadine Naber (2006) found that middle-class Arabs were relatively better protected than lower-class Arabs after 9/11. They were less visible in public spaces, particularly because they were likely to drive to work or school in their own cars rather than taking public transportation (245–6). A similar phenomenon may also be occurring in Canada, where middle-class Muslim Canadians may be better able to protect themselves from harassment in public spaces than those from a lower-class background.

The hypervigilance of Canadian Muslims draws on the legacy of white entitlement, mentioned previously, whereby as the "rightful" owners of the land, white colonizers manage all racial others (Dua, Razack, and Warner 2005). In the post-9/11 era, this management is directed at Muslim Canadians in public spaces; under the guise of hypervigilance against terrorism, white Canadians assert control over public spaces.

Because many white Canadians subscribe to governmental belonging, it is not surprising that the verbal abuse directed at Muslim Canadians often involves being told to leave the country. Zeba and Dawoud mention:

ZEBA: On the subways, I'd have white people make comments to me like, "Oh, you stupid terrorist, leave" or "Why are you wearing that thing on your head? You shouldn't be oppressed in this country." "Go home, go back to your home," stuff like that. I get comments like that on the subway, in grocery stores ... One of my friends, she walks home from

UTM [University of Toronto Mississauga], and she had people drive
by scream and shout at her, "Oh, you terrorist, take off your scarf! You
don't belong in this country." And it's not happened once – it's happened repeatedly. My cousin, she was at the parking lot in the grocery
store; she was putting away her groceries in the car. This white woman
came up to her and said, "You should go home. You're a terrorist, you
don't belong here."

DAWOUD: In different universities, Muslim students' associations have
always had traditions of doing an Islam awareness week. At Wilfrid
Laurier University, someone came up to us and said, "Why are you guys
here? Why don't you go back from where you came from?"

Being told that they do not belong in Canada and asked to leave the
country challenges and devalues Muslim Canadians' citizenship. If they
are not recognized as Canadian, they do not have access to *nationality* –
the recognition of being a part of a people who constitute a nation, an
important component of citizenship. Significantly, Tim Wise (2008) states
that an important component of white privilege is that one's legitimacy
to be in North America is far less likely to be questioned. According to
Wise, when you are white, you are automatically considered as being
part of the nation. Muslim Canadians lack this component of white privilege; as a result, their citizenship is frequently questioned.

These experiences reveal the complexity of citizenship. Academics
have long argued that although racialized minority groups may hold
legal citizenship, they might still be treated as second class citizens
(Young 1998; Sassen 2004). As my research shows, Canadian Muslims'
sense of citizenship is frequently devalued in their face-to-face interactions with fellow Canadians. Treated as second-class citizens, they are
confronted by verbal and physical harassment in racialized and dangerous public places.

As noted above, these experiences also illustrate some white Canadians' sense of entitlement, whereby they believe they have the right
to decide who belongs and does not belong in Canada. Hage (1998)
asserts that the act of telling someone to "go home" is not only a racist
practice, but it is also a nationalist practice. Nationalist practices are
based on the nationalist as a master of national space and the ethnic/
racial other as an object within this space. Hage mentions that when
one begins to worry about the existence of "too many," they are not
only thinking about race and ethnicity but also what they consider a
privileged relationship between their race, ethnicity, and the territory

they occupy. Therefore, when white Canadians tell Canadian Muslims to "go home," they are acting as *nationalist space managers*. As nationalist space managers, such persons consider themselves spatially dominant enactors of the national will and legitimately entitled in the course of everyday life to make governmental/managerial statements about the nation (Hage 1998). The threat of the Muslim other helps substantiate the role of the *national space manager*.

Hage (1998) also points out that nationalist practices, such as telling someone "to go home," cannot occur without an ideal nation being imagined by the nationalist space manager. He notes that the "discourse of home" is one of the most pervasive elements of nationalist practices. What (or who) is classified as undesirable is precisely what is imagined as prohibiting the nation from being what it should be or what it used to be for the nationalist. In the desire to send the other "home," nationalists reveal their own desire to be at "home." In fact, Canada nationalists have always tried to manage the other to create their imagined white community (Dua 2000; Thobani 2007).

While the other has historically been defined using a language of biology and culture, in the present day, a language of security is used to justify the creation of the Muslim other. The act of telling someone to "go home" is nothing new in Canada. Racialized minorities have been subjected to this statement since the inception of the Canadian nation state. However, directing this statement at Muslim Canadians today is justified by the notion that Muslims belong to inferior cultures that support terrorism. As Muslims are increasingly projected as a threat to Western nations, attempts to secure this fantasized nation state may be made by trying to control the Muslim other. Significantly, Hage (1998) mentions that, because the idea of home is a fantasy, it is something that can never really exist. In this context, the other has an important function, as it helps to explain why the fantasized nation state never becomes a reality. This conception of nationalism as a fantasy helps to explain why nationalists get so heated up and why they are always trying to pursue and control the other.

Loss of Religious Freedom

In the Canadian context, the pursuit of trying to control the other in order to achieve the desired white state not only involves telling Muslims to "go home" but is extended to an ongoing disrespect for Muslim cultural and religious practices. Young Canadian Muslims increasingly face stigmatization of their religious practices through both covert and overt actions of other Canadians.

For example, wearing the hijab is a frequently stigmatized religious practice. Haleema, a hijab-wearing Muslim woman, says:

> Sometimes people make comments: "You don't have to go around hiding your beauty" or "you don't have to go around trying to be so modest." People say, "Oh, by the way, you guys are very beautiful. You don't have to wear the hijab, and you don't have to be hiding your looks. You know this is Canada. You're free to do whatever you please. You don't have to wear that."

The Muslim women in my study are often assumed to be forced into wearing the hijab. For instance, Aneesha, a twenty-year-old hijab-wearing woman who was born in Pakistan and came to Canada as a young child, mentions that one time when she went to McDonald's, a person approached her and asked, "Why do you wear it? Are you okay? Do you need help taking it off?" She recalls that she had to spend "a good ten minutes" explaining that it was her choice to wear it and "no one was forcing her." Disapproval of the hijab may be covert as well, as Nashida elaborates:

> I think a lot of things don't need to be said in words. I think a lot of things can be read through the face as well. The way they look at you, ... the way they turn their faces ... it takes more to frown than it does to smile, and it was definitely not smiles. I will experience just, like, looks, like as if I have ... really hurt someone ... like meaningful, hateful looks, you know.

Religious freedom is an issue for Muslim men, as well. Barkat is a teacher; his experience shows that Muslim men also find themselves in situations where religious traditions are not respected:

> I was taught, men and women, they don't shake hands, they don't touch. One parent was quite offended by the fact that I wouldn't shake her hand. She said, "I want to thank you for teaching my son." She put out her hand, and I said, "Oh, I don't shake hands," very awkwardly and uncomfortably. So she said, "Oh, Mr. X, we are in Canada, and you have to learn to be here," and I said, "Yeah, but still." And then she said, "Well, I'm going to give you a hug then." Then she gave me a hug in front of her son, and I just kind of froze and started to walk away. And it was like, "Oh, my

gosh, what was that?" I just felt – I'm going to use the word violated. What I felt was, I told you "No" because of my religious beliefs, and you decided what you thought was more important, so you just step right over that detail that I just told you, and you do what you want to do anyways, because this is Canada. So I suppose my right to be able to practise my religion the way I saw fit, in a way that was not harming anyone else, was not good enough.

As nationalist space managers, white Canadians feel entitled to question the religious practices of Canadian Muslims and to pressure them to assimilate. This illustrates how governmental belonging is expressed as a way to protect Canadians from "inferior" religious practices. Hage (1998) says that the practice of removing someone's scarf or asking them to remove it is a way of imagining one's position within the nation. A person behaving this way believes he/she has the right to manage the space of the nation. This goes a long way towards explaining the behaviour of certain white Canadians towards young Canadian Muslims, who are simply following their religious customs.

These power dynamics raise important questions about multiculturalism in Canada. Ideologically, multiculturalism is supposed to allow a person to express his/her religious and cultural identities without fear of discrimination (Kymlicka 1995). However, this is not how multiculturalism is practised. As noted in the chapter 1, Bannerji (2000) has long argued that multiculturalism maintains hegemonic whiteness by positing Anglo-Canadian culture as the core culture while tolerating and arranging others around it as "multicultural." Because multiculturalism reinforces the dominance of Anglo-Canadian culture, many young Canadian Muslims are stigmatized because of their religious choices and are pressured to assimilate. In fact, since people are still expected to assimilate, Jasmin Zine (2012) considers multiculturalism in Canada to be aesthetic and skin deep only.

Furthermore, the pressure on Muslim Canadians to assimilate reveals an ongoing fear of the other. In trying to understand hostile reactions to the hijab, Yasmin Jiwani (2012) says the hijab has come to symbolize those who are considered culturally and religiously different in Canada. Hage (1998) adds that when someone asks a woman to take off her hijab, he/she sees it as a harmful presence affecting that person's own well-being and invading his/her personal space. Despite the rhetoric of multiculturalism, cultural and religious practices that are not part of the mainstream white culture are seen as a threat and as evidence of the dangerous other.

This lack of respect for different religious and cultural practices points to the incidence of cultural racism, what George M. Fredickson (2002) calls the racism of the new millennium. Cultural racism involves defining the mainstream as "culturally appropriate" and normal and defining racialized groups as culturally incompatible and inferior (Agnew 2007). Cultural racism is increasingly used to marginalize and exclude Muslim Canadians from the imagined community of citizens. It has intensified since 9/11 and is articulated by conflating Muslim religious practices with terror. For example, the North American public has increasingly (and problematically) identified the hijab with Islamic militancy extremism, oppression of women, and anti-Western sentiment (Haddad 2007). This helps to explain the hostility Muslim women experience when they wear the hijab and why they are encouraged to remove it.

But reprimanding Muslim women who wear the hijab is disrespectful of the religion and undermines religious freedom. In addition, the frequent assumption that these women are not exercising individual choice, a notion my interviewees frequently encounter, fails to recognize Muslim women as full citizens in Canada. As noted by Nakano Glenn (2002), *standing* – being recognized as an adult capable of exercising choice and assuming responsibility – is an important facet of belonging.

Furthermore, Jiwani (2012) argues that the desire to liberate a Muslim woman by getting her to remove her scarf and to make her "one of us" is fraught with contradictions. She notes that in the Canadian context, despite the promises of advancement often associated with assimilation, jobs are not forthcoming, and structural discrimination impedes Muslim women's acceptance and inclusion within the dominant culture. Similarly, Hage (1998) comments that people from racialized groups are often led to believe that accumulating national capital or, in other words, adopting nationally valued social and cultural preferences and values will result in being seen as legitimate by the dominant group (53). However, Hage cautions that no matter how much national capital a Third World-looking migrant accumulates, the fact that he/she has acquired it rather than being born into it means that he/she will never reach the same level of belonging. Therefore, although women are frequently encouraged to abandon the hijab, doing so in order to assimilate does not necessarily mean they will be granted the same level of national belonging as white Canadians.

Muslim religious practices have become increasingly contested in Canadian society. As a result, those adhering to them have begun to question their everyday interactions with "white Canadians," even when discrimination is not overt. For example, when Muslim women who wear the hijab are treated rudely by others, they often do not know if they are being treated badly because they are Muslim or if there is another reason. Amineh's experience of poor customer service is an example of this. She says:

> There was this one store, and we wanted a shirt, and we asked if they would call the other stores if they had that shirt, and she just said, "We are too busy, here's the phone number, call yourself," and there was nobody else in that store. There was no line up. You just don't get the standard of customer service that you know that other people are getting and it makes you [wonder] if this is because you are a Muslim.

What is important about this experience is not just whether the store workers discriminated against Amineh because of her Muslim identity; the resulting uncertainty is equally salient. She wonders why she is being treated in this way. Is it her religion or something else? Wise (2008) writes, "No white person, turned away after a store had closed, or given bad customer service, would ever have to consider that perhaps they had been treated that way because of their race. This is a deep privilege and an abiding psychological comfort" (72).

A few interviewees felt their religious freedom was threatened at the institutional level. Dawoud says:

> I was involved with this youth group, and after 9/11, we started getting a lot of emails from various members who were in high school telling us that their prayer space has been taken away for various reasons by the schools. And it wasn't taken away as, "Sorry, we won't let you pray anymore." It was always taken away as, "Well, we need more classrooms. We don't have enough classrooms, so sorry you're prayer rooms are taken away." And there [were] at least four schools in the Peel District School Board which did that, and we worked with a lawyer to basically send a letter saying that, according to the Peel Board of Education at least, that they're required to make religious accommodations, and this comes in under that. We found out later that there were a lot more schools across the GTA [Greater Toronto Area], not just in Peel Board, but across the GTA, where prayer spaces were taken away. And again, the fact that all that

happened just after 9/11, it was the second week of school when 9/11 happened, and they had their prayer space for the first Friday, but they didn't have it for the second Friday. And it's somewhat odd that all of a sudden they need more classrooms.

This incident leads one to question whether any sort of religious affiliation with Islam may be perceived as a sign of aggression and support for terrorism. Tariq Ramadan (2010) argues that since 9/11, a distinction is increasingly made between "good" Muslims and "bad" Muslims. "Good" Muslims are seen as liberal and secularist or religiously moderate. "Bad" Muslims are seen as very religious – as fundamentalists, extremists, and "Islamists." Ramadan states that in Western societies, where the day-to-day visibility of religion is close to zero, the practices of daily prayers, fasting, religiously grounded moral obligations, and dress codes are automatically considered excessive. From this skewed viewpoint, moderate "good" Muslims are those who adopt no distinctive dress, who consume alcohol, and who do not practise their religion publicly.

This categorization of religious Muslims as "bad" and secular Muslims as "good" is not new. During the colonial era, orientalist scholars in Britain and France depicted Muslims in the same binary manner: "good" Muslims either collaborated with the colonial enterprise or accepted the values and customs of the dominant power; the rest, the "bad" Muslims, resisted religiously, culturally, or politically and were dismissed as the other and represented as a danger (Ramadan 2010). A similar phenomenon may be occurring in the present day, whereby Muslims who practise their religion publicly, by wearing the hijab, for example, are deemed as "bad" Muslims and then in turn ridiculed, harassed, and in some cases even institutionally prohibited from practising their religion.

But as Ramadan (2010) correctly points out, the connection between being religious and politically fanatic is weak. He notes that someone who is religiously "liberal" in Islamic practices – such as by not wearing the hijab – can support hard-line dictatorial regimes. Conversely, following the religious practices of Islam is perfectly compatible with a non-violent democratic political stance that rejects all forms of domination, exploitation, and oppression. Therefore, rather than making simplistic binary categorizations, it would be more fruitful to examine the complex dynamics at work in Muslim societies.

To summarize, because their religious practices have been stigmatized, young Canadian Muslims feel unable to openly express their religion. For Muslim women, this expression often involves the hijab, but a few Muslim men speak of a lack of respect for their religious traditions. This lack of religious freedom may be reinforced at the institutional level, as any sort of religious affiliation with Islam may be perceived as a sign of support for terrorism. Because they feel their right to religious freedom is under threat, young Canadian Muslims sense an increasing lack of substantive citizenship (the ability to exercise rights of citizenship).

As mentioned earlier, these negative experiences cast doubt on the state of multiculturalism in Canada. Mackey (1999) claims multi-cultures are fine in Canada as long as they are properly managed and remain loyal to the Canadian project of nation building. For her, multiculturalism is a way for the dominant group to manage differences; members of the group can decide when to "tolerate" cultural differences. The experiences of Muslim Canadians substantiate her assertion. In the wake of 9/11, when Muslims were increasingly projected as the enemies of Western nations, their religious and cultural practices were no longer welcomed. School boards tried to take away Muslim prayer rooms in high schools, and ordinary Canadians pressured Muslim Canadians to abandon their religious practices. Put simply, the dominant group was no longer willing to "tolerate" Muslims.

Sarah Ahmed (2000) argues that multiculturalism can involve a contradictory process of incorporation and exclusion: "It may seek to differentiate between those whose appearance of difference can be claimed by the nation and those that are the stranger's stranger – whose difference may be dangerous to the well-being of even the most heterogeneous of nations" (97). In the post-9/11 era, Canadian Muslims have become the stranger's stranger where any sign of following the Muslim faith is met with ridicule and hostility.

Loss of Economic Security

One of the most significant aspects of racism is that it can lead to discrimination in employment (Agnew 2007). According to Gillian Creese (2007) the Canadian labour market is a diaspora space where otherness is both constructed and contested – it has historically been racialized, and as a result, many groups find themselves precariously situated within it. The often turbulent relationship between racialized groups and the labour market goes back to Canada's early days. For example,

Canada allowed limited migration from Asia in the 1870s and 1880s in order to construct the railway, which was considered vital for the growth of the Canadian economy. Despite their contributions to the economy, however, these new immigrants were put in dangerous work conditions, poorly paid, and regulated to the outskirts of Canadian society (Dua 2000; K.J. Anderson 1991). Put simply, their exploitation was used to expand the Canadian economy.

When Canada eliminated overtly racial classifications during the late 1960s and 1970s, this act was again tied to the dynamics of capitalism, as the Canadian government wanted to capitalize on the economic contributions of immigrants (Dua 2000). Roxana Ng (1996) argues that immigrants are a labour market commodity that can be bought by employers. Many say Canada continues to strengthen its economy by exploiting immigrants; as a result, new immigrants face unforeseen hardships (Creese 2007; Agnew 2007). For example, many racialized immigrants have limited prospects in the labour market compared to their white counterparts. They have higher rates of unemployment and lower wages, and they are concentrated in less desirable jobs (Creese 2007). Furthermore, although today's immigrants arrive with more education and skills than their predecessors, barriers to accessing the professions for which they are trained results in their unemployment and/or underemployment (Agnew 2007). Demands for Canadian educational credentials and Canadian experience constitute major obstacles for these immigrants (Agnew 2007). Significantly, Creese (2007) claims that even if these highly educated immigrants obtain Canadian education and experience, they are still unlikely to reap the same benefits as white Canadians.

Even racialized minorities who are born in Canada and who have Canadian credentials may experience difficulties. For example, they earn less than workers belonging to the white majority (Cardozo and Pendakur 2008). Although some of this gap can be explained by education or labour market choices, a substantial portion remains even after controlling for these characteristics. Andrew Cardozo and Ravi Pendakur (2008) emphasize that the earning differentials faced by Canadian-born racialized minorities are persistent and do not disappear from one census period to another. Krishna Pendakur and Ravi Pendakur (2011) also note that the earnings gaps faced by Canadian-born racialized minorities have not eroded since the 1990s, even though the size of this population has radically increased during the same period.

Discrepancies in earnings exist despite the high post-secondary attainment rate among racialized minorities. Of the working age population,

58 per cent of the racialized minority population hold a post-secondary degree compared to 43 per cent of the non-racialized minority population (Samuel and Basavarajappa 2006). However, racialized minorities have higher rates of unemployment and are more likely to be in precarious work positions. Racialized minority graduates from Canadian universities may be as qualified as other graduates, but they are less likely to find employment (Samuel and Basavarajappa 2006). In fact, even if they are born in Canada, racialized minorities are less likely than foreign-born and Canadian-born non-visible minorities or white people to be in the top 20 per cent of the income distribution (Canadian Race Relations Foundation 2000). Furthermore, racialized minorities with a university education are less likely to hold managerial professional jobs than non-visible minorities with similar levels of education (Jain and Lawler 2004).

Racialized minorities also perceive greater discrimination than white Canadians, especially in the domains of job applications, pay, and promotions (Dion and Kawakami 1996). Muslim Canadians are among this group. Although Muslims adults have the second highest level of education attainment of all religious groups in Canada, more Muslims are in the lower income bracket (earning $30,000 or less) than any other religious group (Beyer 2005).

Grace-Edward Galabuzi (2006) argues that income, sectoral occupations, and unemployment data indicate that a racialized labour market is an endemic feature of the Canadian economy. Characteristic of the racial and gender labour market segmentation is the over-representation of racialized members (particularly women) in low-paid, low-end occupations and low-income sectors, as well as in temporary work. Conversely, they are under-represented in high-paying occupations and high-income sectors. Galabuzi (2006) finds that the racialized employment income gap is observable both among low-income earners and high-income earners. It persists among those with low and high educational attainment (among those with less than high school education and also among those with university degrees).

Overall, there is a clear disadvantage in the labour market for racialized minority groups in Canada, whether they are Canadian-born or not. This disadvantage is reflected in employment patterns, experiences, and earnings. Because Canadian society attributes unequal social value to racialized individuals, their experiences and outcomes in the labour market are impacted (Agnew 2007). Like the rest of Canadian society, the labour market is a space where racialized individuals struggle to gain entry and acceptance (Creese 2007).

How do young Canadian Muslims experience the labour market at a time when their Muslim identities have become so contested and racialized? What are their experiences, and how do they navigate a racialized labour market?

Academics argue that the construction of Muslims as enemies can result in discrimination in employment and financial relations (Macklin 2001; Thobani 2007). In the immediate aftermath of 9/11, stories began to circulate that Muslims were losing their jobs. Zamil, a twenty-nine-year-old man who has been living in Canada since 2005 and has a West Indies background, mentions,

> A friend of mine was fired for making a comment. At their office, they were collecting money for the people post-9/11 at New York. And he suggested to one of his co-workers that they should donate money or collect money for the Afghanistan kids' camps. He was fired for wanting to fundraise for Afghani orphans. His comment had nothing to do with politics, and he was Muslim, and he just thought it would be civil and humane and do some fundraising for the orphans – I guess not. Well, his boss got mad at him for making that comment, and then a week later he was fired. His boss was like, "What the hell are you doing? We are not going to side with the terrorists." And this was in Vancouver.

Ghassan Hage (1998) argues that there is often a limited political spectrum where racialized others can legitimately express their political positions. In fact, they are expected to express total allegiance to dominant viewpoints and gratitude to the nation. In comparison, white citizens have real political citizenship: they can express their views, regardless of how controversial they may be, without comprising their position in the political community (Hage 1998). Being fired for making a simple comment says something about Canadian citizenship in the post-9/11 era. It seems unlikely that if a non-Muslim made such a comment, he or she would have been fired. Because Canadian Muslims increasingly lack access to *allegiance* (Nakano Glenn 2002) and are not considered loyal members of society, any comment perceived problematic or disloyal can have dire consequences, including being fired.

By the same token, many feared that Muslim businesses would lose clients immediately after 9/11. Aamir comments that the textile business of his close family friends "went down at least 30 per cent right after 9/11." Aalia's family was worried that her father's pharmacy would lose clients, though they have not. While the fear of suffering economically may not be as intense as it was in the immediate aftermath of 9/11, many young Canadian Muslims feel the increased discrimination and hostility will spill over into their professional lives, jeopardizing their economic security. Many have difficulties finding work. This is especially a concern for Muslim women who wear the hijab, as Zeba's experience illustrates:

I went to look for a job in the summer, and I went to this hosiery store in Sherway Gardens. It's a very upper-class mall. This lady interviewed me and spoke to me, and then she called her supervisor, and she spoke to her supervisor, and then she told me, she's like, "Frankly, I can't offer you the job, not because you're not capable but just because you wear a scarf, and in this mall there's a lot of rich people. So I don't know how comfortable they'll be with this, so I can't offer you the job. I'm sorry, but this is the case." I was sixteen or seventeen, so it was very heartbreaking. It was the first time that something so large-scale discriminatory had happened to me. I never experienced something like that. I was very upset, very shocked.

J. Helen Beck and associates (2002) argue that discriminatory decisions are often rationalized by references to negative characteristics supposedly applicable to members of a racial minority. Because the hijab has problematically become the ultimate symbol of otherness and is increasingly associated with anti-Western sentiment (Jiwani 2010), wearing it can have serious economic consequences for Muslim women by limiting their opportunities to find work. Some employers are quite open about refusing to hiring someone for wearing the hijab, indicating that negative perceptions about it are now seen as legitimate.

But men also worry about finding work. Dawoud, who was having difficulty finding a co-op work term[2] mentions that he suddenly "began getting more interviews and job offers" when, at his career counsellor's suggestion, he deleted his involvement with Muslim organizations from his résumé. Like other Muslim Canadians, he felt compelled to conceal his Muslim identity when looking for work. A few of my interviewees even altered their Muslim names. Sanya, a twenty-five-year-old woman born in Canada and from an Indian-East African background, notes:

I know of a friend who – he also has a name that's very like obviously Muslim – and he was having trouble finding one [a job], and he just graduated from a really good program at Waterloo. And all his friends were getting jobs, and he wasn't getting anything. And one of the employers told him, you know, he's like, "I suggest that you change your name a little bit so it doesn't seem so obviously Muslim because that's probably one of the reasons why." And so since then he has changed his name. And he has gotten a job.

This type of discrimination is not new; in fact, discrimination in hiring practices has a long history in Canada. In a landmark study, conducted in 1985, Frances Henry and Effie Ginzberg (1985) used a sample of classified ads in major newspapers in Toronto to access employer responses to white applicants versus visible minority applicants. They used direct in-person applications with matched pairs (based on similarity in work experience, skills, and physical characteristics); offers to white people outweighed offers to black people by a ratio of three to one. In another sample of jobs tested by phone inquiries, the percentages of times that white Canadians, white immigrants, and Indo-Pakistani callers were told jobs were open for them were 85.2 per cent, 65 per cent, and 47.3 per cent, respectively (Henry and Ginzberg 1985). More recently, the Ethnic Diversity Survey (Statistics Canada 2002) found that 56 per cent of the participants who perceived racial discrimination or unfair treatment said they most commonly encountered such treatment in the workplace, particularly during job applications and when seeking promotions. In addition, in a field experiment, Philip Oreopoulos (2011) sent out 13,000 résumés in response to online job postings across multiple occupations in Toronto. He found that interview request rates for English-named applicants with Canadian education and experience were more than three times higher compared to request rates for Chinese-, Indian-, or Pakistani-named applicants with foreign education and experience, but rates were no different compared to foreign applicants from Britain. Furthermore, Canadian applicants that differed only by name had substantially different callback rates: those with English-sounding names received interview requests 40 per cent more often than applicants with Chinese, Indian, or Pakistani names. Overall, Philip Oreopoulos (2011) study results suggest that considerable employer discrimination existed against applicants with ethnic names or with experience from foreign firms in the Canadian labour market.

The experiences of my interviewees show that discrimination in hiring practices is still prevalent in Canada. As noted above, some young Muslim Canadians conceal their Muslim identity to find work. For example, Dawoud mentions that Muslim men often "shave their beards." Samir, a twenty-three-year-old man who is a naturalized Canadian citizen with an Indian background, comments that some Muslim women "took off the hijab out of desperation because they couldn't get a job otherwise." This is more than an economic issue: having to hide one's religious identity and customs to obtain work compromises one's religious freedom – and one's sense of self.

A number of Canadian Muslims feel pressured by potential employers to abandon their religious customs. Umar, a twenty-two-year-old man who immigrated to Canada four years ago from India, says:

> I have a friend who is a mechanical engineer, and he went to one of the firms to have an interview, and the last thing they want to know is that he's a Muslim. He goes there wearing a dress pant, and he was wearing the Islamic cap on his head, and he has a long really long beard. And the person interviewing said they encourage their employees to go clean because they meet a lot of people on the job. It's offensive to him because you are calling him dirty because he has a beard, and he didn't want the job after that. So for me, it is discriminatory. I was working at a restaurant, and I was told to shave my beard. I told the owner of the restaurant this is who I am, and it's my right to practice my religion, and you cannot stop me, and I would go behind the store away from the dining area, and I prayed over there. And they finally understood I liked my job because I take my job seriously. I work sincerely as fast as I could. I got a lot of tips. Customers would come to the store manager and say things like, "He's a nice guy, he smiles," and the manager got to know me and understand that I need to pray and dress in a certain way.

Such experiences tell us that assimilation practices are thriving in Canada, despite the rhetoric of multiculturalism. In order to be seen as qualified workers, Muslim Canadians are encouraged to accumulate national capital – nationally valued social and cultural preferences (Hage 1998). By pressuring Muslims to assimilate, employers directly challenge young Muslims' religious freedom. Even on occasions when they are allowed to follow their religious practices at work, they feel they have to earn the right – they are not automatically accorded this right, as Umar's story illustrates.

Racial discrimination can appear in workplace harassment. John Samuel and Kogalur Basavarajappa (2006) find that one out of four racialized minorities has experienced racial harassment in the workplace. A few of my interviewees refer to harassment from co-workers.

Saud, a twenty-two-year-old man born in Canada to a Pakistani family, says the following:

> I worked at Save on Foods. You would have the really loud guys that would sort of try to say things that are inappropriate, like, not come out and directly say that you are a terrorist, they would be a little more careful about it, but they would use the word Bin Laden a lot. I would tell a store manager and call them on it, and I would win the day, and the manager would say, "Apologize." They would apologize in front of the manager, and then they would do it again.

The stereotypes attributed to Muslims, such as being terrorists, can shape how they are treated in the work environment. This is particularly the case for Muslim women. As noted, in the West, the hijab has increasingly been associated with oppression of women and with anti-Western sentiment (Hoodfar 1993; Glavanis 1998; Alexander 2004). This hostility is pervasive and can impact opportunities in the workforce, as Amineh's experience illustrates:

> I know this one girl that never used to wear the hijab, and then she started to wear the hijab, and all of her business jobs got cancelled. Like, her boss was, like, you are not going to go on any of these customer relations stuff. He was like, "You are not the face of business that I want to be sending across the country." My friend was pretty not impressed. She reported it.

Given the reactions, some Muslim women are understandably hesitant to wear the hijab at work. Aaeesha says:

> My sister-in-law wears the hijab, but she doesn't wear it to work. And especially when she was starting her job last year [as a dental hygienist]. Sometimes I think at work, like, with patients that she deals with, she finds that they treat her differently if she does wear it. So she doesn't wear it to work.

Beck and associates (2002) point out that discrimination can take place at any time in the employment process, including during recruitment, screening, selection, promotion, or termination, and it can be either intentional or inadvertent. My research shows that discrimination can also take place in everyday workplace interactions, where one is made to feel uncomfortable simply for following one's religious faith.

Some young Muslim women actually fear that the stereotypical image of Muslim women as oppressed and uneducated can jeopardize their career prospects. Bushra, an eighteen-year-old woman born in Canada and from an Indian-East African background, and Maria (mentioned previously) note the following:

> MARIA: I am a physiotherapist, even with my sisters, one of them is a lawyer the other is a teacher, and we are professional people, but people do not recognize us as that.
>
> BUSHRA: Some of my friends wear the hijab and are trying to get jobs now, and they're not taken seriously, because a lot of my friends wanted to have, you know, a full career, and they were like, "Oh what about time for your family?" and things like that, and she was like, "Well you didn't ask that girl," and you know, just because I'm a traditional Muslim woman doesn't mean that I'm going to devote my entire life to my family either.

Agnes Calliste and George Dei (2000) note that "racially" specific notions of femininity have played an important role in justifying the restriction of black women to menial and physically exhausting jobs, such as domestic work. A similar phenomenon may be occurring with Muslim women. The racialized gendered identity imposed on them as docile, submissive, and oppressed may have serious consequences for their professional lives, as they may be seen as incompetent workers who are not invested in their careers.

In sum, many young Canadian Muslims have trouble obtaining work, face pressure to conceal their Muslim identities, encounter workplace harassment, and worry about their future career prospects. Employment discrimination affects them in multiple ways, and this multifaceted discrimination may explain why there are more Muslim adults in the lower income bracket than any other religious group in Canada, despite Canadian Muslims being highly educated (Beyer 2005). Human rights laws across Canada are supposed to prohibit employers from discriminating against individuals in hiring or firing, or in setting the terms and conditions of employment on personal characteristics including race, ethnicity, and religion (Commission for Labour Cooperation 2010). However, the experiences of my interviewees suggest that these laws are not preventing workplace discrimination. Even more troubling is the fact that many interviewees are still students. Despite their limited time in the workforce, they have already experienced problems, indicating pervasive workforce discrimination.

These experiences point to problems in multiculturalism. A number of academics argue that while multiculturalism promotes the inclusion of multiple identities, the reality is that racialized minorities have lower status, are under-represented, and are less socially accepted in important social institutions (Bannerji 2000; Joppke 2004; Razack 2004). In fact, Sherene Razack (1998) states that multiculturalism promotes "culturalization of racism" by inviting minorities to maintain their cultures without affording them sufficient access to power and resources to do so. The numerous problems faced in the workforce by the interviewees in this study give proof of this.

Racialization of Gender Identities

It is important to note that more women report facing discrimination than Muslim men. Out of the thirty interviewees who reported direct discrimination, eighteen (60 per cent) are women, and twelve (40 per cent) are men. Muslim women also report more threatening forms of abuse. Most incidents of physical intimidation, such as pushing and hitting, involve Muslim women. These findings are echoed by Louise Cainkar (2005), who found, in the U.S., Arab Muslim women to be nearly twice as likely to face verbal assaults as Muslim men three years after 9/11. Although previous literature has found the same thing, what remains unanswered is why this gender difference exists at all. My research suggests the following.

First, due to the hijab, Muslim women are more visibly Muslim than are the men, and they are therefore more easily targeted. In fact, approximately 72 per cent (13 out of 18) of the Muslim women in my study who have experienced discrimination wear the hijab. Similarly, Cainkar's (2005) study found that when assaults against Muslims occurred in a public space, a Muslim woman wearing the hijab was present more than 90 per cent of the time.

Second, and related to the point above, the hijab is seen as a direct challenge to Western notions of modernity, gender equality, and the Western model of cultural behaviour (Haddad 2007). Hence, Muslim women may face more discrimination because of what the hijab has come to represent in the Western world. Dawoud mentions:

I think there can be some frustration [in] the mainstream community, because they do not understand the concept of the hijab. They say, "Why do you continue to put yourself in a state where you are oppressed? Why are you wearing a hijab against your will? Why are you are letting your husband or your brother dictate what you're going to do, how you are going to look, how you are going to dress?" It just boggles their mind. And if you have that idea in your head, that they are doing it against their will, it just boggles your mind.

The hijab, as the ultimate marker of cultural and religious differences, often sparks hostile reactions. In trying to understand these reactions, Jiwani (2012) writes that "the fear of being engulfed by another culture – 'death by culture' – is then the motivating factor that propels a siege mentality in the dominant population and a xenophobic exclusion that is mediated by racism" (381–2).

Third, Muslim women must cope with the racialization of gender identity. In the post-9/11 era, Muslim women are increasingly othered through stereotypical (and negative) conceptions. While Muslim men are perceived to be barbaric and dangerous, Muslim women are imagined as passive and oppressed by their communities, as described by Rubina, a hijab-wearing twenty-six-year-old woman who immigrated to Canada as a young child from Egypt:

They [white people] definitely think Muslim women are oppressed. Muslim women don't have a choice to do anything that they want to do. They are submissive, and that they are domesticated – they just want to stay at home and have all sorts of children. They think that men are the opposite of the Muslim women. The men are oppressors of women and are anti-Western. They think Muslim men are very hard-core and passionate about everything that is anti-Western. They are violent … aggressive.

Academics concur that the primary gender identity imposed on Muslim women is that of the oppressed woman (Hoodfar 1993; Glavanis 1998; Alexander 2000, 2004). Jiwani (2012) points out that the representation of Muslim women as oppressed emerged during colonization. Sadly, this has not changed and is often symbolized by the hijab.

Arguably, because of these gender attributions, some people may feel safer discriminating against Muslim women than Muslim men. Yazeed and Alisha, a twenty-six-year-old hijab-wearing woman who immigrated to Canada at the age of twenty from Pakistan, say the following:

YAZEED: It is much easier for a guy to pick on a woman than it is to pick on another guy. If you look at me, I am intimidating. People are intimidated by me. So you are going to think twice before you come after me. So I guess it has more to do with being coward and just going after the easier target.

ALISHA: People think that a Muslim woman would not talk back to them. She wouldn't raise her voice, she would just walk by, she wouldn't even give it a second thought. People think you can call out against them on the street, and they would not talk back to you, they would just walk by. Whereas a man, they would think, yes, he would talk back, and he would be like, "Why did you call me by this name?" and so on, just that there would be retaliation from them, but not from the women.

Other interviewees agree that Muslim women are singled out because people do not expect them to retaliate. Aneesha says when she speaks out against people who make derogatory comments, they are shocked at her temerity:

They would always be dumbfounded. They'd be just confused. They couldn't think of how a Muslim girl would be able to react to something. I guess they would assume that with the hijab, you would have to be very reserved and shy.

Raewyn Connell's (1987) concept of "emphasized femininity" adds an interesting element to the discussion. Emphasized femininity refers to a range of traditional femininity norms that expect women to accommodate men's power and control. According to Connell, one form of emphasized femininity is passivity, wherein women are expected to accept unhappiness or abuse. In the post-9/11 context, where Muslim women's gender identities have become even more racialized than before, people may expect Muslim women to conform to a heightened form of emphasized femininity by not challenging acts of discrimination. Aneesha's comments, then, would certainly come as a shock.

Homi Bhabha (2004) reminds us that every time we come across a stereotype, we need to calculate its effects, and how it has been produced. Indeed, the gender stereotypes attributed to Muslim men and women are closely tied to political motivations. Historically the creation of stereotypes functioned to enable colonial authority. Colonizers used such ideologies to morally justify eroding the cultures of colonized people (Abu-Lughod 2002; Meetoo and Mirza, 2007). As noted above, the image of the oppressed Muslim women emerged during colonization: saving brown women from brown men allowed colonizers to justify using practices of violence to keep brown men in line (Razack 2004).

By reproducing colonial discourses in the present day, gender ideology retains its earlier function. The notion that Muslim women need saving from Muslim men has fuelled the "War on Terror" and has been used to justify the U.S.-led invasions of Iraq and Afghanistan (Razack 2004, 2005). The perceived oppression of Muslim women is also used to paint Muslim communities in a negative light and to perpetuate beliefs about Western superiority. Once again, gender is used to define the West as an advanced civilization with a unique commitment to women's rights and the non-West (the Orient) as a place yet to progress into the age of gender equality (Razack 2004, 2005).

Interestingly, the image of "oppressed" Muslim women may help Western women feel "liberated," despite the existence of systematic gender inequalities in Western societies. A recent qualitative study (Scharff 2011) finds that European women use the image of the "oppressed Muslim woman" to reject feminism in their lives: "The theme of the oppressed Muslim woman stabilizes [their] positioning as free and emancipated, playing a vital role in the repudiation of feminism as unnecessary to their lives in contemporary western democracies" (Scharff 2011, 131). Similarly, Razack (2004) argues that by comparing their status with their non-Western sisters, Western feminists can draw a line in the sand – of course, their side of the line is "better."

While the image of the oppressed Muslim woman may make some Western women feel better about themselves, my research shows that this racialized gendered identity has serious consequences for Muslim women in their daily lives. Because people assume Muslim women are weak and lack agency, they may feel safer expressing negative thoughts and actions towards Muslim women than Muslim men. Ironically, the focus on the oppression of Muslim women in their own communities makes them more vulnerable to discrimination from the outside.

Strategies of Resistance

Homi Bhabha (2004), in his highly influential analysis of colonialism, highlights the agency of colonized people, which he feels has often been overlooked and underplayed. He argues that colonization is much more than a simple domination of one group over the other, and unexpected forms of resistance can be found in history. In other words, there is a space for strategies of resistance and contestation. This understanding is key to my analysis of young Canadian Muslims' experiences.

   The previous sections reveal that many interviewees feel increasingly victimized in the post-9/11 era. They no longer feel safe in Canada, they face harassment in public spaces, their religious practices are stigmatized, they suffer a loss of economic security, and their gender identities become racialized and stereotyped. How do they deal with this? How do they contest the dominant conceptions imposed on them, including the assertion that they are a threat to Canada and do not belong in the country? As I found during the interview process, young Canadian Muslims are resourceful: they employ multiple strategies of resistance and attempt to acquire national capital in various ways.

   Some counter verbal and physical abuse by contacting the police. When Zeba's friend was verbally harassed and called a terrorist by people driving by, she called the police. Zeba comments that the police officer was very helpful: "He calmed down my friend and said he would try to identify the people in the car." While the police were helpful in this instance, this is unfortunately not always the case. For instance, Abdual says that the police did not help when his wife, who wears the hijab, was verbally and physically harassed on the street:

> It's happened two times to my wife. One time, it was a real attack from a homeless individual. He was swearing a lot and saying, "Muslim – you're friends of Bin Ladin, get out of my country," and he's trying to touch my wife; he's trying to attack her. Even my son was there, he's like six years old, and he was scared and nobody tried to help her on the street. She was on Bay Street, a very lively area, at around five p.m., all the people are going, and nobody tries to help her, and she called the police … The really bad thing is that she was waiting at the place for one whole hour, waiting for the police to come so she could report what happened, and they didn't come. And she called me here, and I said to her "Just go home," and they went to home, and I called 911 again, and they came around eleven p.m. – which is six hours after what happened. We had thought that we are in a country that is safe. It can't be that you call the police and say "Somebody is attacking me," and police don't come. It's something similar to what happened in rural areas in Egypt, which we are always making fun of. It was really a bad experience. We are not living in the best of place, as we should be.

Abdual says that after this experience, he started to regret his decision to move his family to Canada from Egypt.

Other institutions may refuse to help as well. Maria talks about how the administration at the University of Toronto failed to respond when she and a friend were verbally and physically harassed at Hart House, a student athletic centre at the university:

> This woman starts shouting, "Go back to your country." I was born in Kitchener. And she continues, "You terrorists." She looked so mad. She's screaming at the top of her lungs. It is 12:20 p.m., and Hart House is full, and there are tons of people there in that room, and not one person got up to say anything. I told my friend "Let's just get out of here." When we get to the Hart House desk, we told them that there was this angry woman shouting at us, and asked them to call the campus police. They called right away, and the police did not show up. They just didn't respond. We went to the campus police ourselves – you have to cross campus ... and they said, "Oh we got that phone call," and I was "Like that didn't sound urgent to you?" And we were actually scared because she looked so angry. I'm generally not scared of people, but if you have the guts to touch me in public, you have the guts to do much more. So we went to the police ourselves, and gave the description of the two women and what they did. But nobody called us, nobody contacted us, and nobody asked us anything ... We assumed that they would. We thought there would be a protocol when something happens ... At least a call from the diversity officer or the campus police or Hart House or somebody, but nobody really contacted us.

Frustrated by the lack of university response, Maria and her friend went to the Muslim Student Association, which later organized a workshop about Islamophobia on campus. They invited the university administration to discuss the incident, Maria remembers:

> The workshop was good, but it was just odd because it was put on by students and not by any administration. The University of Toronto diversity officer at the workshop told us "not to make a big deal," and we said, "We wouldn't have made a big deal out of it if you guys had done something." And then we went talk to him personally, and then he did apologize as well. The ironic thing is that there should be university protocol when something like this happens, like there's university protocol when there's sexual harassment. There is still not a protocol for racial harassment.

As Scott Poynting and Barbara Perry (2007) remind us, "hate-motivated vilification and violence can only flourish in an enabling environment," and discrimination is often conditioned by the activity or inactivity of the state (161). By failing to reprimand hate crimes, law enforcement agents and major institutions like universities enable those who commit them and reinforce discrimination. But as my research shows, interviewees like Maria refuse to be silenced, courageously challenging institutions that fail to respond to discrimination.

My interviewees fight back in other ways as well, for example, by being on their "best behaviour." Samir says:

> If you make one wrong comment … you've kind of screwed yourself over. It might be something as small as a joke. If it's taken the wrong way, people are going to paint Muslims with the same brush. I have to be on my best behaviour. Like, I have to be the best Muslim possible. If not, it's going to affect all Muslims. If I do something, people are going to expect that all from all Muslims. So for example, if that Muslim guy lied to me … that means all Muslims are liars … Let's say if I was a Christian Caucasian male, and I just happen to lie to somebody, it's seen as you know – he lied – he is a bad person. Whereas, you know, if it's a Muslim, it's like, "He lied, he's a Muslim – it's part of his faith."

Clearly some young Canadian Muslims feel pressure to represent their faith in a positive light. Muslim women who wear the hijab are especially vulnerable to this, as Rubina and Atiya note:

> RUBINA: I always feel that I have to be on my [best behaviour]. Because I know that people look at me, and I know that I represent my religion, and I worry about everything that I do know – that this is what I represent, and I know what people think about it, and on every occasion if it's possible maybe I try to change their minds about Islam.
>
> ATIYA: I feel like I have more responsibility. Like, if I was experiencing road rage before, and I wanted to flip the bird, I would have done it before. But now I am wearing the scarf, and now they are going to look at me and feel that all Muslims are like this, and so I feel that I have to be more aware of my actions. I had to be more careful because I know that people are not going to be, "Oh she is a crazy driver." They are going to say, "That Muslim is a crazy driver." So I have to be on my best behaviour all of the time. So yeah, it has made me more aware of my actions and how people would react. So even if I am having a terrible day, I will still smile at people because people are just going to think that I am a crappy Muslim. And because I wear the scarf, I am representing my faith the entire time.

In short, to present a positive image of Muslims, the interviewees may conceal their negative emotions and work to display a positive image. Haleema, who wears the hijab, says she wears bright colours to look more positive and "less oppressed":

> I try not to wear all black because I think that that is another stereotype or idea, that Muslims are so gloomy and that they always dress that way ... So I try to put a positive image to kind of counter that negative image.

Alisha, who also wears the hijab, tries to be on her best behaviour while using public transportation:

> Yeah, like, when you walk on the subway, you want to get up [from] your seat every time an old lady passes by. I really want to get up and let her have the seat – yes, it's a part of my religion – but it's also so people don't think that I am rude.

Through small efforts of this nature, women challenge the label of the "bad" Muslim, so often attributed to Muslims who practise their religion publicly. They try to refute the idea that they are barbaric, uncivilized and oppressed.

While trying to represent a positive image of Muslims is a strategy of resistance, it is also tied to what Nadine Naber (2006) calls the "internment of the psyche." This concept refers to the fear Muslim communities internalize as a result of state surveillance and the everyday acts of discrimination directed towards them. Because of the internment of the psyche, Naber argues that individual Muslims may start self-regulating their behaviour. This has clearly happened among some of my interviewees, where they feel they have to be on their best behaviour to counter negative stereotypes. This self-regulation is also tied to my interviewees' efforts to accumulate national capital (Hage 1998). In order to be seen as legitimate by the dominant group, my interviewees try to show that they are "good" and safe Muslims.

Because their gender identities have been racialized, there are also gender variations on how my interviewees try to acquire national capital. As previously discussed, in the post-9/11 era, Muslim women are increasingly imagined as passive and oppressed by their communities, while Muslim men are perceived as barbaric and dangerous. As a result, Muslim women try to establish themselves as educated and independent individuals in order to be seen as legitimate by the dominant group; meanwhile,

Muslim men project themselves as being liberal, egalitarian, and peaceful to be viewed as legitimate. Alisha and Haleema say the following:

ALISHA: I'm doing biochemistry. And professors, they don't expect a girl wearing a hijab to walk into their class. They think someone like me wouldn't be interested in university life, or if I was, I'd more interested in social sciences. A lot of us try to shatter these stereotypes, but yes, we do carry an added burden of having to shatter them. I try to be more outgoing in class and be nicer to non-Muslims. In class, I try to give it my best. I try to impress the prof. I try to ask [smart] questions and just try to be intelligent. Even when I am talking to a white person in general, I try not to ask dumb questions. I also try to be more outgoing – something I am not – but just to shatter their image of me being obedient and, you know, just staying at home and not doing anything. It makes my life more difficult because I have to shatter these stereotypes. So in that sense, it makes life harder on me.

HALEEMA: Me being in school should show you that Muslim women can be smart, they can be intelligent. And don't stereotype us in that way, that we should stay home, and cook, and clean, and you don't stereotype us in that way ... I think a lot of minorities feel, especially when you are the only minority in class, you feel that you have to excel because you feel that extra burden. You have something to prove. Like speaking up more in tutorials and whatnot, especially when you are the only Muslim girl.

Some Muslim women who wear the hijab challenge gender stereotypes by directly confronting their detractors. Aneesha's and Atiya's ability to fight back is noteworthy:

ANEESHA: First, I would not just reply back if someone said something mean, and ... the other time, someone said I was "making soldiers die in Afghanistan." I actually went up to the person and said, "How I am causing anything?" And I had a discussion with that person. I said, "How can I, as a Muslim practising my religion in Canada, be causing people to join the army and cause them to die?" I tried to be rational with them. The person was dumbfounded. They couldn't believe how a Muslim girl was able to react to something like that.

ATIYA: My mom and us, we often get people giving us these weird looks, and I have this very aggressive character, and so sometimes, I say, "Hey, what are you looking at?" and that kind of freaks them out because they are like, "Oh, wow, she is really speaking out against us." But it is me saying you are not going to intimidate me.

By doing the opposite of what is expected, these women attempt to construct alternative meanings about what it means to be Muslim women.

A few Muslim men challenge the racialization of their gender identities. This includes contesting the notion that they are dangerous and violent, as Abdual and Dawoud say:

> ABDUAL: I am the father of two daughters. I want people to know that we are good Muslims. I want people to see that I am not some crazy and tough Muslim guy with my daughters. So it's a lot of burden. I feel like we need to show others that I actually do listen to my wife. So yes, I have this burden.
>
> DAWOUD: My outreach work in a non-Muslim community has been more about being an example. Being a visible practising Muslim, who would fit the profile otherwise of someone that they would be scared of. But then behaving in a manner, they should learn to accept me and not be afraid of me.

These experiences also speak to issues of white privilege. Tim Wise (2008) notes that an important component of white privilege is that one's daily life is freed from the need to fight racial stereotypes. Muslim Canadians do not have this luxury.

Conclusion

Most of my interviewees grew up in Canada feeling like outsiders because of their racial and "immigrant" identities. This worsened after 9/11, when the simple fact of being Muslim garnered attention; Muslims were increasingly perceived as dangerous and their religious identities racialized. These dominant conceptions have serious consequences.

They lost their sense of safety and security; simply stated, they lived in a climate of fear. They particularly felt vulnerable in public places and were often afraid to display their Muslim identity in public. Public places, especially public transit, are racialized spaces where they experienced verbal and physical abuse, simply for being Muslim. The abuse these young Canadians encounter often involves being told they do not belong in Canada. The vilification of Muslim identity goes hand in hand with a lack of respect for Muslim traditions and customs. Young Muslims feel their religious freedom is threatened when their religious practices, such as wearing the hijab, are ridiculed by other Canadians.

The hostility directed at Muslim communities spilled into their work and professional lives. Immediately following 9/11, many feared they would lose their jobs and that Muslim businesses would lose clients. Because Muslims sense their identity as a disadvantage when looking for work, some conceal it or are pressured by others to do so. Many speak of workplace harassment. They also worry about their career prospects.

Gender identities are racialized as well, and this can be particularly dangerous for Muslim women. Because people assume them to be weak and less likely to retaliate, they may face more physical harassment than Muslim men. They are also highly visible if they wear the hijab, and given the general hostility towards the hijab, discrimination may be heightened.

The lived experiences of Muslim Canadians give us the opportunity to reflect on how multiculturalism functions as a daily reality. Enakshi Dua and associates (2005) argue that multiculturalism actually creates structures that keep racialized Canadians in a marginal social, political, cultural, and economic position. To this, Jasmin Zine (2012) adds that multiculturalism has not guaranteed equality in acceptance and instead obscures relations of power and privilege that shape the nation. The experiences of my interviewees certainly support these arguments. My findings reveal that multiculturalism reinforces and supports white privilege. David Goldberg (2002) says "whiteness" appears in social institutions and social spaces in subtle and overt ways to maintain white dominance; multiculturalism does not challenge this. This can be seen in my interviewees' limited access to important social institutions, including the workplace. Put simply, multiculturalism fails to challenge issues of power and privilege in Canada.

When Canada introduced multiculturalism, it helped create a myth of Canada as a nation innocent of racism. In this ideology, Canada has moved beyond a white settler state to a liberal democratic one (Mackey 1999). However, this is just a story that Canada has been telling itself and the rest of the world. In reality, Canada has a long way to go before it becomes a nation that equally values all citizens regardless of 'race', religion, and ethnicity.

What Canada remains is a colonial nation that is now using the othering of Muslims, as a way to exalt its national identity as belonging to a superior order of humanity, as Sunera Thobani would put it (2007). While in the formation of the Canadian state, this exaltation was made possible through the figure of the lawless and savage native; in the post-9/11 era, the crystallization of Canadian national identity is achieved by mixing issues of security, culture, and gender with religion, resulting in the racialization of Islam. As a result, Muslims are seen as belonging to inferior cultures that are barbaric, outside the realms of Western civilization, and therefore a threat to Western nations. In the post-9/11 era, the positioning of Muslims as the new racial other allows the white Canadian national subject to be exalted as liberal, modern, democratic, and egalitarian. This privileged subject, in turn, expresses *governmental belonging* by trying to protect Canadian society from dangerous "Muslim terrorists" who are physical and cultural threats to the national hegemony. Acting as *nationalist space managers*, many white Canadians feel entitled to banish Muslim Canadians from public spaces, to verbally and physically harass them, to question their religious practices, to pressure them to assimilate, and to ask them to leave the country.

Thobani (2007) argues that the acts of telling someone to "go home" or ripping off someone's hijab should not simply be seen as isolated hate crimes. She categorizes them as rituals and rites of citizenship, similar to the national anthem and the rising of flags (80). She maintains that these rites of citizenship have remained consistent throughout Canadian history and are often passed on from generation to generation:

> Identifying these practices as rites of citizenship directs attention to their important function in reinforcing their legitimate belonging, in reinforcing their incontestability of citizenship as they act their insider status ... They reflect who is power and who is prohibited from exercising such power. (80)

Though acts of discrimination, self-exalted Canadians express their superiority over Muslim others. They reaffirm their historically privileged positions and express their own belonging by excluding the other. This revival of the Canadian national subject is particularly dangerous for Muslim women, who face the brunt of many hate crimes.

Moreover, Thobani (2007) notes that exaltation does only work symbolically; it also gives rise to insiders' desire to protect the perceived sparse resources and entitlements of the nation (such as land, employment, mobility, citizenship rights, etc.) for themselves and to limit others' access to them. It should not be surprising, then, that in their interactions with fellow Canadians, my interviewees increasingly experience infringement on their rights as Canadians, including their right to use public transportation without harassment, their right to religious freedom, and their right to employment equity.

As noted in the previous chapter, Hage (1998) says that in day-to-day living, certain Canadian citizens are made to feel more or less national than others. The incompatibility between the state's formal accept-ance of new citizens and their lived experiences of national belong-ing becomes most apparent in the every day. Although young Muslim Canadians have formal legal citizenship, this has not guaranteed their recognition as a part of the nation. Instead, they feel like outsiders within the nation. Hage sees legal citizenship only as an entry into "the game of achieving an embodied citizenship that is recognized as legitimate by the dominant national community" (55). This "game" is played by acquiring national capital in order to be seen as legitimate by the dominant group. Perceived as dangerous others, young Canadian Muslims make various attempts to convert themselves into a state of national belonging. They present themselves as "safe" citizens, give a positive representation of their religion, conceal any negative emotions, and counter gender stereotypes. However, as the othering of Muslims is now an essential mechanism of national identity in the post-9/11 era, such attempts most likely will yield limited results.

Nakano Glenn (2002) argues that when individual actors from the dominant national community define and redefine citizenship bounda-ries, they draw on social norms and values established by the larger societal structure. Poynting and Perry (2007) emphasize that state practices that stigmatize or marginalize historically oppressed groups, whether at the institutional or local level, legitimize the mistreatment of these same groups on the streets. Therefore, I dedicate the follow-ing chapter to examining how state-sanctioned surveillance practices at airports and border crossings impact young Muslims' sense of belong-ing and citizenship in Canada.

3 States of Exception: Young Canadian Muslims' Experiences of Security and Surveillance

Introduction

In the summer of 2006, Maria and her friend, both Canadian-born Muslims who wear the hijab, went to Egypt for the summer to take part in a special training practicum for their master's program in occupational therapy. While they had a great time in Egypt, their travel back to Canada was anything but fun. When they were connecting through London and were in line for the security check, two male security guards shouted, "You two get out of line." After taking them aside, the security personnel told them to "leave the airport." When the young women replied that they couldn't leave because they were going to Canada, they were "further checked and ... interrogated for five hours." This interrogation involved security personnel looking though their belongings, including "extensively" looking at Maria's MRI X-rays, which she had with her for medical reasons. Maria found this "quite intrusive" and had to stop them from putting her X-rays through the scanning machines, as this would have ruined them. The security personnel asked questions about their background, why they had gone to Egypt, and why they didn't just do the special school program in Canada. When Maria finally decided to protest, the following happened:

> Finally I got a little upset, and I asked them why they are asking me this, and why they didn't ask anybody else, and in front of everybody, the security guard said, "Why do you dress like that if you don't want to be questioned?" And so I didn't say anything; I just shut up. 'Cause if somebody is going to say something like that, no matter what I say, they are going to

refuse everything I say based on what I'm wearing. The only thing I said in response was, "It's sad to know that racism still exists."

This is one example of the mistreatment Muslims are subjected to at airports and border crossings and how they feel forced to comply with such surveillance, despite attempts at resistance.

During the course of the fifty in-depth interviews I conducted, I heard a number of similar stories. Many emphasize that for them, one of the most profound consequences of 9/11 has been this increased surveillance; they report racial profiling, hostile questioning, and intrusive searches by security personnel. The fear of being harassed and having citizenship rights undermined by state officials causes them to experience great anxiety when travelling.

State surveillance practices at airports and border crossings are one of the most troubling aspects of young Canadian Muslims' post-9/11 experiences. As shown in this chapter, these practices give meaning to the interviewees' identities as both Muslims and Canadians and to their citizenship rights in Canada, ultimately impacting their sense of belonging in Canadian society. In order to give these experiences the attention they deserve, I focus on three key issues. First, I explore how Canadian Muslims experience surveillance at airports and border crossings. This includes how they experience the targeting of their Muslim identity through extensive questioning and searches, the undermining of their sense of Canadian citizenship, racialization, and gendered surveillance. Second, I examine how young Muslims have handled and responded to state surveillance. Third, I investigate how they experience surveillance in their daily lives.

States of Exception

To fully understand Maria's experience of being harassed at the airport and similar experiences, we need to locate them within the complex web of the "War on Terror" and the intensified state surveillance of post-9/11. Michel Foucault (1977) argues that throughout time society has used various disciplinary technologies to domesticate populations and turn individuals into docile citizens – with penal institutions being prime examples. Foucault adds that modern states have increasingly moved away from exceptional disciplines such as arrest and prison to more generalized and diffuse forms of state, mutual, and self-surveillance. Yasmin Jiwani (2012) elaborates that in the post-9/11 era, heightened and persuasive surveillance has taken disciplinary technologies to an entirely new level, and modern states have widened their powers to regulate citizens' lives by punishing behaviours deemed a "threat" to national security. As in previous disciplinary technologies, racialized bodies are more vulnerable to punishment and containment through state surveillance practices than other bodies. Jiwani likens the treatment of Muslims in the wake of 9/11 to that of black and native populations. But the rhetoric surrounding the "War on Terror" overshadows (using Jiwani's words) the colour line in which disciplinary technologies operate and gives modern nation states a free pass to do whatever they want in the name of national security.

Michael Williams (2003) reminds us that security is not an objective condition, but the outcome of specific social and political processes. The "War on Terror," which is premised by a language of national security, needs to be understood in similar terms. Richard Jackson (2005) emphasizes that the "War on Terror" is both a set of institutional practices and an accompanying set of political narratives. He argues that the language of the "War on Terror" is not simply a set of neutral or objective policy debates about realities of terrorism and counter terrorism; rather, it is a discourse specifically designed to make the war seem reasonable, responsible, and "good," and to silence any counter-arguments questioning state power. Central to this discourse is an imagined struggle between "barbarism" and "civilization" – wherein Muslims are imagined to be outside of modernity and posing a threat to Western civilizations (Jackson 2005).

A hyperbolic language of threat marks this discourse. Jackson (2005), for example, notes that it goes beyond a threat of sudden violent death to threaten "our way of life" and the "peace of our world." Instead of reassuring the nation that 9/11 was an exceptional and unique event, Jackson says, the George W. Bush Administration chose to construct it as a new age of terror – the start of a deadly form of violence directed at Americans and civilized people around the world, including a threat to principles of freedom and democracy. The "War on Terror," then, becomes one of "good" versus "evil," wherein Muslims are envisioned as inhumane, violent, and extremist. Jackson notes that this construction is convenient and liberating for Western states; if an enemy is removed from the moral realm of human community, any action taken against him/her cannot be judged on moral terms. In other words, potential terrorists are not only ejected from our political community, they are removed from humanity itself.

Sherene Razack (2008) provides a similar account of the "War on Terror" through two interlinked arguments. First, there is *race thinking* – the denial of a common bond of humanity between people who are of European descent and those who are not. According to Razack, race thinking is a structure of thought that divides the world into the deserving and the undeserving, according to descent. Second, this colour line is increasingly governed by what Giorgio Agamben (2005) has termed the *state of exception*. The state of exception refers to the suspension of human and legal rights in the interests of national security; it involves the voluntary creation of a permanent state of emergency, leading to measures that curtail civil liberties and freedoms, creating categories of people who lack rights (Razack 2008). In states of exception, the rule of law does not apply. Since there is no common bond of humanity, there is no common law. In other words, because Muslims are marked as a different order of humanity, they enter a legal and bureaucratic zone where the full law does not apply. As a result, increasing numbers of people (mostly Muslims) are evicted from the political community, and categories of people who do not have rights because they do not deserve them are created, with inmates at Guantánamo Bay prison serving as a prime example (Razack 2008).

Razack (2008) elaborates that these states of exception are underpinned by the idea that modern enlightened secular people (the West) must protect themselves from premodern religious people (Muslims) through any means deemed necessary. The logic is a colonial (and orientalist) one: they are not like us and are likely to erupt in violence. The suspension of rights is justified by the logic that the colonized cannot be governed through the rule of law as Europeans can. Prevention of assumed violence justifies the state of exception. Race thinking becomes so embedded in law and bureaucracy that the suspension of rights appears not as violence but as the law itself. Razack argues that the eviction of Muslims from a political community is ultimately a racial process begins with Muslims being marked as a different level of humanity and being assigned a separate and unequal place in law.

At the heart of the state of exception is the notion that only unlimited state power can properly confront threats to the nation and that governments can do anything in the interest of governance (Razack 2008). We are led to believe that our security is such a priority that the suspension of civil liberties is necessary for the greater good (Khan 2012). Iris Marion Young (2003) adds that states of exception are justified through the logic of masculinist protection, wherein "state officials adopt the stance of masculine protector – telling us to entrust our lives to them, not to question their decisions and what will keep us safe" (9). Young says that through this logic of masculinist protection, Western states offer to ensure the protection of their citizens, as long as they obey and agree to the states' actions in the name of security. This obedience is deemed necessary to ensure the safety of the state. She argues that this yields an unequal relationship, where citizens come to occupy a position subordinate to the state.

As a result of their subordination, citizens are stripped of their ability to question state practices or demand independent reviews of their decisions, while officials working on behalf of the state are accorded a wide range of discretionary powers (Young 2003). Furthermore, security states do not justify their wars by appealing to sentiments of greed or desire for conquest; they appeal to their role as protectors. They claim that special measures of unity and obedience are required to ensure protection from unusual danger. Because they take the risks and organize the agency of the state, it is their prerogative to determine protective action. In such security states, there is no room for shared powers – or for questioning the protectors' decisions and powers (Young 2003).

Fear validates the state of exception. Since 9/11, citizens have been led to think of any bombing in any part of the world as an immediate threat to their own personal security (Fekete 2004). Liz Fekete says, "The constant reference to spectacular events, like those of 9/11 serves a wider political arena; that of manufacturing consent to increasingly intrusive surveillance and the circumscription of personal freedoms through the evocation of fear" (2004, 7). Muslims are depicted as threats, becoming scapegoats to garner support for the increased security and surveillance being perpetrated by Western states upon their citizens.

Two assumptions remain unchallenged in the state of exception. One is that we can always tell who the enemy is, and second is that the suspension of law will not affect those of us who are deemed to be within the political community (Razack 2008). In fact, Young (2003) notes that the majority of citizens in Western democracies have not strongly opposed the infringement of civil rights because they believe such practices will not be directed at them but will be used against others who are deemed to be threatening.

In sum, post-9/11 Western countries have been adopting enhanced security measures, with governments expanding their powers and reach to create a state of exception. The suspension of civil rights and liberties is presented as a necessary step to protect the nation from dangerous Muslim others who are deemed unworthy of belonging to the political community. Muslims are stigmatized, put under surveillance, denied full citizenship rights, and detained on the basis that they are uncivilized people located outside of modernity.

Canada's Anti-Terrorist Legislation

A key element in the securitization of Western states has been the introduction of a wide range of anti-terrorist legislation. After 9/11, Canada joined the U.S. and the U.K. in introducing and strengthening anti-terrorism legislation. Canada's anti-terrorism Bill C-36, adopted on 7 December 2001, modified twenty-two existing laws, including the Criminal Code, the protection of personal information, access to information, and the request for evidence. This new legislation also led to the creation of criminal offenses such as facilitating and enticing terrorist acts (Helly 2004; Poynting and Perry 2007; Hameed and Nagra 2015). Initially, these amendments were subject to a sunset clause and were to be time limited. However, in April 2013, Bill S-7, the Combating Terrorism Act, was passed in the House of Commons to extend these powers. This act reformed many of the provisions of early anti-terrorism legislation; it also imposed stiffer penalties and introduced a new prohibition against individuals leaving Canada to commit terrorism abroad (Parliament of Canada 2012). In the past year alone, Canada has also introduced Bill C-24 and Bill C-51, with the former allowing for the revocation of citizenship for committing national security offenses (Black 2014), and the latter for broadening surveillance power of CSIS and enhancing the internal sharing of information across all government departments (Forcese and Roach 2015; Hameed and Nagra 2015). Both have been highly controversial and have been highly criticized by academics and legal experts alike (Forcese 2014; Macklin 2014; Forcese and Roach 2015; Hameed and Nagra 2015).

Canada's new security configurations have been accompanied by protests from Canadian human rights groups and Canadian Muslim organizations, which caution that these measures not only make Muslim individuals vulnerable to intrusive surveillance but also reinforce public perceptions that Muslim communities are a threat to Canada (Helly 2004; Poynting and Perry 2007). Canada's anti-terrorist legislation has been criticized for being conceived with little time for thoughtful reflection or public debate (Poynting and Perry 2007). The legislation has also been accused of allowing security services at border crossings and airports to profile Muslims. Academics argue these new measures enable the Canadian Security Intelligence Services (CSIS) and the Royal Canadian Mounted Police (RCMP) to collect intelligence from people active within the Muslim community and from Muslims whose immigration status is uncertain (Helly 2004; Poynting and Perry 2007). Scott Poynting and Barbara Perry (2007) write that Canada's anti-terrorist legislation "allows for an unprecedented extension of intrusive law enforcement activities on one hand, and contraction of individual and collective rights on the other" (163).

According to Christopher Murphy (2007), Bill C-36 has transformed the governance of policing and security in Canada. Murphy argues that the bill "makes it easier for public police to get search warrants, detain without charge, compel testimony, expand the scope of legal surveillance, establish 'reasonable suspicion" instead of 'reasonable belief' as grounds for police action, and create new private 'investigative hearings'" (8). Murphy mentions that the recent "securitization" of public policing in Canada has broadened the police mandate, expanded the police role, and increased police power and resources. In fact, Murphy mentions that prior to 9/11 many political theorists were predicting a declining power and significance of the modern state. In the years before 9/11, the cost of policing had become a serious fiscal problem for governments at all levels, resulting in lean spending on public policing in Canada. In the wake of 9/11, this scenario dramatically changed. Police-administrated data indicate that from 2000 to 2005 aggregated police spending grew from $6.8 billion to $9.3 billion (in current dollars), representing an impressive 37 per cent increase (Murphy 2007). In comparison, between 1995 and 2000, there had been only a 17 per cent increase. Ultimately, the threat of terrorism has given the Canadian governments and the police new arguments to reassert the centrality and importance of the state. This has led to new national security policies, significantly increased security and policing expenditures, and the creation of new security oriented ministries and agencies (Murphy 2007).

The changes made in the anti-terrorist legislation and the expansion of policing are tied to the potential fears of terrorism that have been conjured up in Canada. For example, Murphy (2007) notes that in the immediate period following 9/11, a highly politicized "insecurity discourse" emerged in Canada that was constructed to convince Canadians to be supportive of a more aggressive national security agenda. Much of the initial public discourse was designed to bring forth the fragility and vulnerability of the Canadian state to both external and internal security threats. He writes,

> A new group of instant security experts filled the airwaves, TV screens and newspapers, and lecturing Canadians about their smug complacency, naive liberalism and false sense of security. They warned that Canada had become a hiding place for sleeper terrorist cells, a haven for illegal and smuggled immigrants, a source of illegal passports, a conduit for terrorist money-laundering and fund-raising, the creator of a dangerously liberal immigration system and the keeper of an under-policed border which posed a security threat to its powerful neighbour, the United States. (3–4)

Fears surrounding terrorism drastically changed the discourse surrounding racial profiling in Canada. The central concern was no longer whether racial profiling was taking place in Canada or how to prevent it. The discussion now became whether Canadian society could morally, legally, or politically condone racial profiling (Bahdi 2003).

The introduction of anti-terrorist legislation and the increase in surveillance in Canada is connected to Canada's geographical proximity to the United States. The United States is Canada's primary political, military, and economically. Not surprisingly, then, after 9/11, the United States demanded that Canada align its policies on immigration control, political asylum, and security with American ones (Choudhry 2001; Macklin 2001; Morgan 2001; Helly 2004; Lyon 2006). The pressure to harmonize with U.S. policies is tied to the widely held belief that Canada's liberal immigration and border policies pose a real security threat to the U.S. In fact, in the immediate aftermath of 9/11, some American senators suggested that Canada should suspend its immigration programs entirely and that the U.S.–Canada border be closed (Murphy 2007). Fear of a weakened alliance with the United States played an important role in the Canadian adherence to its demands. Under the leadership of former prime minister Stephen Harper, Canada became tied even more closely to the U.S. through various trade agreements and the conservative government's attempt to turn Canada into a nation similar to the U.S. where military history and militarized interests defined our values (Khan 2012).

In fact, the Canadian government has complied with American practices of extraordinary retention and has aided foreign security services in the detention and torture of Canadians travelling abroad (Khan 2012). Jasmin Zine (2012) notes that Canadian Muslims travelling abroad have been arrested and detained without charge and sometimes even tortured on information provided by Canadian officials. For example, Maher Arar was illegally deported to Syria by U.S. officials, with the consent of the Canadian government, where he was later tortured. Abdullah Almalki, Muyyed Nureddin, and Ahmad Abou El-Matti are other Muslim Canadians who were detained in Syria based on information provided by Canadian authorities, and later subject to violent beatings and solitary confinement (Zine 2012).

Perhaps the most high profile case of Canadian collusion with U.S. security forces to the detriment of a Canadian citizen is that of Omar Khadr. Omar Khadr, a Canadian citizen, was only fifteen years old when he was captured on 27 July 2002 by American forces following a four-hour firefight in Afghanistan (Williamson 2012). The U.S. military claimed he had killed a U.S. solider and provided material support for terrorism. He was later detained in the Guantánamo Bay detention camp where he was severely tortured. After several years of solitary confinement, he was convicted for war crimes under the United States Military Commissions Act of 2009 (Williamson 2012). However, the U.S. military commission played by its own rules. Under international law he should have been guaranteed rehabilitation and not imprisoned.

His case is the first modern-day prosecution of a child solider. Disregarding his status as a child solider, Canada chose not to seek extradition or repatriation, despite the urgings of Amnesty International, UNICEF, the Canadian Bar Association, and other prominent organizations (Williamson 2012). In April 2009, the Federal Court of Canada ruled that the Charter of Rights and Freedoms made it obligatory for the government to immediately demand Khadr's return (Williamson 2012). Similarly, in January 2010, the Supreme Court ruled that Khadr's constitutional rights had clearly been violated, but did not order the government to seek his return to Canada (Williamson 2012). Khadr was returned to Canada in 2012 to serve the remainder of his sentence, a decade after being unfairly confined in Guantánamo Bay.

Khadr's case provides a disturbing example of how the Canadian government has given the U.S. and other nations free reign to do whatever it wants to its Muslim citizens in the "War on Terror." This raises important concerns about what Canadian citizenship is supposed to mean for Muslim Canadians, if anything. When the Canadian government turns a blind eye to other nation states that are torturing its Muslim citizens, it renders them stateless, leaving them without a nation state to turn to (Edney 2012).

Canada has not only supported the U.S. in the torture of its Muslim citizens but has also subjected them to surveillance within its own borders. For example, through the use of the new anti-terrorist legislation, Canada has invoked "national security" to block incarcerated Muslims from learning what evidence is being used against them (Dossa 2008). Since 2001, security certificates have been used by Canada to jail six Muslims suspected of potential terrorist activity, with no trial and without any evidence shown to them, their lawyers, or the public. Furthermore, on 3 June 2006, when seven Toronto Muslim men, five under the age of eighteen, were arrested for having "intent" to engage in terrorism, no evidence was made accessible to their lawyers or the public (Dossa 2008). A 2004 report published by Canadian Council on American-Islamic Relations (CAIR-CANADA) documents that many Canadian Muslims have been questioned by law enforcement agents. Out of 467 respondents, 80 per cent had been contacted, and among those not contacted, about half (45 per cent) knew at least one Canadian Muslim who had been (CAIR-CANADA 2004). These encounters with law enforcement agents often involve the following: aggressive and threatening behaviour; threats of arrest; problematic and suggestive questions; improper identification; attempts to recruit participants as informants; and interrogation of minors (CAIR-CANADA 2004).

Simply stated, these and other measures of social control, policing, and legislative regulation that have emerged in the post-9/11 era undermine Muslim citizenship and sense of belonging in Western nations. Liz Fekete (2004) writes that "new legislation, policing and counter terrorist measures are casting Muslims, whether settled or immigrant, as the enemy within" (3). Eleanor Stein (2003) notes that racial profiling dehumanizes Muslims and constructs them as the enemy. Henri Thaler (2004) emphasizes that social control, policing, and legislative regulation have resulted in the racialization of Islamic personhood. What is further problematic is that the use of security and surveillance practices to construct Muslims as the enemy can result in discrimination in domains such as employment, financial relations, and personal relationships (Macklin 2001; Thobani 2007).

Inderpal Grewal (2003) adds that the construction of Muslims as the enemy provides an effective way to shore up nationalism. Grewal points out that the categorization of Muslims as the enemy has allowed the resurgence of American nationalism: "Thus within the racial hierarchies of the US, another racial formation was created that produced a new other that could produce 'Americans' through their solidarity with those who died or suffered in the attacks and through their difference from the terrorists" (548). The targeting of Muslims through state surveillance procedures performs a similar function in Canada, where the vilification of the Muslim other works to reaffirm Canadian national identity at the expense of Canadian Muslims.

Sunera Thobani (2007) and Fauzia Ahmad (2002) argue that the racial profiling of any minority group is indicative of the problematic relationship that all racialized people, immigrants and non-immigrants alike, have with Western democracies. Thobani says that racial profiling puts racial minorities "back" in their place as outsiders in the West. Ahmad and Audrey Macklin (2001) note that racial profiling and the detention of "Muslim-looking" individuals fall in line with past racialized Canadian immigration policies. Similarly, Shahnaz Khan (2012) argues that if we look at our history, we see a pattern wherein collective rights of an identifiable group have been trampled in the name of security, with the internments of Japanese and Ukrainian communities during the world wars being prime examples.

During the First World War anything or anyone seen as non-British was considered dangerous, unpatriotic, and possibly treasonous, and many groups faced internment (Boyko 2000). One group that faced internment was the Ukrainian population in Canada. As a result, with the enactment of the War Measures Act, the Canadian government sent Ukrainian immigrants to internment camps. Ukrainian schools were banned, cultural centres were closed, and it became illegal to speak Ukrainian in many towns. Furthermore, thousands of Ukrainians across the country were fired from their jobs simply because they were Ukrainian. This mistreatment has had long-term impact on Ukrainian immigrants in Canada (Boyko 2000).

Another group that faced internment under the guise of security were Japanese Canadians. During the Second World War, 22,000 Japanese Canadians were forced to leave their homes and were imprisoned in camps deep in the interior of British Columbia. This recast Japanese Canadians as being outside the imagined white collective space of the Canadian nation and marked them as an enemy (Oikawa 2002, 77). The construction of Japanese Canadians as uncivilized hinged upon the orientalist notions of their otherness, which was then used as a justification for the violent actions committed against them (Oikawa 2002). While the suspension of citizenship in a moment of crisis separated Japanese Canadian families and destroyed an economically vibrant community, it helped to consolidate the economic domination of white nationals at a time when both state and national formation were still in a state of flux (Thobani 2007). The internment of Japanese Canadians was an extension of a fifty-year history of discrimination against them (Oikawa 2002). For decades, Japanese Canadians had faced popular political resistance against their access to fishing licences, their ownership of land, and their access to employment and educational opportunities. While they were already excluded from the many rights of citizenship prior to the internment, the processes of dispossession and displacement served to strip them of any legal resources and legal rights well into the future (Oikawa 2002; Thobani 2007).

These two cases show us that in the past Canadian policy makers did not hesitate in the name of security to revoke citizens' rights. It is important to note, however, that the implementation of racist policies and laws has not been limited to moments of crises in Canada. Charles Smith (2007) argues that, throughout its history, the Canadian government has developed and implemented laws, policies, and procedures that have been racist – ranging from the sanctions of slavery and segregation to the racialization of law enforcement, criminal justice and immigration, and refugee determination processes.

The increased surveillance of Muslim communities in the wake of 9/11 is an extension of the racial profiling that has historically been directed at racial minorities in Canada. Roy Coleman and Michael McCahill (2011) remark that surveillance practices demarcate and reinforce social borders, with racial categories being one of the borders policed. In other words, by marking some as worthy of the entitlements and considerations associated with citizenship and others as unworthy, surveillance practices reinforce racial boundaries. In this chapter, I show how surveillance practices place Muslim Canadians on the periphery of the nation by stigmatizing them as racial others. Exploring these experiences also allows for the opportunity to consider how the logic of *states of exception* can impact a number of Muslim Canadians through their encounters with state surveillance practices at airports and border crossings. The purpose of this chapter, then, is not to evaluate the procedures of racial profiling but to consider what these experiences mean for young Muslims' sense of belonging and citizenship in Canada.

As mentioned earlier, my interviewees are extremely disturbed by the surveillance they experience at airports and border crossings. These sites have a profound impact on Canadian Muslims because these are the sites where Muslims directly interact with state policy and state agents. Sujit Choudhry (2001) writes:

First there is the use of profiling at the border, with respect to the degree of scrutiny that travellers-be they citizens, permanent residents, or visitors – receive by customs and immigration officers as they enter Canada. Second, there is the use of profiling by airport security, prior to boarding, on both domestic and international flights. (370)

Although racial profiling is not officially sanctioned at Canadian border crossings or at Canadian airports, racism as a racialized discourse is manifested in the articulation of state policies and practices (Bahdi 2003). Kent Roach (2002) elaborates that even when the law does not specify racial discrimination, potential for discrimination exists in the implementation. In this work, I contend that a racialized discourse is implicit in government attempts to ensure safety and security. More particularly, by authorizing "differences" and "similarities" between individuals at airports and border crossings, state practices are deeply involved in undermining individuals' sense of citizenship.

Airport security has become an increasing concern in Canada since 9/11 (Lyon 2006). Through section 4.7 of the Aeronautics Act,[1] employees of commercial airlines and airport security personnel have the discretion to decide if a person or his/her possessions should be searched (Choudhry and Roach 2003; Bahdi 2003). They can also remove someone from an aircraft. People who appear to be Muslim or Arab may face more scrutiny as a result of this discretionary power (Bahdi 2003). Furthermore, under section 4.83 of the Aeronautics Act, airline carriers can provide information about their passengers to governments. As a result, Reem Bahdi (2003) notes that individuals who are Muslim or look Muslim may be subject to surveillance in the U.S. despite having Canadian citizenship. Hence, Muslims are affected not only by Canadian laws but also by international policies. However, Bahdi also says that because racial profiling takes place on the ground and is often the result of discretionary decision-making, it is difficult to determine the extent to which it occurs. By exploring how young Muslims understand their experiences at airports and border crossings and how they attempt to deal with them, I hope to contribute to the limited knowledge about racial profiling at these sites. While no official legislation calls for profiling at border crossings in Canada, Anna Pratt and Sara Thompson (2008) find that, despite official denials, many border officers admit that racial profiling does occur. Border officials use the ambiguity about what actually constitutes racial profiling to engage in it without repercussions. Some define racial profiling as the explicit and official directive to target specific racial groups. Pratt and Thompson say that officials use this narrow definition to deny that profiling occurs. Racial profiling also involves "less official patterns and organizational mechanisms of racialized decision making that include 'race' but that extend also to other eclectic blends of ethnicity, culture and religion" (621). Pratt and Thompson find that border officials use an awkward mix of racial, national, and regional indicators to profile individuals. While they explore the strategies used by border officials, however, they do not document how these counter-terrorism measures impact the experiences and lives of young Canadian Muslims.

David Lyon (2006) notes that social sciences know relatively little about those that are under surveillance. In a bid to contribute to this knowledge, I focus on three key issues in this chapter. First, I explore how Canadian Muslims experience surveillance at airports and border crossings. This includes examining how they experience the targeting of their Muslim identity through intrusive questioning and searches, the undermining of their sense of Canadian citizenship, racialization, and gendered surveillance at airports and border crossings. Second, I examine how young Muslims have handled and responded to the surveillance they face at these sites. Third, I investigate how they experience surveillance in their daily lives. Exploring these issues helps us understand what surveillance practices mean to young Canadian Muslims and how they use individual agency to resist dominant conceptions attached to being Muslim.

Young Muslims' Experiences of Surveillance at Airports and Border Crossings

There is a widespread belief among the interviewees that Muslims are subject to extra surveillance at airports and border crossings. When asked whether they thought Muslims underwent extra searches at these sites, 49 out of 50 interviewees responded yes. Sixty per cent of the interviewees (30 out of 50) recalled feeling unfairly treated by security personnel while travelling. Meanwhile, 78 per cent (39 out of 50) say their family and friends have faced similar problems. This high percentage is important. Having people close to you face discrimination can be just as troubling as facing discrimination personally. Therefore, I examine not only the experiences of my interviewees but also the experiences of their friends and family.

Overall, the young Muslims in this study described in detail eighty-one incidents[2] in which either they or people they knew experienced unfair treatment at airports and border crossings by security personnel. Fifty-seven (70 per cent) of these incidents occurred at airports, while twenty-four (30 per cent) occurred at border crossings. The higher percentage of incidents at airports may be a result of the interviewees travelling more through airports than through border crossings. Forty-seven (58 per cent) of these incidents occurred while the interviewees were in the U.S. or trying to enter the U.S. Twenty-six incidents (32 per cent) occurred in Canada, six (7 per cent) occurred in England, and one each in Italy and Israel. These findings suggest that Canadian Muslims are indeed impacted by state practices at airports and border crossings in the U.S.

Arguably, the majority of the incidents occur in the U.S. Because of its close proximity to Canada, many young Canadian Muslims travel more to the U.S. than to Europe or other parts of the world. And because the U.S. substantially increased security and surveillance after 9/11, it is possible that Canadian Muslims are more vulnerable to discrimination at airports and border crossings when travelling there. However, since 32 per cent of the incidents occurred in Canada, the extra surveillance of Muslims at these sites is not restricted to the U.S., but is a problem in Canada as well.

In what follows, I examine young Canadian Muslims' experiences at airports and border crossings. I first explore how, feeling they are questioned and searched more than others, gives young Muslims the sense that they are perceived as a security threat as opposed to a peace-abiding citizen. Next, I examine how they feel their Canadian citizenship is threatened through surveillance practices. Then, I look at their experiences of racialization. I conclude by focusing on how young Muslims experience gendered surveillance at airports and border crossings.

Experiencing Invasive Questioning and Intrusive Searches

By and large, my interviewees say that state surveillances practices treat their Muslim identities as dangerous and as potential security risks. There is a prevalent feeling that Muslims are subject to greater physical intimidation at airports and border crossings, and this intimidation involves intrusive questioning and searches. Samir, a twenty-three-year-old man who immigrated to Canada from India as a young child, and Aatifa, a twenty-four-year-old woman who is a naturalized Canadian citizen with a Saudi Arabian background, say:

> SAMIR: I have had a number of bad experiences at the airport. If you're travelling with a group, you'll be taken in separate interrogations and you'll be asked really specific questions. Even if one question happens to be a little bit off from maybe one of your peers, even if it's the most irrelevant thing like, "How long have you lived at your current residence?" Maybe your sister will say three years, and maybe you'll say two years. Something as insignificant is taken as "Oh, maybe they're hiding something. This is their story, they messed up" ... So the whole being interrogated, one thing. Two, being interrogated separately from your peers, and three, just that fact you're being interrogated for travelling. Like, you haven't done a crime in the air, you're just travelling.
>
> AATIFA: This was very recent when I had a weird border experience. The [security] guy, first of all he couldn't say Bangladesh; instead he read it as Baghdad. I don't know if he was having fun or not. But he asked where we were going, so my dad said we were going to visit my uncle's place. And he started asking how long have you known them? How long have they lived there? Where do they live there? Do they rent a house or have they bought the house? All these nitty-gritty things, which I didn't think they were important, but he started asking these. We kind of got a little cynical at that point thinking the only reason he might've asked all those questions is just because he was waiting for an opportunity for us to get angry or say something like, "Why do you need to know all this?" so then they can justify pulling us over maybe.

As these comments show, young Muslims react with anger and frustration at being treated as potential security threats just because they are Muslim. Worse, they think security personnel try to trick them into saying something damaging or into acting hostile so they can be detained even further.

In addition to extra questioning, the young Muslims in this study believe that they and their belongings undergo extra searching at airports and border crossings. Muslims from diverse cultural backgrounds and different genders recall being singled out by security personnel. For instance, Sakeena, a twenty-seven-year-old woman who is Canadian-born with a Pakistani background, and Zaahir, who is a naturalized Canadian citizen with a Saudi Arabian background, say:

SAKEENA: Oh, in the airports actually, I've noticed a lot in the airports. I've done quite a lot of travelling post-9/11. And for instance I'll be with all Caucasian people, and I'll be the one that's stopped to go through my luggage and things like that.

ZAAHIR: When my brother and I were about to board the plane [in the U.S.], we were asked to come on the side for a security check by TSA agents where they checked our luggage again. They say it is random, but to me it doesn't seem very "random." I think people who are working there are privileged with exercising their judgment, which I think might be discriminatory.

Post-9/11 the George W. Bush Administration constructed the "War on Terror" as a response to an imminent threat to the safety of all civilized people all around the world – terrorist attacks could happen at any time and any place (Jackson 2005). The enemy that was conjured up in this war were Muslims that needed to be identified, classified, and destroyed in the name of Western civilization (Khan 2012). Since Muslims are imagined as the enemy presenting the "imminent" threat to Western nations, they are treated as dangerous others at airports and border crossings, and face the brunt of the increased securitization that has taken place post-9/11.

Being treated as potential terrorists can result in traumatic experiences for my interviewees, thus impacting their sense of safety and dignity. One of Amineh's friends who wears the hijab was strip-searched at the Washington, DC, airport despite not triggering the metal detector; she later successfully sued security officials for violating accepted procedures. To this, Zeba adds:

My friends when driving down to the States through the border, and they've had their entire car searched; they've had dogs come around their car. They have small children in their car, and they've had the dogs come around their car, scaring the kids. They've been held for about two, three hours at security.

The distrust of Muslims is so high that security personnel may have no regard for children with Canadian citizenship; they may even violate official surveillance procedures. The complete disregard towards Muslim children that are Canadian citizens brings to light the fundamental flaws in the "masculinist protectionist logic" used by state officials to justify state surveillance procedures. For example, Young (2003) mentions that Western leaders have used their role of protector of women and children to justify consolidating their executive power at home. What has been overlooked, however, is how this extension of state security can actually result in the victimization of Muslim children who are Canadian citizens.

Also as noted above, many interviewees feel that official attempts are made to downplay discriminatory practices at airports and border crossings. Most mention that when they are interrogated at airports and/or border crossings, they are told it is a "random" search. Yazeed, a twenty-one-year-old man who was born in the Sudan and came to Canada when he was twelve years old, says:

> They say they have "random" checks, but they don't seem "random" to me because I do get checked every time I go through them. They say it's a "random" check, but I do always get checked. Chance alone says it shouldn't be happening.

Many interviewees express frustration at being picked out of a line and told it is a "random check," when they firmly believe they are being targeted due to their Muslim identities.

It is important to question the purpose of classifying these checks as "random." Does it allow security personnel to conduct checks under the guise of fairness? Does it silence potential protests? Does the classification of searches as "random" bolster the official discourse, which states that no racial profiling occurs at airports and border crossings in Canada and the United States? Or does it help to hide the violation of Muslim's citizenship rights?

Although security personnel classify these checks as "random," they don't hesitate to question Muslims about their religious practices. Maria says she has been "questioned" about her faith, a fact that she finds "ironic." She notes that security personnel will ask "if you're practising" or "what you believe in," which is "funny cause what does it have to do with searching my bag?" This type of questioning illustrates that security personnel at airports and border crossings equate Islam with suspicion and terrorism, a point also made by academics (Helly 2004; Fekete 2004; Thaler 2004). The practising of the Muslim faith is then seen as a justification for subjecting Muslims to extra surveillance. This can also be seen in Maria's experience described at the beginning of this chapter when she was asked at the London airport by security personnel, "Why do you dress like that if you don't want to be questioned?"

Razack (2008) argues that secularism can function as governmentality. Foucault's (1977) concept of governmentality refers to the ways in which individual subjects are governed through various institutions and processes that organize modern life. Razack (2008) argues that secularism operates as governmentality when Muslims are sanctioned by state practices for simply following their religious faith. Maria's experience illustrates how surveillance practices can be used to control and punish those that follow a religion that is increasingly imagined to support a violent hatred of the West. By targeting those that publicly practise Islam, surveillance practices also reinforce the categorization of "good" Muslims versus "bad" Muslims. As mentioned in chapter 2, Muslims that adopt no distinctive dress and who are secular are often considered as being "good" Muslims. Conversely, those that are very religious or publicly practise Islam are often envisioned as "bad" Muslims, presenting a threat to Western nations (Ramadan 2010).

Overall, most interviewees believe that their Muslim identities are treated as security risks, and as a result, state surveillance practices are targeted towards Muslims. Because airports and border crossings have become such a hostile environment for them, even when Muslims undergo standard searches, the emotional experience of being searched at airports and border crossings is different for them than it is for others. This can be seen in Aaeesha's account of her father's experience of being searched after 9/11: "My dad was really angry. Because he wouldn't have any trouble, he'd go through fine, and now it's, like, he is stopped. He has to take off his belt and everything, and before (9/11) he didn't have to do that."

It may be argued that since 9/11 non-Muslims also have to take off more of their belongings while going through security check points. However, when Muslims are searched at airports and border crossings, they fear they are being targeted because of their religious identity, and this affects their emotional experience of being searched. This is the cost of vilification of Muslim identity. There has been so much targeting of Muslims that they end up questioning their every experience at airports and border crossings, even when discrimination may not be easily apparent.

Experiencing Their Citizenship Being Challenged

Ghassan Hage (1998) mentions that practical national belonging (the everyday acceptance or non-acceptance as a subject of belonging) can have consequences for one's official status. Similarly, Vijay Agnew (2007) argues that different forms of belonging do impact on actual citizenship. Hence, the discourse surrounding Muslims as being dangerous others and not real Canadians can present real consequences for them when they try to actualize their citizenship rights as Canadian citizens. This can be seen in my interviewees' experiences.

For example, surveillance at airports and border crossings is often experienced by the interviewees as a direct challenge to their Canadian citizenship. Seventy-three per cent (22 out of 30) of the interviewees who recall facing discrimination at these sites are Canadian citizens; 40 per cent (12 out of 30) were born in Canada; while the remaining 33 per cent (10 out of 30) are naturalized citizens. When these interviewees and their family members face surveillance at airports and border crossings in Canada, they see it as a direct challenge to their Canadian citizenship. Aaeesha and Farah, twenty-year-old Canadian-born Muslim women who do not wear the hijab and who come from East African and Indian backgrounds, comment:

AAEESHA: You could be a Canadian citizen, and you could have lived here for years, and yet they will stop you. I don't agree with that. And I find that they do that more and more. I think that the trust citizens had before 9/11 is not there anymore.

FARAH: It is saddening that a country that you live in would do that to you [profile you], that they would do that to a loyal citizen that had been living here for so long.

Clearly, Muslims' sense of citizenship and belonging in Canada is impacted by the surveillance procedures at airports and border crossings within Canada. They feel *allegiance,* an important component of citizenship, is not allocated to them (in other words, they are not viewed as loyal members of society) and, as a result, they face intrusive questions and searches.

A few interviewees are especially troubled about the difficulty some Canadian Muslims experience re-entering Canada after travelling abroad. Asima and Zaahir describe the following:

ZAAHIR: Coming back to Canada has always been a problem. People would see that I am born in Saudi Arabia, that I am Muslim, my family is all Muslim, so based on that they spend a lot of time going through our belongings or doing security checks. The reason why I see it as unfair is that we have been Canadians for eighteen years without a blemish or any bad records.

ASIMA: When my dad was coming back, it was not actually in the States, it was in Canada. In the airport, they stripped all of his stuff, went through everything, and they made him take off his shoes. And he was a Canadian citizen. He has been here for twenty-three years. They checked everything, and they still kept him there for so long for questioning. And to everybody else was they were saying, "Just go through." He was really upset about that, especially because it happened in Canada. He was not expecting something like that to happen in Canada. It kind of scared him. Flying after an incident like that and then being harassed just got to him, and he got really upset about that.

Blackwood and associates (2012) remark that while in most other places national identities are taken for granted, airports are one of the few places where they are made implicit. Through these experiences Muslims are directly made to feel as though they are potential threats to Canada – not its citizens. According to Macklin (2007), an unconditional right of legal citizenship is the right to enter and remain in one's country of citizenship. Although Canadian Muslims have legal citizenship, some feel they have to fight for this unconditional right, to enter, which is reluctantly granted by security personnel. Although these interviewees have formal legal citizenship in Canada, they do not always feel they have substantive citizenship – that is, the ability to exercise rights of citizenship. Even though they are Canadian citizens, they fear their rights can be revoked.

Another significant way my interviewees' experienced blatant disregard of their Canadian citizenship was by the questioning techniques employed by security personnel. For instance, Dawoud, a twenty-five-year-old who was born in Saudi Arabia, says:

They start off with a simple, "What do you do? When did you move to Canada?" I normally get picked up after they say, "Where were you born?" and I say, "Saudi Arabia," and you see their expression change, and they immediately send me inside. So they ask questions like, "Why did you move to Canada?" and I'd say, "Well, my parents moved." And, "Why did they move?" "Well, they wanted a better education for their kids and a better future." "You're done your education now?" "Yes." "Why haven't you gone back?" Like, "I'm not a Saudi citizen. I never was." I was a Pakistani citizen because Saudis don't give citizenship. And I am a Canadian citizen now. It's my home. I look at it as my home. So sometimes the questions become very annoying. And I've been asked that question every single time, "Why don't you go back?"

By continuously questioning their citizenship, border officials can make the participants feel like illegitimate members of the nation despite their Canadian citizenship.

Furthermore, many interviewees also feel that their Canadian citizenship is not recognized when trying to enter the United States. The vast majority of the interviewees recall experiencing problems when travelling to the United States. A few interviewees recall being refused entry into the United States because they have names similar to individuals on the U.S. no-fly list, while some have been refused entry without specified reasons. Others refer to only entering the U.S. after overcoming major challenges. For example, Amber, a twenty-four-year-old woman born in Canada to a Pakistani father and a German mother, recalls a "humiliating" and "traumatic" experience of surveillance when she and two friends, a "white" Christian man and a Lebanese Muslim man, tried to cross the border from British Columbia into the United States. The Christian friend was left alone, but the Lebanese friend was strip- and cavity-searched by U.S. customs, and Sakeena was interrogated for an hour. Similarly, Rashid, a twenty-two-year-old man who came to Canada at the age of fourteen and who comes from an Indian background, recalls the following:

A friend of mine was going to a conference in Washington from Vancouver. He went to the border wearing a turban and they stopped him and asked him where he was going. He took them aside and strip-searched him. They detained him for eight hours and then they sent him back to Canada. This happened at the border.

Davina Bhandar (2008) says the U.S.–Canada border is constituted differentially, depending on the racialized, classed, and gendered bodies passing through it. Up until 9/11, it was a "friendly" border in public discourse, although it was not such a friendly one for migrants and non-white immigrants. The "War on Terror" radically altered this public image by conflating border management with security issues (Bhandar 2008; Hiller 2010). The tightening of the U.S.–Canada border is tied to beliefs that Canada's liberal immigration and border policies make it a safe haven for terrorists and a security threat to the U.S., claims exaggerated by media reports (Hiller 2010; Murphy 2007).

Not surprisingly, my interviewees experience the border as difficult to navigate. This is particularly troubling as they quite rightly believe their Canadian citizenship should allow smooth entry into the U.S., given the close relations between the two nations. However, Bhandar (2008) points out that while crossing the U.S.–Canada border is often understood as a shared sense of entitlement for both Canadians and Americans, it has historically "not been a friendly point of entry and exit for those who fit uncomfortably within the boundaries of a national sense of belonging on either side of the border" (284). Similarly, Jane Helleiner (2010) says border crossings between Canada and the U.S. are stratified according to "perceived racialized, classed, gendered, regionalized and citizenship positionings," reinforced and expanded since 9/11 (96). With the racialization of Muslim identity as a security threat, the citizenship of Muslim Canadians has lost currency, especially at the border. This has many consequences for my interviewees, disrupting their travel plans, limiting their employment prospects, and restricting their access to family and friends.

Evelyn Nakano Glenn (2002) argues that citizenship is often localized, and the actions of state agents at the local level determine whether certain groups have substantive citizenship. By specifically targeting Canadian Muslims, security officials at airports and borders actively participate in the interviewees' sense of citizenship and belonging in Canada. Many of my interviewees are troubled about the manner in which they are treated by security personnel. Two women who wear the hijab, Alisha and Zora, mention:

ALISHA: They [security personnel] just direct you more. They try to be more rude. And they just try to have this thing, like this, not superiority, just ... just try to be hard, just try to be more ... I don't know ... try to be more rude ... just 'cause you're Muslim they try to be more rude so that you'll feel intimidated.

ZORA: When I flew one time, and I was entering the U.S., I was asked questions like, "Have you ever been to the Middle East?" "Are you from Iraq?" And "Have you ever been to Baghdad?" ... um, "Do you support the regime there?" ... um, "What is your religion?" You know? It was not the questions themselves but the manner in which they were asked that was quite aggravating. They were trying to provoke us. The guy was pretty sarcastic in his tone. Like, it's obvious that I am Muslim, but he's like, "What's your religion?"

State officials at border crossings and airports have the discretion to determine whether an individual or their belongings should be subject to higher scrutiny than others. Pratt and Thompson (2008) remark that this widespread discretion is "enabled by protectionist and quasi-chivalrous narratives that represent frontline borders officers as benign guardians of public safety – whose pre-emptive and morally charged work protects the endangered nation, local communities and innocents from harm" (625). Bahdi (2003), however, reminds us that when security personnel search Muslims, they do not approach them with a clean slate; instead, "decision makers operate against a backdrop of ingrained, but often unconscious stereotypes," including the notion that Muslims are fanatical and prone to violence (306). The discourse surrounding the "War on Terror" posits Muslims as barbarians threating the Western way of life. As a result, security personnel don't just impose extra security checks on Muslims, they also treat them with hostility and anger. They engage in the victimization and harassment of Muslims that go much farther than just performing extra security checks. Racial profiling, hence, gives security personnel the legitimacy to express racist attitudes and their own hatred towards Muslims.

Nakano Glenn (2002) also notes that the maintenance of citizenship boundaries relies on "enforcement not only by designated officials, but also by so called members of the public" (52). In the southern United States, for example, bus segregation was made possible not only by white drivers but also by white passengers who imposed sanctions on blacks when they violated boundaries. A similar phenomenon may be occurring at airports and border crossings. Amineh and Aneesha, who both wear the hijab, say:

AMINEH: One thing that I noticed after 9/11 is that flight attendants, especially Air Canada's, were very rude to me. They were giving out pops, and I just wanted another pop, and she was just like, "Oh, so you are the one that is all picky about it that you just should be happy that I am giving you a pop." She was very rude and plus [gave me] a dirty look on top of that. As for other passengers, there was this one time that we were told by the passenger to go back to our country. We were travelling, and this lady beside us was pregnant, and the chair was bothering her and touching her stomach, so my mom just asked the lady in front of her to "pull up the chair," but that lady was like, "No why don't you just go back to your country? You have no right to speak and make demands," and my mom called out a flight attendant, and she was, like, "There is nothing that I can do for you," and she just basically sided with the woman.

ANEESHA: A guy I knew was praying before going on a flight [and] a woman felt uncomfortable and complained. They wouldn't allow him on the flight. For us in Islam it's mandatory to do five prayers a day, and you don't disturb anyone. He went to pray, and he wasn't allowed to go on the plane.

The undermining of Muslims' sense of Canadian citizenship has multiple dimensions. They feel their negative treatment is reinforced by fellow passengers, security personnel, and other airport workers. In their view, Muslims are seen as undeserving of common courtesy and face animosity from the general public. The wearing of the hijab, in particular, seems to result in hostile reactions from both security personnel and the public, an issue explored later in the chapter.

Peter Nyers (2006) argues that, post-9/11, the birthright citizenship of individuals born in the U.S. to non-citizen parents, particularly Muslims, is now deemed simply "accidental." And this concept of "accidental citizenship" has been used to undermine the ability of some native-born citizens to claim the rights and entitlements of birthright citizenship. A few of the interviewees believe that they are experiencing this phenomenon, as Maria's sentiments illustrate:

Muslims who are born in Canada to everybody there are not considered Canadian; they are considered Canadian-born. Which is a difference, because as a Canadian, you are part of this country, you contribute to society, you have some sort of pride. Canadian-born means you were just born in Canada. A Muslim born in Canada is considered Canadian-born. They are not considered Canadian, which is so different.

Thus, although born in Canada, many young Muslims feel that their birthright citizenship is being challenged and that they are seen as not belonging to Canada. This reinforces Thobani's (2007) view that racial profiling does not distinguish between those born in North America and those here temporarily, thereby illuminating the precarious nature of citizenship for all racial minorities.

Experiencing Racialization of Muslim Identity

Since citizenship boundaries are often drawn along racial lines, it is important to look at how young Muslims experience racialization at airports and border crossings. Nadine Naber (2006) argues that, in state surveillance practices, Muslims are perceived as the other, through the melding of multiple characteristics such as skin colour, name, country or origin, and clothing. My interviewees' experiences support this assessment.

To begin, many interviewees believe that state surveillance practices racialize Muslim identity by using physical markers such as skin colour, as described by Fareeda, a nineteen-year-old naturalized Canadian citizen with a Bangladeshi background:

> There are so many different kinds of Muslims. Muslims range from being the darkest skin tone to the whitest, blue eyes. But it is naturally the quintessential Middle-Eastern guy who has dark skin and a beard that they [security] are targeting.

Academics such as Robert Miles (1989) note that the characteristics used to racialize people vary historically; for example, in the post-9/11 era, beards are used to racialize Muslim masculinities. (The role of gender in how Muslims are treated at airports and border crossings will be discussed in more detail later in this chapter.)

Margaret Chon and Donna Arzt (2005) argue that because Muslim identity has been racialized to accord with dark skin colour in the post-9/11 era, non-Muslims of Middle-Eastern and South Asian descent, along with other people of colour, are lumped together with Muslims. As my research shows, these groups may also be targeted at airports and border crossings, implying that surveillance practices at airports can impact non-Muslim racial minorities. For instance, Bushra, recalls that in 2007, when her high school class went on trips to places like Vancouver, Los Angeles, and Hong Kong, during security checks at these airports, a non-Muslim Indian student was always picked out, along with her and other Muslim students for extra security checks, while the rest of her class was left alone. Similarly, Leela, a twenty-year-old Canadian-born Muslim woman from an Indian background, says:

> My family and I were stopped, and, yeah, my dad got very upset. Like, there were a few other families, but all the people that were pulled aside [at the airport] were "brown." And not necessarily Muslim, but we were all just "brown," the colour of our skin. And my dad got angry, and asked the guy who pulled us aside ..., "Why are you pulling only brown people aside? This is discrimination," and he's like, "No, no it's a random check."

Because Muslim identity has been racialized, people who simply look Muslim due to their skin colour may be treated with the same suspicion as Muslims. The use of skin colour to differentiate between individuals at airports and borders suggests lingering differences in how citizenship rights are allocated to racial minorities. It also suggests that security and surveillance procedures play a role in the racialization of Islamic personhood.

However, the racialization of Muslim identity is complex. Chon and Arzt (2005) argue that although physical markers such as skin colour are used to profile Muslims in the post-9/11 era, perceived religious difference is the critical component of racial formation of the other. In this context, light-skinned Muslims may not be easily identified as Muslims, but once they are, they will be seen as belonging to an inferior racial category and will be subject to extra surveillance by security personnel. As a result, markers such as country of birth, names, and clothing are also used to undermine Canadian citizenship and can lead to extra surveillance. Sanya, a twenty-five-year-old woman born in Canada to an Indian–East African family, mentions:

> I have a friend who is very, very light skinned; she always gets told that she's Jewish, but she's actually Persian, and she was born in Iran. Just looking at her, and even her name, is very anglicized, like, it's not a Muslim name really. But when they [airport security] see that she's from Iran, they sort of have to second-guess, and then they start to question her a bit more. So I think that the country that you were born in or that you're coming from might also have an impact.

Since religious difference is now the crucial component, being born in the Middle East is used in the racialization of Islamic personhood. Fahad, a twenty-eight-year-old man who is a naturalized Canadian citizen born in Syria, conveys: "I think for me, one of the reasons I'm being questioned every time is because it says on my passport I'm born in Syria, and it says when I got my Canadian passport." These experiences raise concerns about how citizenship functions for those individuals who acquire citizenship but are not born with it. Macklin (2007) argues that "the fact that Canadian passports still identify place of birth reveals something about the lingering differences in the heft of citizenship for the birthright versus the naturalized citizenship" (365). In the post-9/11 era, this information may be used by security personnel to racialize Muslim identity and to subject Canadian Muslims to extra surveillance.

An individual with a Muslim name can also lead to the racialization of Muslim identity, as Zaahir mentions: "Actually one time I went to the airport with my brother-in-law. It was in Buffalo, and the lady actually pick[ed] up the phone and said 'I have one of those people with names,' so that sort of stuff. I think it's kind of silly." Zaahir's experience captures how once someone is identified as Muslim, he/she is treated with suspicion. The fact that Zaahir has been a Canadian citizen from the age of four loses meaning when he is assigned the identity of a dangerous Muslim.

Traditional Muslim clothing may be an identity factor in racialization as well. Consider Sakeena's experience returning to Canada from Pakistan while wearing a Pakistani shirt:

> I remember at immigration they gave me a huge hassle, and as I walked out, my sister asked what took me so long, and as soon as she looked at me, she said, "It's because you're wearing that." And I did realize that at that time. I was like, "You know what, I should've worn a Western shirt."

Sakeena's experience, however, illustrates that anything seen as foreign, even a simple Pakistani T-shirt on a Canadian-born citizen, may be treated with suspicion and is used in the racialization of Muslim identity. For Canadian Muslims, then, being born in Canada or holding Canadian citizenship is not enough to be recognized as Canadian. They also have to act and dress in a certain way to be recognized as Canadian, thereby calling into question the much-vaunted Canadian multiculturalism.

Ultimately, these experiences show that state surveillance practices mark Muslims as the other through the use of multiple characteristics; skin colour, name, country of origin, and religious markers meld together to make Muslims highly visible as suspect figures (Jamil and Rousseau 2012). The suspicion of the other then sticks to their bodies, resulting in them being seen primarily as objects of fear (Ahmed 2000).

Experiencing Gendered Surveillance

What role does gender play in the surveillance of Muslim communities? Claire Alexander (2004) notes that, in the Western world, Muslim women are seen as oppressed and submissive, and Muslim men are projected as radical and violent, thereby resulting in the racialization of Muslim gender identities. She argues that Muslim masculinities are racialized as deviant and dangerous, and as acting against the hegemonic norms of male behaviour. This gender ideology is then used to justify the regulation and social control of Muslim communities (Alexander 2004). In my research, I wanted to see if this gender ideology could explain my interviewees' understandings of their treatment at airports and border crossings. When I asked if there are differences between Muslim men and women, a general feeling is that Muslim men have more difficulty. Saud says:

> I would have a reason to believe that women would not be as discriminated against as men because simply on the basis that all of the hijackers were men, and it is typically perceived that within the patriarch[al] gaze that men are the ones who are more apt to be militant, more apt to be violent, and to promote these kind of organizations which promote violence. So I would say that the males are more feared.

The experiences of Kareena, a hijab-wearing twenty-one-year-old Canadian-born woman with a Bangladeshi background, and Sanya correspond to the feelings expressed by Saud. These women say that while travelling with their male relatives, the men were aken aside for extra questioning, while they were left alone by airport officials.

Despite this difference, my research shows that Muslim women are extensively searched at airports and border crossings. Among my interviewees, there is an equal split among men and women reporting problems at these sites. Out of the 30 interviewees who report problems themselves, 15 are men and 15 are women. However, when I examined all 81 incidents that involved both the interviewees and the people they know, a slightly different picture emerges. Out of these incidents, 23 involve women, 40 involve men, and 18 involve both men and women. Men are involved in 71 per cent of the incidents compared to 50 per cent of the incidents involving women. This suggests that Muslim men, at least in my study, face more problems at airports and border crossings than do Muslim women. There may also be differences in the nature of searches between men and women, an issue for future research.

However, my data do not show a large difference between the male and female experience per se. This may seem surprising given the general perception of Muslim women as passive and weak. When asked why they feel Muslim women face intrusive questions and searches at airports and border crossings, my interviewees come up with three possible reasons. The first of these is that Muslim women are seen as a threat simply because they are Muslim, despite their gender, as discussed by Yaman, a twenty-five-year-old man who was born in Canada and comes from Saudi Arabia: "I think the perception behind that ... is that if you're Muslim you could be involved in a terrorist attack [so] there's not really much differentiation between Muslim men and Muslim women." When it comes to security and surveillance, the attribute of being dangerous is not restricted to Muslim men but extended to the entire Muslim community. This helps to explain why elderly Muslims and Muslim children are subjected to hostile treatment, although they do not fit the image of a young male terrorist.

The second reason for the surveillance of Muslim women could be tied to the hijab. Out of the fifteen women who have experienced problems at airports and border crossings, ten (67 per cent) wear the hijab, and these women recall frequently being asked to take off their hijab when going through security check points. When discussing their experiences, Maria and Zeba say the following:

> MARIA: I think it has to do more with making you feel discomfort. After going through ten security check points, what are you going to hide in your hijab? What about sweaters, shirts? You are asked about your hijab. You're not asked about your pants. Does it make any sense? But I think its discrimination. Although I comply, I know there's no reasoning behind it.
>
> ZEBA: I think there's an inherent fear in society about something that you don't know. Anytime you don't know something, you're going to be scared about it. Because a lot of times Eastern cultures or the Islamic culture seems very foreign, it's not very common in a supposed secular world, so when a woman is wearing a hijab, she's an overt sign of religion, and a religion in a society that you know determines itself on a secular nature. I think there's a fear involved. There's a tension about religion, and there's a tension about the foreign. The idea of the other, that's an issue as well.

Like Maria, a few interviewees say they are frequently asked to take off their hijab when travelling because security personnel treat it with suspicion and fear. This reaction echoes what is said in the literature. In Ahmad's (2002) view, the hijab has become a site of confrontation in the Western world because it is problematically perceived as representing the evils of Muslims, Islam, and the Middle East, including the oppression of women. So, too, security personnel may interpret the hijab, a sign of religious difference, as an indicator of aggression conveying anti-Western sentiment and, hence, may subject Muslim women wearing it to extra surveillance (Fekete 2004).

Jiwani adds (2005, 2012) there is a structured ambivalence surrounding the hijab. On the one hand, it is perceived as a sign of premodern ultrapatriarchal system. On the other hand, it is considered something that is dangerous and threatening – for example, "as the suicide bomber hiding her bomb beneath the folds of her burqa" (2012, 382). Jiwani (2005) elaborates that the victim status of Muslim women derives its meaning from a counter-construction: that of Muslim women as callous, militant, and fanatical mothers of terrorists. She adds that both these representations then help justify imperialist conquests and behaviours. This two-dimensional approach to the hijab may help to explain why women wearing the hijab are thoroughly checked at airports and border crossings.

Finally, the third reason is that some state agents may fear that Muslim women are being used as tools for terrorism. Zeba says:

> Because people think they are influenced by the men, so if the men influenced them in a negative way, they are going to have the negative actions. So they could be a potential terrorist as well, because they're influenced by the men, so there's that issue.

Other racialized women have been perceived in a similar manner. For example, Mexican women and black women may face extra surveillance: because of the way their identities are racialized, they are often seen as drug mules. Muslim women may be a new addition to the list of racialized women whose citizenship rights are undermined because it is assumed that they don't have agency. Like other racialized women, they may not have access to a crucial component of citizenship, *standing*, which as noted above, refers to being recognized as an adult capable of exercising choice.

Young Canadian Muslims' Response to Surveillance at Airports and Border Crossings

The focus of this chapter thus far has been on how young Muslims experience surveillance at airports and border crossings and what meanings these state practices impose on them. How do young

Canadian Muslims react to and attempt to handle this surveillance? Their responses are complex. Some report heightened anxiety when travelling; others try to conceal their Muslim identity to avoid surveillance. While a few try to resist harassment, by filing official complaints, for the most part, interviewees feel forced to comply with security officials.

One consequence of facing surveillance is heightened anxiety related to travelling. Samir and Asima comment:

> SAMIR: Honestly, I'm a little bit hesitant to fly as much. Like, I feel like I don't want be caught in a bad situation, maybe they're having a bad day, maybe some guy's just going to pull me in. Like, I've heard stories about people being called in and just kind of disappearing ... I mean, every time I travel, like before travelling was just like, you're going on a plane. But it's like, "Oh God, what if I get stuck in the airport?" Let me go there four hours early. Let me write a will before I leave. So you never know what's going to happen.
>
> ASIMA: Oh yeah. Every time. Every time. My father gets very anxious [about travelling]. He gets very uptight when we have to go across the border or even if we have to go to the airport. Even if he's not traveling, even if he just has to go the airport, he gets very uptight. So, um, yeah. He's very anxious. He can't handle it. He loses his temper really easily about the whole situation.

To deal with this anxiety, many interviewees go to the airport hours earlier than what is required in case they are held up by security and come close to missing their flights. They make sure they "do not have anything extra on them," such as jewellery, which could result in security personnel stopping them.

Similar feelings of anxiety are expressed by other groups. Bahdi (2003) notes that African Americans who experience racial profiling while driving have reported feeling fear and humiliation. Zuhair Kashmeri (1991) has found that during the Gulf War, children in the Arab and Muslim community in Canada experienced psychological harm when they and their communities were considered dangerous. A similar phenomenon seems to be occurring with some of the interviewees in this study. When young Muslims are perceived as potential threats at airports and border crossings, their own sense of safety and security are jeopardized. They experience what Naber (2006) calls an "internment of the psyche," which involves a sense of internal incarceration that any moment one could be harassed, beaten up, picked up or locked up, or disappear.

How do Muslims react to this undermining of their safety and security? Some protest mistreatment through individual agency. Recalling the experiences of her father, Aatifa says:

My dad, ever since that episode we had at the border, at the Canadian–American border, he just kept saying, "I'm never going to the States ever again unless it's very, very important." Because he just felt humiliated and insulted. So he feels a little more strongly that he doesn't want to go to the States.

Like Aatifa's father, a few interviewees say that they now refuse to travel to the United States because of problems with security personnel. Although young Muslims cannot control how they are treated by security personnel in the U.S., they can control whether they go there. Others respond to mistreatment by becoming more politically active. Twenty-two-year-old Rashid wrote an article about the mistreatment of the Muslim community after airport officials at the "Washington airport detained and strip searched a good friend" for eight hours.

I heard of two incidents where individuals consulted the government after being mistreated. Samir recalls that when one of his friends was told that he was on the no-fly list in Canada and was therefore unable to enter the U.S., he "managed to get off the list by contacting his MP." However, contacting the government did not prove beneficial for another man. Amineh says:

After a bad border experience, my dad actually asked for an investigation from the commission that deals with discrimination in BC. We have it at home. They sent back the report saying that "there was no discrimination there." But they quoted an officer saying that "I saw that they looked very Islamic so I pulled them over just to make sure." If that is not discrimination, then what is? I think a lot of people just don't realize what they are doing is discrimination ... They quoted the officer saying that but they still said they found no evidence of discrimination.

The failure of the government to recognize this as discrimination is illustrative of how the racial profiling of Muslims is systemic. Although some interviewees, such as Rashid, speak out against the mistreatment of the Muslim community, most comply with security personnel, even though they feel their rights are being violated. Barkat, a thirty-year-old man who came to Canada as a young child from South Africa, and Samir mention:

> BARKAT: The last time I travelled on an airplane was in 2003, and it was to Europe. And I think that I was a little bit anxious. I was anxious going to Paris and then when I got to the U.K., I was asked all sorts of weird questions at the airport. He asked who I was staying with, and I was staying with my friend. And he said, "Where does he live?" And I said, "I don't know, close to Baker Street station." And he says, "How long are you planning to stay?" "A week and a half." "Why are you here?" "Going to a friend's wedding." And then he started asking questions like, "How much money did you bring? How much money do you have in your bank account? Do you plan on finding work here?" And a whole bunch of other really bizarre questions that I just wasn't even expecting at all. But again I complied instead of, "Why the hell are you asking me this for?" I really wanted to. There was this voice inside me that says: "Ask him why?!" But I didn't do it because you don't want them to detain you because you're being difficult, so you just go ahead and answer their questions in as few words as possible and move on.
>
> SAMIR: I think you just tend to comply, because if you don't comply it's kind of seen as, "Oh, what's he hiding?" So you just kind of comply, you have no other choice. What do you want to do? You don't want to get detained, right?

The reasoning behind this compliance is complex. One is the fear of being detained or interrogated further by speaking out. The fear of missing flights or being refused entry into another country also plays a role. Dawoud says: "I've always complied. Because I always have to travel, you know. Turning back would have resulted in personal or economic consequences."

Furthermore, a few interviewees feel that security personnel are provoking them to speak out to "justify pulling us over." They believe that by complying they are not likely to be further interrogated.

For some interviewees, the extra searches have become routine practice; in their view, complaining would only prolong the experience. Leela says, "I just go with the flow. Like what are you going to do, argue with them every time?" Others mention that they would like to complain, but they do not know how to do so. Fahad notes, "I haven't actually complained, and my brother also has not, because there is nobody to call and complain to. I don't know who I'd complain to, and I don't think it would change anything."

In short, although their citizenship rights are undermined at airports and border crossings, a myriad factors force Muslims to comply with mistreatment rather than speak out against it. The fear of being detained, potentially being refused entry into the countries they are travelling to, not knowing who to complain to, all work to silence them. The fear that they will be further stigmatized for voicing their objections to state surveillance practices also point to the lack of political citizenship that Muslims have in Western nations. Hage (1998) comments those that have real political citizenship (often whites) can question state practices and still be considered a part of the political landscape. Muslims increasingly don't have access to political citizenship and, as a result, fear that any questioning of state surveillance procedures will mark them as disloyal citizens who are hiding something.

Foucault (1980) has argued that those are under surveillance can often begin regulating their own behaviour in order to avoid suspicion. For example, he writes:

> There is no need for armed, physical violence, material constraints. Just a gaze. An inspecting gaze, a gaze which each individual under its weight will end by interiorising to the point that he is his own overseer, each individual thus exercising this surveillance over and against, himself. (155)

Since many Canadian Muslims don't feel they can report the problems they face, some interviewees and their families deal with the undermining of their Canadian citizenship by trying to acquire national capital when encountering state surveillance at border crossings. As mentioned previously, the aim of accumulating national capital is to be seen as legitimate by the dominant group (Hage 1998). Because at airports and border crossings they are seen as potential security threats as opposed to loyal Canadian citizens, my interviewees try to acquire national capital by making physical changes to their appearance and trying to conceal their Muslim identity. This is particularly the case for women wearing the hijab. Atiya says:

> I will not wear the black scarf because that always has negative connotations. Um, and also pink lipstick seems to help because it looks friendly, like light colours and pastel colours. It is less intimidating and foreign. The image they get of a Muslim woman is in all black and, yes, colours really seem to help with travel.

Atiya acknowledges that wearing the hijab presents difficulties and admits that her parents have asked her to remove it for safety reasons when she travels. She refuses to do so, choosing instead to play with colours to make herself look less foreign to security personnel, even though she was born in Canada.

Other women take off the hijab when they are travelling. Asima and Amineh recall:

ASIMA: When my dad was in the States, and my aunt who was originally in Africa, and she wears the whole hijab and everything. And they were going to the States, and she took off the hijab just to avoid [problems], and that was a big thing. We were like, "Was that a good thing or was that a bad thing?" Do you fear something like that, and then take off something that you really believe in? So yeah, there are issues like that.

AMINEH: My mom takes it [the hijab] off. The first time she took it off was a few weeks ago, and she just wore a hat. And she was, like, there was a huge difference in the way she was treated. My mom has been harassed a lot more than I have. They have held her up for an hour and grilled her and honestly all sorts of stuff. Honestly, my mom has been through a lot more than I have. So my mom has had a lot of bad experiences. So this time she just did not feel like going through it, so she just took it off, and she said, like, no one bothered her, and no one harassed her. None of the border people said anything.

Some Muslim women recognize their lack of religious freedom and take off the hijab to avoid problems. However, this is not an easy decision. Are they being disloyal to their religion and to themselves by doing so? Or is taking off the hijab warranted in these circumstances?

Making physical changes to one's appearance is not restricted to women. It is an issue for Muslim men with beards, as noted earlier. Ali is a nineteen-year-old man who was born and raised in Bangladesh and has been in Canada since 2003, and Radi is a twenty-five-year-old man who was born in Canada and comes from a Pakistani background. They say the following:

ALI: My father, when he came to America, he trimmed down his beard because you know what you have to face. You can't fight against something like this. You are going into their country, so you have to do what they tell you to do. When I travel internationally, my dad tells me to shave properly and to look decent.

RADI: Well, we were all told by our fathers: "If you're going to travel, wear a suit. If you have to keep that beard, trim it down as low as you can. Look as Canadian as you possibly can."

Surveillance procedures at airports and border crossings force some young Muslims to give up symbols of their religious roots and follow the social norms of North American society. Samir says, "Although I choose to wear traditional clothes at times, I'm not going to travel in it because I know it's not going to make it any easier for me." Yet Samir refuses to trim his beard when he travels, and Asima says her father has the same response. They both comment:

SAMIR: I don't shave my beard when I travel. I don't really choose to alter my religion for other people. I keep a beard because I feel like it's something that I want to do. And you know a lot of people keep a beard. If it is going to get me stopped, it's going to get me stopped. I'm not going to change my lifestyle, but at the same time, I will be more careful. You're a lot more careful of what you say and what you wear, you don't want to look suspicious, you don't want to avoid eye contact, at the same time, you don't want to be staring at somebody because it might be seen as being suspicious.

ASIMA: As much as my dad is paranoid about travelling, I think he almost purposely does not shave his beard, and he avoids that. I remember my mom once said, "You should dye your beard," because when his beard is white, he looks completely Muslim. You better dye your beard, and blah, and he's like, "No, I am not going to dye my beard. What are they going to do? I have nothing to hide." He avoids trying to change himself. Um, one thing he has done is that he has started to use his middle name more than his first name. That's because his middle name is not as Muslim as his first name. I think that is something that has just evolved. I think that is one thing that he has changed about himself.

Muslims' reaction to surveillance at airports and border crossings is complex, as Muslims are constantly negotiating with themselves about appropriate ways to handle extra surveillance without jeopardizing their religious beliefs. While some try to gain national capital by adopting more of a Western look, some refuse to give up their religious roots because they believe by doing so they may be disrespectful to their religion and are yielding to the pressure to confirm to Western norms. However, men who refuse to shave their beards and women who refuse to take off the hijab may utilize other practices to avoid being interrogated at airports and border crossings; they may be extra cautious, not drawing any attention to themselves, and may use their middle names. Hence, they may also try to gain national capital by engaging in alternative practices of self-regulation in an effort to manage their outward Muslim identity.

Foucault (1977, 1980) argues that state surveillance practices work to domesticate populations. In this context, targeting Muslim signifiers through surveillance practices can be seen as an attempt to discipline Muslim citizens. The adopting of Western clothing or other signifiers of non-Muslim by some Muslims, in order to avoid extra surveillance and to gain national capital, can be interpreted as an acceptance of state discipline. However, there are also instances where some Muslims refuse to be disciplined and to let go of their religious identities. Not all conform to the gaze of surveillance and instead show signs of resistance.

Overall, young Canadian Muslims cope with extra surveillance and the undermining of their citizenship in a variety of different ways. Some express feelings of humiliation and anxiety related to travelling; in these instances, their sense of safety and security has been jeopardized. Others demonstrate individual agency, refusing to fly into the U.S., for example, where much of the discrimination towards Muslims occurs. A few become more politically active. Some try to conceal their Muslim identity to avoid problems, causing conflicting emotions. However, for the most part, interviewees comply with airport and border-crossing personnel because they do not feel they have political citizenship: not wanting to be detained further, fear of being refused entry to the countries to which they are travelling, trying to avoid being tricked by security personnel, and not knowing who to complain to, all result in the silencing of Muslim communities.

Young (2003) notes that, in the present-day security state, citizens have lost the ability to question state surveillance practices and to hold state officials accountable for their actions. This is indeed the case for many of the young Canadian Muslims in this study who feel powerless and forced to comply with state surveillance practices that are discriminatory. Considering the wide range of problems Muslims face, a way to deal with discrimination at airports and border crossings is urgently needed.

Experiences of Surveillance in Daily life

The targeting of Muslim communities is also seen in the overall surveillance of the Muslim community in Canada, even though this may not be as extreme as in the United States.[3] Bill C-36, adopted in 2001, increases the power of police and government agencies to conduct secret searches, use electronic eavesdropping, monitor overseas communication, conduct inquiries without warrants, and so on (Helly 2004; Poynting and Perry 2007). Murphy (2007) elaborates that since 9/11 some urban communities have been transformed into security problems, "changing communities from partners to suspects and from communities at risk to communities of risk" (461). The securitization of Muslim communities is based on the idea that the ordinary domestic lifestyles of imported or homegrown terrorists make all citizens in some Muslim communities either potential suspects or informants. Murphy writes that "this enemy within logic distances local police from the community, increases mutual suspicion and undermines previous trust based relationships established through community policing strategies" (462).

Particular areas facing increased surveillance after 9/11 are mosques and other Muslim organizations. Dawoud says:

CSIS [Canadian Security Intelligence Services] has openly said, for example, they have an informant in every mosque and every organization. We, a bunch of Muslim youth activists, had a meeting with CSIS after the eighteen guys were picked up. And they said, "Oh, we know very well what's happening in the Muslim community. We have informants in every mosque and every organization."

The securitization of Muslim communities directly impacts the lives of Canadian Muslims. For one thing, it labels them as dangerous others that cannot be trusted, thereby prohibiting Muslim communities from having *allegiance* (being seen as a loyal member of society), an important facet of citizenship, as noted above. Umar comments:

Muslim students have been approached by Canadian security authorities. RCMP officials have showed photographs of other Muslim youth to them and have questioned if they know about terrorists, questions like that. I know of a lot of Muslim youth who have been occasionally approached by security authorities and are asked questions which sometimes can be quite offensive. That's a regular phenomenon.

In a similar vein, Dawoud mentions the bugging of the prayer room at Ryerson University. He recalls that "they found recording devices behind the curtains near the top of the windows." As a result, fear spread throughout the Muslim university community. In such instances, young Canadian Muslims are not treated like regular university students but are viewed as a threat. Although universities are supposed to be venues for learning and self-exploration, some young Muslims see them as places where they face scrutiny and pressure to demonstrate their loyalties by becoming informants for the police.

In some cases, government surveillance may be more invasive and traumatic. Yazeed recalls the invasion of his friend's house and business by the police because of their suspicions about one of his workers:

> One friend of mine, his place of business got hit [by the police]. It was a printing shop in Toronto. The police hit simultaneously their home and their business, and that was a really bad situation. I think that is a stain on the Canadian government, because from what he was telling me, there were guns pointed at his sisters who were five and six. I think they were screaming. It is not really nice to have, like, thirty or forty people coming into your house and business with guns and to force you to go into the floor and put you in handcuffs and treat you like you have done something already. Part of the reason was that one of his workers was sending money to his mom, and it wasn't even large sums of money; it was a small sum of money he was sending to Algeria, I think. So they guy was deported. This happened within the first year [after] 9/11.

Clearly, such measures jeopardize Canadian Muslims' sense of security in Canada. Murphy (2007) notes that, while community policing may appear beneficial from a security standpoint, the heavy handed use of local police may destroy trust and further alienate Muslim communities.

The deceitful practices of Canadian security agencies play an important role in the breaking of this trust. Rashid says:

> My friend, he was a part of this Muslim organization, and I was also part of this organization, and I was, like, his right-hand man. He was given a call saying that the Governor General would like to meet with you. The motive seemed really nice. It was like we are getting good publicity – like the Muslim perspective on something. Then he goes and comes back to me at the end of the day. "Yeah it wasn't the Governor General. I went, and there was a CSIS woman that told me that 'the Governor General thing, that's not true, and I am from CSIS. I would like to ask you some questions.' So there was deceit right from the very beginning. Then he started feeling very uncomfortable. She would ask questions like this, "Is

there anyone in your organization that prays excessively?" and this was a theologically religious organization, right. Or, "Is it quite religious?" and "[Does it] follow certain sects like the sect that is dominant in Saudi Arabia?" And then he was, like, "No." My point is that even if we do, who cares and so what?

Muslims who are religious and who belong to Muslim organizations are treated with suspicion and are subjected to extra surveillance. This, along with the extra surveillance of mosques and other Muslim organizations, illustrates Muslims lack of religious freedom. The fixation of finding Muslims that are "excessively religious" once again show that those that strictly follow Islam are categorized as "bad" Muslims by security personnel.

The surveillance of the Muslim community by government organizations undermines their substantive citizenship (their ability to exercise rights of citizenship). However, as noted previously, this undermining may be supported and enforced by their fellow Canadians. Amineh and Maria recall:

AMINEH: CSIS came to the Muslim school I worked at. They came and checked everything out and they did not even have a search warrant and we were just like, "We have nothing to hide, you can come and look." The neighbours had just reported us. They said that we had suspicious activity. We were building an extension to the gym, and CSIS came and checked it.

MARIA: There is this Muslim help line that came up in Mississauga; it's a hotline for Muslim children who have parental problems or abuse, having troubles at school, or with drugs or alcohol. It's just a helpline. An article was published in the *Toronto Star* and the *Globe and Mail* that claimed it was jihadist or something (laughs), which is so dumb because it's a helpline.

Nakano Glenn (2002) argues that the maintenance of citizenship boundaries is often enforced by the general public at the local level. In the post-9/11 era, when citizens are encouraged to be hypervigilant towards potential terrorism, the surveillance of Muslim communities can also occur through the gaze of individual citizens.

Naber (2006) argues that anti-Muslim state policies create a "culture of fear" within Muslim communities where they feel highly visible in negative ways. According to Naber, this fear can lead to silence, avoidance, and self-censorship at both the individual and community levels.

This can be seen in my interviewees' experiences. A constant fear of being under surveillance exists regardless of whether this is actually the case. Nashida, a hijab-wearing, twenty-three-year-old woman who was born in Canada to a Pakistani background, and Dawoud say:

> DAWOUD: We actually have a friend, who works for Bell, and we were having some troubles with our phone. We would pick up our phone at home, and it'd be like about three seconds before the tone would come. And we called him and said, "Something's wrong with the phone, what's happening?" He looked into it and said, "Your phone is bugged." And a lot of people felt that their phones were behaving differently.
>
> NASHIDA: I'm involved in the MSA [Muslim Students Association]. One of the girls whose husband is in jail for the Toronto 18, she was involved in the MSA, and she asked me to join one of the events taking place at the University of Toronto Mississauga. She called me on my cell phone, and I noticed that my cell phone had this flashing thing after she called me. It said forwarding online, and it had the weirdest [feel to it], like, you know your own phone, and you know when something appears that you've never seen before. I wasn't sure what it was, but I think I can use my own judgment on it. I believe that my phone was being bugged.

This fear of phone tapping illustrates the level of insecurity Muslim communities feel about their citizenship rights in Canada, in this case, the right to privacy.

In addition to being fearful of using the phone, some Muslims are fearful of using the Internet. For instance, Zeba says:

> Post-9/11 my dad was very concerned. For the longest while, we wouldn't talk on the phone about anything related to 9/11. We'd talk in person. Like, he was insistent that we be careful of our emails, MSN messages, anything Internet-related just in case, because there was this rumour that CSIS was tapping all Muslim phone lines. I don't know how much of that is true, and there's scare tactics involved in that as well. But I know, like, for the Toronto 18 that was a real case, and a lot of their families' and friends' phones were tapped.

Simple things such as using the Internet, taken for granted by most, become problematic for young Muslims.

In some cases, interviewees mention a fear of being followed. Aneesha says:

I have heard people follow Muslims in malls with security cameras, but I don't know how true that is. Like there's always rumours too, that's the other problem. Because there's so much random stuff happens in the Muslim community, they're all about conspiracy, so they assume things. They'll be like, "Oh, it's a conspiracy. You're being followed," and stuff like that. But I do know phone tapping happens. I'm pretty sure sometimes there are people that go to our conferences just to make sure they're not promoting terrorism in any way and stuff.

Other interviewees are fearful that expressing their political opinions could result in surveillance. Amber, a twenty-four-year-old woman born in Canada to a Pakistani father and German mother, notes:

I have been to a number of protests, and I have been very politically active, and I know very well that my name is on some file somewhere put away. Like, I have seen people take pictures of me when they have no reason to take pictures of me. Even in our mosques, we were afraid of saying the simplest things such as prayers for our brothers and sisters in Palestine because we were afraid we would get reported. There was just this climate of fear that you could just not say anything without being labelled as a terrorist sympathizer if not a terrorist.

Some interviewees are afraid of showing allegiance to other Muslim communities in the world or of supporting certain political issues, revealing their lack of political citizenship in Canada.

To sum up, due to actual experiences of surveillance, the fear of surveillance is quite persuasive in the Muslim community. This involves being fearful of phone taps, belonging to Muslim organizations, using the Internet, being followed, and expressing political opinions. What does this say about Canadian citizenship? Safety and security are supposed to be important components of citizenship. However, Canadian Muslims do not always have access to this. While they hold formal citizenship, on many occasions they lack substantive citizenship.

Conclusion

Canada has historically policed its borders through racial lines (Dua 2000; Helleiner 2012; Thobani 2007; Sharma 2006; Bhandar 2008). This can be seen in the rigid border controls put in place during the first half of the twentieth century to limit the entry of Asian and South Asian immigrants into Canada, the mobility restrictions placed on indigenous populations, and the creation of immigration policies favouring "white" immigrants (Simpson 2008; Sharma 2006; Bhandar 2008; Thobani 2007). Bhandar (2008) says the practice of crossing borders reveals "the production of differentiated racial ontologies of immigrant/migrant communities situated within the nation state" (281).

Since 9/11, a number of scholars have raised concerns about the use of racial profiling in the name of national security (Akram and Johnson 2002; F. Bhabha 2003; Bahdi 2003; Choudhry 2001; Choudhry and Roach 2003; Sharma 2006; Bhandar 2008; Razack 2008; Jamil and Rousseau 2012). Sharma (2006), for instance, stresses that in the post-9/11 world, the threat of "Muslim terrorists" has become the strongest rationale for increasing regressive border policies throughout the global North. These policies include the racial profiling and targeting of Muslim identity (Sharma 2006; Bhandar 2008; Bahdi 2003). Bahdi (2003) elaborates: "9/11 forced a fundamental shift in the racial profiling discourse. The central contention was no longer whether racial profiling was in fact taking place ... but whether Canadian society can morally, legally, or politically condone racial profiling" (295).

Bhandar (2008) remarks that the "experiences of border crossings is an ontological one whereby both the technologies used in border security and the mode of securitization are understood to have a profound effect on immigrant and migrant communities within nation states that may range from feeling of not belonging or being external to the nation project, to being forcibly made external, policed and detained" (281–3). The experiences of my interviewees backs this up. For most, one of the most troubling consequences of 9/11 has been the heightened surveillance at airports and borders. In other words, state surveillance and racialized border practices do much more than just perform security checks. They give meaning to one's identity and citizenship. By directly targeting Muslims for extra searches and questioning, security procedures vilify and stigmatize Muslim identities. My interviewees experience surveillance as a direct attack on their Muslim identity. Having their religious faith seen as a potential security threat is troubling. They also feel their religious freedom is threatened when they are racially profiled because of their religious practices.

Bhandar (2008) remarks that border crossings in North America have supported a variety of nationalist myths and ideologies that simultaneously contribute to and adhere to racial discourses. Not surprisingly, central to my interviewees' experiences is that racialized border practices worked to punish their Muslim identities. Racial profiling at border crossings in the post-9/11 world is complex and includes a new security architecture that targets and racializes a host of ethnicities, Islamic religious traditions, and cultures as the Muslim other (Zedner 2010). Within this architecture, Muslims experience risk subjectification, "a process through which they become defined as dangerous by virtue of sharing some characteristic of the 'typical terrorist'" (Mythen 2012, 390). This is reflected in my interviewees' experiences. While physical markers such as skin colour may be used to other individuals, perceived religious difference is the most critical component of the other.

Racialized border practices have serious repercussions for national belonging, as claims to citizenship are arbitrated in these spaces (Salter 2007; Helleiner 2010). Salter (2007) writes, "Travelers are reduced from citizens, foreigners, refugees, with complex identities and claims to home into objects of danger or benefit" (59). Borders become ways to create multiple differential exclusions (Sharma 2006) with those seen as "us" or as "real" citizens granted entry and those designated "dangerous" and "others" subject to scrutiny (Mythen 2012). In the post-9/11 world, key targets of coercive border practices are those constructed as non-members of Canadian society, regardless of their citizenship status (Sharma 2006).

My interviewees' experiences suggest Canadian Muslims no longer enjoy the rights of Canadian citizenship at airports and border crossings. They are more likely to be perceived as "suspects" than Canadians with rights. They fear they will never be treated as "real" Canadians with full and legitimate citizenship but will always be considered "accidental" Canadians or "Canadian-born."

Various mechanisms at border crossings undermine the citizenship of my interviewees. Bhandar (2008) and Bannerji (2000) say that by asking populist nationalist questions during interviews, state officials can discipline national identities. My interviewees spoke of being asked questions about their nationality, their loyalty to Canada, their association with the Middle East, their religious beliefs and practices. Not surprisingly, this was upsetting, as it undercut their sense of citizenship. For Thobani (2007), even if phrased politely, such *requests* to prove legality are, in fact, *rites of citizenship* that "reflect the common sense of knowledge shared among nationals that strangers need to prove their legality before they should allowed to access their rights of citizenship" (100). As mentioned in the previous chapter, rites of citizenship reinforce notions of legitimate belonging, whereby "real" Canadians enact their insider status. They demonstrate "who has power and who is prohibited from exercising such power" (Thobani 2007, 80).

Significantly, Sharma (2006) notes that during the last decade of the "War on Terror" differentiations between the various types of legal status have become more important. This can be seen in attempts to differentiate between citizens born in a national state and those who hold legal citizenship status through naturalization. An unconditional right of legal citizenship is the right to enter and remain in the country of citizenship (Macklin 2001). However, some of my interviewees, particularly naturalized citizens, feel they have to fight for this right at border crossings. If their passports reveal they were born in places like Saudia Arabia or Pakistan, they say they risk losing their rights as Canadian citizens. Lyon (2006) says state-produced passports and identity documents not only regulate population movements but also categorize populations by distinguishing between outsiders and insiders or "legitimate" citizens and others. By the same token, Macklin (2007) argues, "The fact that Canadian passports still identify place of birth reveals something about the lingering differences in the heft of citizenship for the birthright versus the naturalized citizenship" (365).

My findings point to the role of racialized border practices in how young Canadian Muslims experience national identification and citizenship. My interviewees' experiences support the broader literature documenting how the Western citizenship status of Muslims is often discounted. My findings support Lucia Zedner (2010) and Benjamin Muller (2004) who argue the citizenship status of Muslims who are Canadian, American, or British is often perceived as "irregular" or "flawed; they are treated as sub citizens who are considered 'outsiders inside.'" Despite their Canadian citizenship, my interviewees are treated as illegitimate members of the nation and have become securitized citizens. They often lack access to substantive citizenship, as evidenced in their difficulties re-entering Canada. To them, these experiences suggest Canadian citizenship may not have equal value for all citizens, not only in Canada but internationally. Their sense of citizenship, including their birthright citizenship, is threatened because they lack access to *allegiance* (being viewed as a loyal member of society) and *nationality* (being recognized as Canadian), important facets of citizenship. Even more troubling, surveillance practices displace their sense of citizenship because they are often supported and enforced by the general public. Confirming this impression, Thobani (2007) writes, "The political practices of the Canadian nation state have likewise stamped the citizenship of people of colour on our faces, so that our rights to cross borders and to make claims to social entitlements are met with greater suspicion and vigilance" (101).

State surveillance practices leave many young Canadian Muslims feeling powerless. While some try to resist or avoid surveillance by refusing to fly, challenging security personnel, or reporting their discriminatory treatment, many feel forced to comply. They say they are even fearful of surveillance in their daily lives, again illustrating the lack of substantive citizenship.

These findings bring to light how the coupling of Islam with terrorism has disrupted the relationship between the Canadian state and Canadian Muslims. Since now the very presence of Muslims within Canada is considered a threat to the nation, Canadian citizenship is losing its ability to provide protection for Canadian Muslims. Anti-terrorism measures adopted by the Canadian state have reshaped the meaning of Canadian citizenship. Similarly, Thobani (2007) writes that by "casting the nation as primarily as western in nature, these measures enable the citizenship rights of those who are Muslims (or look Muslim) to be suspended by the Canadian state and even stripped away by the American state" (221). In the eyes of the Canadian state Muslims are guilty by religious and cultural association, regardless of their actual stance on international politics. The racialization of the category Muslim has resulted in Muslims inside the country to be linked directly with the enemy outside the borders of Canada, thereby changing the relationship of Muslim Canadians with the nation state. According to Thobani (2007, 242), this inscribing of suspicion and illegality onto the bodies of those who look Muslim works to make the legal citizenship of Canadian Muslims irrelevant. Whatever protections citizenship was supposed to accord Canadians have now become depleted for Muslim Canadians because of the way Muslim identity has been racialized and politicized. Because the figure of the Muslim is used to represent a threat to national security (Thobani 2007), all Canadian Muslims are seen as potential threats regardless of their legal status, thereby justifying the stripping of their legal protections and exposing them to states of exception.

My interviewees' experiences suggest the logic of states of exception – the suspension of civil liberties and citizenship rights in the name of security – is not limited to rare cases such as Maher Arar or Omar Khadr. It can impact Muslim Canadians in more subtle ways. They may be selected for extra searches and questioning just because they are Muslim. They may not be recognized as Canadian citizens and are treated as "dangerous" simply because of their religious identity.

Drawing on Foucault, Zine (2012) argues the surveillance of Canadian Muslims has led to a panoptic effect whereby people enforce a type of self-surveillance, cautiously avoiding suspicion by second-guessing and curtailing otherwise innocent actions for fear they might be misread as subversive. "Within a 'panoptic society,' individuals objected to surveillance begin to regulate their own behavior and actions in accordance with the dominant norms and codes" (Zine 2012, 398). In her research on American Muslims, Naber (2006) refers to a similar phenomenon with the concept of the "internment of the psyche" – a fear Muslim that communities internalize as a result of state surveillance and the everyday acts of discrimination directed towards them . As a result of the "internment of the psyche," Naber argues that individual Muslims may start self-regulating their own behaviour. This is occurring among my interviewees wherein they frequently alter or manage their visibility as Muslims at border crossings (removing the hijab, for example) in order to avoid state surveillance. However, as will be shown in the next chapter, this disciplining of Muslim identity through state practices has the opposite effect in the long run. As a result of being treated as securitized citizens by state practices, Canadian Muslims develop reactive identities, whereby they affirm their Muslim identities. They show individual agency by asserting their Muslim identity in everyday life and resist pressures to conform. As described in the next chapter, through "reactive identity formation," my interviewees resist the racialization of Islam and reclaim their religion by highlighting their Muslim identity in an anti-Muslim climate. However, there are limits to their reactive identities and to their political agency. As illustrated in this chapter, my interviewees do not feel safe in expressing their reactive identities at airports and border crossings because these are sites where their citizenship rights are most at risk of being eroded by the state.

Overall, while some literature argues state surveillance practices turn Muslims into docile citizens (Naber 2006; Zine 2012), I find the impact of state surveillance on identity formation is much more complex. While my interviewees experience "internment of the psyche" (Naber 2006) or the panoptic effect (Zine 2012), as will be shown in the next chapter, being treated as securitized citizens by the state and by the general Canadian public can lead to the development of reactive identities.

4 "Our Faith Was also Hijacked by Those People": Reclaiming Muslim Identity in a Post-9/11 Era

Introduction[1]

Thus far, I have shown how young Muslims in the post-9/11 era are victimized by fellow Canadians and the state. While I was interviewing young Canadian Muslims, I was particularly interested in whether they had stepped away from their religion in the post-9/11 era as a result of such experiences. One of my first interviewees, Mohammed, a nineteen-year-old who was born in Canada and who comes from a Bangladeshi background, says:

> I have seen the opposite effect. Girls were being extra religious and wearing proper traditional clothes after 9/11. They were being more religious than before. You would think they would do the opposite because they did not want to be discriminated against, but they became more religious. But I don't know why.

Like Mohammed, I had expected that young Canadian Muslims would distance themselves from their religious background to avoid discrimination post-9/11. I was intrigued to learn that the opposite might be occurring. Studies in the United States and the United Kingdom concur with Mohammed's observations (Kundnani 2002; El-Halawany 2003; Peek 2003; Gupta 2004), but they do not provide a theoretical explanation. My encounter with Mohammed and the gap in the literature leads me to ask a key question: How can we theorize young Muslims' assertion of their identity in a post-9/11 world?

To address the issue, I draw upon and extend Alejandro Portes and Rubén G. Rumbaut's (2001) theory of reactive ethnicity, which posits that when people experience racism, they increase their identification with their ethnic group. Portes and Rumbaut focus on ethnic identity, but I extend their work by arguing that the formation of reactive identities is not limited to ethnic groups. Rather, as evidenced in the reactions of young Muslims in the post-9/11 era, religious minorities can do the same thing, something I choose to call "reactive identity formation."

Muslim Identities

In recent years, academics have conceptualized "Muslim" identity in various ways. Some understand Muslim as an ethnic identity. For instance, Oliver Roy (2004) views Muslims in contemporary Western Europe as a neo-ethnic group that has largely been socially constructed. For him, "'neo' means that culture of origin is no longer relevant, and 'ethnicity' (means) that religion is not seen as faith but as a set of cultural patterns that are inherited and not related to a person's spiritual life" (125). He sees the acceptance of the label Muslim by individuals who are not religious as substantiating his argument. Others see Muslim as a racial identity. Claire Alexander (2000) argues that Muslim identity has undergone a process of racialization, which is both ascriptive and naturalized. As a result, she feels that Muslims are now a stigmatized racial group: "Muslims have ... become the new 'blacks' with all the association of cultural alienation, deprivation and danger" (15). For her, the emergence of Islamophobia in the British context is less a new phenomenon than an extension of earlier concerns around the presence of "black" communities in Britain. Alexander argues that when religion is naturalized and essentialized it becomes synonymous with "race." In other words, when Muslim identities are seen as fixed and absolute, they begin to take the form often associated with race.

While Roy and Alexander make interesting arguments, they neglect to take into account that, for many Muslims, religious faith still plays a large role in their identity formation as Muslims. A scholar who incorporates religious faith into Muslim identity is Jytte Klausen (2005). She uses the label Muslim to refer to both faith and identity, which she argues is similar to how labels of Christian or Jewish are often used. Her approach, however, does not give due attention to the role social forces play in ascribing identity.

For my part, I understand Muslim as a religious identity that has been racialized in the post 9/11 era. I use this approach because barring a few outlier cases, the vast majority of my interviewees are religious.

Contradicting Roy's findings, my interviewees do not use Muslim as a label without ascribing to the religious faith and they do not adopt an atheistic form of a Muslim identity. For example, a frequently expressed sentiment was that Islam was a guiding force in their lives. Aatifa and Radi say the following:

AATIFA: Being Muslim is a way of life. You actually live your religion, whether it is praying five times a day or wearing the hijab ... believing in Allah and believing in the prophet Mohammed. Islam is part of my every day. Everything I do or the judgments I make always have to reflect back on my religion. So it's very important that the way I live reflects back on my religion.

RADI: To me being Muslim is pretty much everything. It is who I am. Islam is a way of life – it is who I am as a person, what I should practise, what I should follow, and how I should live my life is shaped by Islam. It is my connection to God and to the Muslims all around the world.

The vast majority also adhere to the religious practices advocated by Islam. For example, Barkat says: "I pray five times a day. I don't eat pork and I do not eat meat that is not halal. I do not drink alcohol. I don't gamble. I don't do things that my religion prohibits me from doing." Aalia also says, "It's just a daily practice. Like daily life. We pray five times a day. The month of Ramadan just passed, where we fast for a month from sunrise to sunset."

In short, Islam plays a significant role in my interviewees' lives. However, religions are complex and religious texts can often be interpreted in various ways (Casanova 1994). Accordingly, my interviewees may interpret Islam in unique ways. But exploring the different religious interpretations of Islam is beyond the scope of this study. Instead my intellectual interest is focused on exploring how young Canadian Muslims make sense of their Muslim identities, in light of the discourse surrounding the Muslim other, which posits Muslims as inferior, dangerous, and a threat to Western civilizations. For this reason, I understand Muslim identity as a racialized religious identity. In other words, following Alexander (2000, 2004), I see Muslims as vulnerable to the same social processes of systematic inequality, external labelling, inferiority, and otherness as other "racial" groups.

Because conceptualizing Muslim identity as being both a religious and racial identity allows for the recognition of both the religious component and the external ascription nature of identity, I use this approach here. While this advances our understanding of Muslim identity formation, however, it does not give guidance on how to study the impact of discrimination on identity formation among marginalized groups.

Identity Formation

Scholars such as Stuart Hall (1990) and Nira Yuval-Davis (2011) provide important insights into the role of external conditions in the construction of identities and the fluid nature of identity. Hall (1990) writes, "Perhaps instead of thinking of identity as an already accomplished fact, we should think instead, of identity as a 'production,' which is never complete, always in process and always constituted within, not outside, representation" (222). Self-identifications are complex, always in flux and vulnerable to social forces:

> Identity is formed in the "interaction" between self and society. The subject still has an inner core or essence that is "the real me," but this is formed and modified in a continuous dialogue with the cultural worlds "outside" and the identities which they offer. Identity, in this sociological conception, bridges the gap between the "inside" and the "outside" – between the personal and the public. The fact that we project "ourselves" into these cultural identities, at the same time internalizing their meanings and values, making them "part of us," helps to align our subjective feelings with the objective places we occupy in the social and cultural world. (Hall 1996, 597–8)

For Hall (1996), identity then helps to stabilize the cultural worlds subjects occupy, by allowing both to reciprocally become unified and predictable (598). He mentions that while the subject has historically been thought of as having a unified and stable identity, the modern subject actually holds multiple identities, which are often unresolved and contradictory. Identity should no longer be considered fixed, essential and permanent:

> Identity becomes a "moveable feast": formed and transformed continuously in relation to the ways you are represented or addressed in the cultural systems which surround you. It is historically, not biologically, defined. The subject assumes different identities at different times, identities which are not unified around a coherent "self." Within us are contradictory identities pulling in different directions, so that our identifications are continuously being shifted about. If we feel we have a unified identity

from birth to death, it is only because we construct a comforting story or "narrative of the self" about ourselves. The fully unified, completed, secure, and coherent identity is a fantasy. Instead, as the systems of meaning and cultural representation multiply, we are confronted by a bewildering, fleeting multiplicity of possible identities, any one of which we could identify with – at least temporarily. (598)

Hence, when societies and communities are held together, it is not because people are intrinsically unified but because, under certain circumstances, some elements of identities can be articulated together, although this is always open to change (Hall 1996).

Yuval-Davis (2011) has similar thoughts about identity, arguing identities should be understood as narratives and are therefore malleable. They are stories people tell themselves and others about who they are and who they are not:

Identity narratives can be individual or they can be collective, the latter often a resource for the former. Although they can be reproduced from generation to generation, this reproduction is always carried out in a selective way. The identity narratives can shift and change, be contested and multiple. They can relate to the past, to a myth of origin; they can be aimed at explaining the present and, probably above all, they function as a projection of a future trajectory. (14)

At the same time, Yuval-Davis (2011) recognizes identities are frequently intertwined with social locations: "When it is said that people belong to a particular gender, race or class ... what is being talked about are social and economic locations, which at each historical moment have particular implications vis-à-vis the grids of power relations in society" (12–14). As a result, identity becomes an important dimension of one's social location, with both becoming more intertwined (12–14). Taking this argument a step further, Yuval-Davis says in certain historical contexts, constructions of self and identity can be forced on people. Kwesi Appiah (2005) says imposed identities have real consequences for how people come to perceive themselves:

Once labels are applied to people, ideas about people who fit the label come to have social and psychological effects. In particular these ideas shape the ways people conceive of themselves and their projects. So the labels operate to mold what we may call identification, the process through which individuals shape their projects – including their plans for their own lives and their conceptions of the good life – by reference to available labels, available identities. (66)

Hall (1991) also pays close attention to how external forces help shape identities. He holds that the process of identification is constructed

through splitting – between which one is and which is the Other ... this is the Other that belongs inside one. This is the Other that one can only know from the place from which one stands. This is the self as it is inscribed in the gaze of the Other. And this notion which breaks down boundaries, between outside and inside, between those who belong and those who do not, between those whose histories have been written and those whose histories they have depended on but whose cannot be spoken ... the notion that identity has to do with people that look the same, call themselves the same, is nonsense. As a process, as a narrative, as a discourse it is always told from the position of the Other. (48–9)

There are two important dimensions to this splitting. First, it defines the other and by defining the other, also defines the self. To illustrate his point, Hall (1991) uses an interesting example of "British Identity." He notes that while tea has become a symbol of British social identity, not a single tea plantation exists within the United Kingdom. Instead, tea comes from places like India. According to Hall, "that is the outside history that is inside the history of English history. There is no English history without that other history" (49). Second, through this splitting, Western regimes hold the power to label colonized people as the other; at the same time, they have the power to make the colonized see and experience themselves as the other:

It is one thing to position a subject or set of peoples as the "Other" of a dominant discourse. It is quite another thing to subject them to that "knowledge," not only as a matter of imposed will and domination, by the power of inner compulsion and subjective con-formation to the norm. (226)

Both Hall and Yuval-Davis stress the role of power relations in the construction of identity. They pay close attention to how politics of representation can emerge among marginalized populations. Yuval-Davis (2011) argues identities are not just about social locations but also about the ways they are valued. As a result, identities reflect people's desire to belong and their desire to share emotional attachments, with some having more weight than others:

> Of course not all belongings are as important to people in the same way and to the same extent. Emotions, like perceptions, shift in different times and situations and are more or less reflective. As a rule, the emotional components of people's constructions of themselves and their identities become more central the more threatened and less secure they feel. In the most extreme cases people are willing to sacrifice their lives/and the lives of others in order for the narratives of their identities and the objects of their identifications and attachments to continue to exist. After a terrorist attack, or after a declaration of war, people often seek to return to a place that is less "objectively" safe, as long as it means they can be near their nearest and dearest, and share their fate. (15)

Hall (1991) sees identity as a kind of representation, which plays a central role in identity politics. At times, collective identities can be constituted as a form of defence against the practices of racist society, as for example, the collective "black identity." In this instance, Hall sees black as a politically and culturally constructed category. People identified themselves as black not because of skin colour but for historical, social, and political reasons (Hall 1991). Simply stated, the first wave of black immigrants in England used a unifying and singular framework to articulate a positive identity across ethnic and cultural differences (Hall 1991, 1990). "Black identity politics" had two principal objectives (Hall 1992). The first was to reference common experiences of racism in Britain so a new politics of resistance could emerge among communities with very different histories, traditions, and cultural backgrounds. The second was to contest stereotypes and exotic images of blacks by creating a counter position. These two strategies formed the politics of representation (Hall 1992).

Black identity politics was not without its own problems, contradictions, and challenges. First, it silenced Asians who also were subjected to processes of racism and marginalization. Second, some blacks could not identify with this collective identity. Hall (1992) notes that in forming itself in reaction to white domination, it at times concealed multiethnic distinctions and pushed aside many of the people it wanted to include. It threatened to overlook the "extraordinary diversity of subjective positions, social experiences, and cultural identities, which compose the category of 'black'" (225). In addition, other systems of social stratification were embedded in the movement, for example, affirming black masculinity over black femininity.

Hall (1990, 1991) calls for conceptualizing identity through difference by recognizing the differences in values, lifestyles, beliefs, and family networks which distinguish one ethnic group form another and by acknowledging the differences that arise from people's multiple social identities. His politics of representation would go beyond trying to reverse one discourse of identity by constructing another. Instead, it would investigate the diversity of all experiences in relation to social locations (Hall 1990, 1991).

Yuval-Davis (2011) and Hall (1990, 1991, 1992, 1996) lay the ground-work for much of what I see in Muslim identity formation in the post-9/11 era. Following them, I conceptualize identity as an ongoing, fluid social process shaped by self-attribution and societal ascription alike. Like all other identities, Muslim identities can be produced, reproduced, and transformed in different social settings. In the post-9/11 era, Muslim identity can function as "a form of representation" (Hall 1990) or a "narrative" (Yuval Davis 2011), trying to counteract the vilification of Islam by providing an alternative image of what it means to be Muslim. Of course, like black identity politics, there are limits and challenges.

Reactive Ethnicity

As theorizing the formation of Muslim identity among second-generation Muslim Canadians in the post-9/11 era is complex topic, I turn to the work of Portes and Rumbaut (1990, 2001, 2006) who have used the theory of "reactive ethnicity" to understand the experiences of second-generation immigrants in the United States, and their work is also quite useful to understand the experiences of second-generation Canadian Muslims. The term "reactive ethnicity" is used to explain how youth from marginalized ethnic groups can intensify their ethnic identification when they experience or perceive racism. The authors suggest that "reactive ethnicity" enables them to cope with discrimination. They use their social similarity to or dissimilarity from reference groups close to them, often in terms of gender, language, nationality, and ethnicity, to define their social identity. This type of self-definition carries an "affective meaning implying a psychological bond with others that tends to serve psychologically protective functions" (Portes and Rumbaut 2001, 151). Hence, when youth are in a mainstream supportive environment, they may take their ethnic self-identity for granted. However, when they feel they are facing discrimination because they belong to a certain ethnic group, though they may cope by trying to assimilate with mainstream society, an alternative is to reaffirm their ethnic solidarity (Portes and Rumbaut 2001).

Portes and Rumbaut (2006) say that, like ethnicity, religion can become reactive among first- and second-generation immigrants. But they believe religion only becomes "reactive" when immigrants begin disassociating themselves from their native religious traditions to fit into their host country. This happens when immigrants feel that their native religion is not fulfilling their needs, and they are exposed to alternatives, as for example, Japanese and Korean immigrants in the United States who have embraced Protestant Christianity (Chen 2008).

In my view, religious identity may become reactive in the same manner as ethnic identity, and Portes and Rumbaut (2006) overlook some important aspects of identity formation. First, identity is not merely a feature of ethnicity, and other important social attributes such as gender, class, and age can impact identity formation. Second, religious identities can be racialized and prone to the social processes of discrimination, inequality, and external labelling.

Taking these insights about identity into account, my research suggests that people may experience reactive identities when any one of their dimensions of identity is threatened. Portes and Rumbaut's (2006) theory of reactive ethnicity can help to explain the experiences of religious minority groups. But a better term to describe the social process by which marginalized individuals assert their identities is "reactive identity formation," a concept developed more fully in the following sections of this chapter.

My research shows how multiple factors, including both societal ascription and individual agency, can lead to the formation of reactive identities. Trying to cope with multifaceted discrimination plays a role in the reactive identity formation of young Canadian Muslims, as reactive ethnicity theory would suggest. Increased societal interest in Islam, which leads to more self-learning about Islam, coupled with resistance to mainstream ideologies, also contributes. But when young Canadian Muslims begin to build closer ties to Muslim communities and to each other, they experience a host of difficult challenges.

Impact on Muslim Identity

Many of my interviewees speculate that individuals can deal with the negative perceptions of the Muslim community in Canada by stepping away from the faith. However, only one participant has chosen such a path: immediately after 9/11, Falak stopped telling people that she is Muslim because she feared for her personal safety. Others do not recall having this kind of reaction. Fifteen interviewees indicate that their Muslim identity was a focal part of their identity before 9/11 and has remained so; thirty-four say they have come to identify themselves more strongly as Muslims and feel a deeper connection to their faith in the post 9/11 era. Overall, forty-nine out of fifty interviewees maintain a strong Muslim identity or have affirmed their Muslim identity since 9/11. Saud and Zora comment:

> SAUD: I think that largely 9/11 did change how I saw myself as a Muslim ... It has made me more aware of the nature of Islam. It has made me more aware of myself as a Muslim. My general awareness has increased. My involvement with Islam increased.
> ZORA: I am sure there are Muslims that have decided to abandon their own faith [after 9/11]. However, I believe many Muslims have decided to become more educated about their own faith because they realize this is a time where they have to protect their faith. So, in some ways, I believe that many Muslims have become more religious.

In short, many young Muslims assert their Muslim identity in the post 9/11 era (see Kundnani 2002; El-Halawany 2003; Peek 2003; Gupta 2004). I find that they do so in various ways: some assert their Islamic faith and religiosity, as demonstrated by Saud and Zora. As will be shown shortly, others build closer ties to Muslim communities, become more educated about Islam, and start reflecting on what it means to be Muslim. Still others assert their Muslim identity publicly to resist the demonization of Islam. However, it is not yet clear why this affirmation is occurring.

Reactive Identity Formation as a Way to Cope with Discrimination

Thirty-one out of the fifty Muslims I interviewed indicate direct experience of discrimination related to their Muslim identity post-9/11, and forty-one (82 per cent) told stories of family members or close friends being victimized. This high percentage is important; having people close to you face discrimination because of their religious identity can be just as troubling as facing discrimination personally.

The young well-educated Muslims in this study clearly feel a heightened sense of discrimination since 9/11. They face hate crimes from strangers in public places, stigmatization of their religious practices, and racialization of their gender identities. They encounter state discrimination at airports and border crossings, as well as employment discrimination. This multifaceted discrimination has a host of consequences for them, impacting their sense of safety, their daily routines, and employment prospects, not to mention their sense of belonging to Canada.

How do they deal with this? According to theories of reactive ethnicity, when people experience or perceive discrimination, in order to cope, they are likely to intensify their identification with their ethnic group and build closer ties to their ethnic community (Portes and Rumbaut 1990, 2001). So, too, the Muslims in this study are strengthening their Muslim identity. Asima and Nashida comment:

ASIMA: I have not met any Muslim that has disassociated with the religion. I have met people that became stronger in the faith. I think Muslims feel that there has been an attack on their religion, and when something like that happens, you need that closeness to feel secure and to maintain your faith and your power. Your faith has to become much stronger.

NASHIDA: I feel the Muslim community got closer after 9/11. We went to the Mosque more, just to make each other feel more confident that we should not be blamed for this, and that we are not the problem.

As the women's comments show, to handle post-9/11 discrimination, some Muslims are strengthening their Muslim identity through a reassertion of faith and active participation in Muslim communities; in other words, like ethnic identities, religious identities can become reactive. As mentioned previously, Yuval Davis (2011) maintains that the less secure people feel about their identities in society, the more salient they become in their lives. This is clearly happening in the case of my interviewees. Because they feel their Muslims identities have been threatened in the post-9/11 era, they engage in attempts to strengthen it.

Building closer ties to Muslim communities plays an important role in coping with discrimination in the post-9/11 era. Deborah Schildkraut (2004) has found that "while seeing oneself as discriminated against can have a negative impact on mental and physical health, this negative impact can be mitigated if the perception of discrimination also promotes self-identification with the aggrieved group" (4). Radi says:

Yeah I would say that I have definitely (have come closer to the community). Yeah people came closer. Something else that I noticed, that at the Friday prayers there were people that would come that would definitely not have come before. More students would come then before. They would come, and want to learn more about their faith. They would want to become religious and feel more acceptance into their own group. I guess. Yeah I would say, that as a community as a whole, it became stronger and more connected.

Amber, who is half-Pakistani and half German, also indicates that she has come closer to the Muslim community and now goes for Friday prayers on a regular basis. She describes her reasoning:

Because I have it easiest than others because no one would assume right away that I am Muslim because of the way that I dress, not very conservative, and because of my features. So I felt that I had to be close to my community and support those that had the outward signs of being a visible minority and that would face more discrimination than I have.

Significantly, Yuval-Davis (2011) mentions that identity narratives are often constructed as specific forms of practices. She writes "specific repetitive practices relating to specific social and cultural spaces, which link and individual and collective behavior are crucial for the construction and reproduction of identity narratives and constructions of attachment" (15–16). In the case of my interviewees, regularly attending religious prayers and gatherings of their Muslims communities may work to help solidify their Muslim identities. Furthermore, for my interviews these repetitive practices may also take the form of constantly being asked questions about Islam by others and then feeling the need to constantly learn more about it to answer such queries.

Reactive Identity Formation and Learning More about Islam

Some interviewees say that their assertion of a Muslim identity is both triggered and reinforced by society's increased interest in Islam and Muslims. Salman, a twenty-four-year-old man who came to a Canada in 2003 from Bangladesh, and Ayesha note:

SALMAN: In a way, it has brought more unity and has brought about more curiosity within our religion. Like, it has made me more say, like, religious. People ask me questions right, left, and centre, so I feel obligated to learn more about my religion, so I know what to say and what not to say, you know.

AYESHA: After 9/11, we had more group meetings in mosques to be able to understand and learn more about Islam and what's behind it and why we practise certain things. So we had more general education about Islam. I read the Quran more after 9/11 because before I kind of had taken it for granted.

As these experiences show, the formation of reactive identities is not solely the result of discriminatory acts. Rather, it has links to the increased interest in Muslims and Islam after 9/11. These young people want to learn more about Islam for themselves. They also want to be able to explain its tenets to others.

In fact, many go out of their way to educate others about Islam. They even attend conferences to learn how to better answer questions. Rashid and Atiya describe the special training they have received:

RASHID: They have the Islamic Speakers Bureau based in California and they came down here for some talks. They train you to go to high schools and sensitivity training for university professors and stuff like that. You go and do power point presentations on Islam. So there is an institutional response.

ATIYA: We recently attended a Speakers Bureau. It is an organization that helps Muslims give answers to questions that are asked of them. And answers that are unbiased. So when people say that you guys did this and you know how to rephrase, it back it sounds inviting and yet it is truthful and it does not sound too much like you guys do this and we do that. Um, so we have been receiving that kind of education.

Significantly, some say that becoming more educated about Islam has led to them to become more religious and affirm their Muslim identity. Aamir and Aatifa says:

AAMIR: I think that people would naturally want to learn more about their religion after 9/11. When you actually learn more about it, you feel closer to it, and then you can start to understand it better. From then on, you naturally progress into trying to observe Islam more actively and taking an active role in Islam, like wearing the hijab.

AATIFA: I also started learning more about the religion because people were asking more questions about the religion. I actually became more religious because I learned more about the religion. So I think that actually became a catalyst for a lot of people. To stand up for what they believe and to also let others know what is real and what is not. I think that made me more religious.

The nuances of reactive identity formation are reflected in these comments. Some Muslims in this study affirm their Muslim identity not only because they have faced discrimination but also because they have become more educated about their religion and are now more appreciative of it. Hence, individual choice and learning can play a role in the formation of reactive identities, something not explored by reactive ethnicity theorists.

For these young Muslims, the post-9/11 era provides an opportunity to think and learn about Islam, which, in turn, raises their individual sense of Muslim identity. This suggests that one positive outcome of the spotlight put on Muslims after 9/11 is its creation of an opportunity for young Muslims to reassess what it means to be Muslim in a North American context. Alisha says:

> After 9/11 I started to think, okay, I'm a Muslim because my parents are Muslim, but what does it really mean to be Muslim? I know what these guys [terrorists] calling themselves Muslims are doing is wrong. But then what is right? I started reading the Quran to figure this out. Because some people are saying Islam is wrong, but what is wrong with it? People keep on telling me you are Muslim, so yes I am Muslim but what does it mean to be Muslim? So what does Islam expect of me, in that sense? You just become aware of it more. Before 9/11 I had taken Islam for granted.

Interestingly, an in-depth exploration of Islam often leads young Muslims to question what is essential to Islam and to criticize the practices of previous generations. They particularly reject what they believe to be cultural forms of Islam (practices specific to certain regions such as Bangladeshi Islam) and instead try to embrace perceived "true" and "basic" elements of Islam (things fundamental to Islamic beliefs), a phenomenon Kibria labels "revivalist Islam." A discussion of how young Canadian Muslims move towards revivalist Islam and how this leads them to advocate for a collective Muslim identity appears in the next chapter.

Reactive Identity Formation as Resistance

As mentioned earlier, Muslim identity has increasingly been racialized as the new dangerous other threatening Western nations. As a result, young Muslims in this study affirm their Muslim identity as an act of resistance. In trying to counter the negative discourse surrounding Islam, they try to portray a positive Muslim identity in public. Asserting a Muslim identity in public becomes a way to resist the racialization of Muslim identities. In this way, Muslim identity becomes a "representation" and functions similarly how a collective black identity functions as a political category to resist racism and to create a counter-positive black image (Hall 1991).

Frustration over the portrayal of Islam as a violent religion is expressed by almost all interviewees, as voiced by Zora:

> There was sadness that innocent people are dying and a tremendous sorrow that Muslims would do this in the name of Islam. It was really devastating and hard to deal with. It was the exact opposite of what our faith teaches us. All the efforts that our community had been trying to put forth a positive face of Islam – in one moment that just vaporized. We felt like just how those planes were hijacked – our faith was also hijacked by those people.

Zora's comments reflect the wide range of emotions Muslims feel about 9/11, a finding supported by other studies (Ahmad 2006; Gillespie 2006). They see a beautiful religion suddenly (and negatively) reinvented and associated with terrorism. Zora's feeling that her "faith was hijacked" indicates the deep sense of betrayal and anger many well-educated young Muslims feel towards the perpetrators of 9/11.

However, non-Muslims do not necessarily differentiate between ordinary Muslims and terrorists, and the negative image of Islam as violent is perpetuated by the media. Aamir says: "Since 9/11 the media are just focusing on the negatives and the very small group and it gives the perception, indirectly at least, that the whole faith promotes violence and terrorism." Interviewees feel the media plays a substantial role in portraying Islam as a violent religion by attributing 9/11 to the entire Islamic faith, an impression backed up by a number of studies (Ahmad 2006; Harb and Bessaiso 2006; Korteweg 2008). When asked whether they feel the media contribute to discrimination, all fifty interviewees say "yes."

How do those who have grown up believing in the Muslim faith deal with this sudden turn of events? As noted, they frequently affirm their Muslim identity, making their affirmation an act of resistance. For instance, Radi says the following:

> After 9/11, I was more proud to be recognized as a Muslim than before. When I would be with Muslim sisters who would wear the headscarf, I

would want to be recognized as a Muslim compared to anything else. I was proud. I wanted people to know that I was not going to be drawn away from the faith. I wanted people to know that this is not Islam. The true Islam is not what happened with 9/11.

Similar to Radi, other young Muslims in this study are also demonstrating individual agency and attempting to "reclaim" Islam by asserting their Muslim identity. This reclaiming of Islam involves broadcasting their Muslim identity in public and resisting pressures of assimilation. In others words, Muslim identity becomes intertwined with what Hall (1996) has identified as "politics of representation."

This representation also involves trying to create a positive image of what it means to be Muslim. For example, Aatifa says the following:

Most Muslims do want everyone to know that not all Muslims are like that, and it's just a couple of people with a warped idea in their head giving all Muslims a bad name. Especially after 9/11, I try to be the best Muslim that I could. Both at home and outside, my behaviour with Muslims, or especially with non-Muslims, I try to be on my best behaviour or the best person that I can be.

Interestingly, this attempt to create a positive impression of Muslims in their interactions with other Canadians shows how there can be contradiction in reactive identities. On the one hand, my interviews try to define Muslim identity on their own terms and resist the vilification of Islam. However, these attempts to show a positive image of Muslim identity to other Canadians is still partially tied to wanting to be accepted by mainstream society. Therefore reactive identities can at times still function as a way to acquire national capital (Hage 1998). In other words, by trying to illustrate that they are "good" Muslims, my interviewees may be trying to acquire legitimacy as Canadian citizens.

Nonetheless, resistance and reclaiming Islam take many forms. Some young Muslim women wear the hijab to assert their identity. Aamir comments:

Actually close family friends, they have a huge textile business in Canada, and their business has gone down at least 30 per cent after 9/11. The textile company name has a very Muslim name. The wife goes to all of the meetings, and she wears the hijab. Before 9/11 she didn't – now she does. A lot of Muslims after 9/11 want to broadcast that they are Muslim – so she goes to these meetings wearing the hijab. If she loses the business – she says it's fine because she knows now who is being ignorant and who is discriminating against her, and she does not want to do business with them anyways.

Wearing the hijab is so important for this woman that she does so despite potential economic consequences. Two other female interviewees, Atiya and Zeba, also began wearing the hijab after 9/11. They both emphasize that while there are many reasons for their decision, above all, they want to represent a "positive image of their religion." The hijab is not imposed on these women, despite popular assumptions. Rather, it becomes a political tool, helping create an identity of resistance. My findings are similar to those of Homa Hoodfar (1993), who says that while the hijab has been used as a mechanism to control women's lives, women have also used it to free themselves from patriarchy.

Interestingly, I found no examples of Muslim men making changes to their physical appearance after 9/11, such as growing a beard or wearing traditional Muslim clothing. This difference may be due to the special meaning of the hijab in Western society. Since the hijab is a clear visible indicator that someone is Muslim, by simply wearing it, Muslim women become ambassadors for the religion.

A few interviewees try to reclaim Islam by becoming more politically active, another form of resistance. Amber says that the biggest impact of 9/11 is her increased involvement in political issues: "If anything else, it made me more passionate about my causes because of the backlash that took place ... I was always very politically active, but I did it even more, you know, so that it is not going to stop, we are not going to back down." Similar to Amber, other interviewees also spoke out against the policies and legislation that unfairly target Muslims. For these and other young Muslims, individual agency plays a role in the formation of reactive identities, something that reactive ethnicity theory does not consider.

Many of my interviewees make conscious decisions to affirm their Muslim identity to counteract negative stereotypes perpetuated after 9/11. However, it is important to note that the attribution of identity by society plays an important role in reactive identity formation. As described earlier, both Yuval-Davis (2011) and Hall (1990) hold that external labelling can play a powerful role on the internalization of identity. This is also occurring among some of my interviewees. For instance, Zeba mentions:

I think to a degree my faith has been defined by others. The way I view myself, the way others view me has been defined by others not by myself because of the political nature of how Islam has become. I think others have determined me Muslim, have labelled me Muslim, so I internalize that experience, and I call myself Muslim. Post-9/11, I saw a dramatic change right away. As soon as I left my high school, I knew right away that I was Muslim. That's how society defined me, and then I accepted that. Initially, I was kind of put off by that because, I mean, that's not how I identified myself, but as it became more [natural], I accepted it, and now it's my identity.

Zeba points to the impact of social ascription on how people see and locate themselves in society. Her experience along with other interviewees, are reflective of the splitting process described by Hall (1990, 1991), wherein hegemonic powers not only assert the power to label some groups as the other but also succeed in getting these individuals to identify themselves using the same categorization, which then marginalized groups attempt to convert into a positive identity.

Similar to Hall (1990), Micheline Labelle (2004) and Mary Waters (1990) shed light on why this occurs. Labelle (2004) notes that racialized and marginalized groups often utilize attributed identities as a form of resistance: "Negative stereotypes of minority groups, labeling diverse ethnic groups as black, and of inferior social status, had led to racialized groups, in turn – re-appropriating this attributed identity, subverting it and using it to define an identity of resistance" (46). Waters (1990) argues that African Americans in the United States have been socially constructed to identify themselves as "blacks" and have used this identity as a way of resistance, although they know their ancestors include many non-blacks. A similar phenomenon is occurring among the young Muslims in this study. Like Zeba, many feel they are stereotyped as belonging to a monolithic Muslim community. Like American blacks, their assertion of Muslim identity then serves as an act of resistance and a "form of representation" (Hall 1991).

When the interviewees began asserting this identity of resistance, they were being encouraged by community leaders and parents to keep a low profile for safety and security reasons. Salman says, "My mom [right after 9/11] was in tears. She would tell me not to go to the mosque, to have a clean-shaven face, and to keep away from any Muslim groupings. In a way, she was telling me to compromise my everyday routine or even my being a Muslim. I'm like, 'No, I'm not going to compromise my beliefs.'"

Atiya, describes her parents' fearful reaction in the following way:

> I thought they were proud of me because I was practising more and
> becoming wiser, but they also were more fearful. They were, "Well, why
> don't you just wear it [the hijab] when you go to the Mosque instead of
> wearing it all of the time?" They did kind of want to talk me out of it. But
> I did not. I had made up my mind to wear it.

As Atiya's comment makes clear, in addition to encountering discrimination from mainstream society, many young Muslims face parental
pressure to hold back from practising their religion. Thus, their ongoing resistance indicates the importance they place on reinforcing their
Muslim identity in a post-9/11 era.

Muslim religious affiliations have become a politically charged issue
not only in Canada, but also globally. Islam is increasingly portrayed
as an inferior religion that is barbaric, outside the realms of Western
civilization, and a security threat to Western nations. In such a hostile
climate, reactive identity formation may allow young Muslims to challenge hegemonic forces that demonize their religion, thus tying the
affirmation of Muslim identity to political resistance against the racialization of Islam.

This is occurring across gender lines, although there may be slight
variations in the form it takes. There is no evidence of variations between
the Muslims born in Canada and those born elsewhere; regardless of
country of birth, many indicate an intensification of their Muslim identity. Nor does age appear to play a role: both younger interviewees,
ages eighteen to twenty-three, and older interviewees, ages twenty-
four to thirty, speak of affirming their Muslim identity post-9/11. They
do so in various ways: becoming more religious, building closer ties to
Muslim communities, educating themselves in the Islamic faith, purs-
ing advocacy work to educate the public, reflecting on what it means to
be Muslim, asserting a Muslim identity in public, and becoming more
politically active.

Limits to Reactive Identities

Thus far in this chapter, I have shown my interviewees are building
reactive identities in the post-9/11 era. However, what remains unanswered is how these reactive identities play out for young Muslims as
they live their everyday lives. While previous literature has theorized

why reactive identities emerge, little is known about how second-generation minorities manage them as they continue to live in hostile climates that help trigger these reactive identities. Do they always feel safe expressing reactive identities? How do others respond? Do they ever feel forced to conceal their reactive identities in certain social institutions? In this chapter, I take an important step to answer these questions by exploring how young Canadian Muslims manage their reactive identities when faced with state surveillance at airports and border crossings.

The mistreatment of Muslims at airports and border crossings can play a part in the emergence of a reactive identity. Rashid, a twenty-two-year-old man who came to Canada as a young child, feels quite strongly about the new the security measures:

> You can go crazy at airports but it is not looking at the root of the problem. The root of the problem is poverty and terrorism. The root is economic deprivation and systematic mass murder and sanctions, like 500,000 Iraqi children killed. Targeting Muslims is not the solution.

He says the first time he wrote an article about the mistreatment of Muslims was after airport officials at the "Washington airport detained and strip searched a good friend" for eight hours. Incidents like this inspired him to learn more about Islam, become more politically active about Muslim issues and ultimately to affirm his Muslim identity: "All of a sudden I could write about stuff that I was learning about. I started to feel very confident and I learned what it meant to be Muslim Canadian. This spurred my Muslim identity."

The targeting of Muslims through increased surveillance also played a part in Asima's decision to affirm her identity following 9/11. Talking about airport and border-crossing surveillance, Asima, a twenty-three-year-old woman born in Canada and who comes from an Indian-East African background, says:

> I think that if there is a bomb scare or something like that then everybody should be stopped because I think that everybody is equal. I just don't think that it should be just Muslims because of one incident or because of two incidents. There are so many incidents were other people are involved with other religions. Do you all of the sudden just stop all of the white people? You don't just isolate one religion and do that. I do not think that is right.

In such a climate, Asima feels the need to protect her religion; her solution is to affirm her Muslim identity.

However, many young Muslims do not feel safe expressing a reactive identity at airports and border crossings because this is when they are at most risk of being stripped of their civil rights. For instance, Radi, a twenty-five-year-old man who was born in Canada to a Pakistani family, mentions that he has been extensively searched and questioned by security personnel at the airport. One way he has coped with the increasing stigmatization is by becoming closer to his community. While Radi feels safe expressing this reactive identity in public at his university campus or public places like the mall, he does not feel the same way expressing it at airports and border crossings. He actually does the opposite and tries to conceal his Muslim identity. He says: "My dad has told me that when I fly I should shave my beard. He says he does not want me to have a more Muslim look. He doesn't want me to take a chance – he says I should be clean shaven. I listen to him because I'm not stupid." Radi listens to his father's wishes because he fears being targeted at airports and border crossings.

Zora, a twenty-two-year-old woman who wears the hijab and has been living in Canada since she was eight years old, mentions her negative experiences when travelling:

> When I flew one time, and I was entering the U.S., I was asked questions like, "Have you ever been to the Middle East?" "Are you from Iraq?" "Have you ever been to the Middle East?" "Do you support the regime there?" "What is your religion?" It was not the questions themselves but the manner in which they were asked that was quite aggravating. They were trying to provoke us. The guy was pretty sarcastic in his tone. Like, it's obvious that I am Muslim, but he's like, "What's your religion?" And I have to say that I even lied because he asked if I had ever lived in the Middle East and I had. I did live in Saudi Arabia for eight years but I said "no.'" I said, "I am from Bangladesh and I am Canadian." I just wanted to avoid trouble. I was fearful that if I said yes he would ask me even more questions.

Zora finally decided to take off the hijab when travelling, but it was not an easy decision. She has conflicting feelings and asks rhetorically, "Ultimately, I feel that love for your religion should come before your fears, but what can you do?" Although she conceals her Muslim identity when travelling, she affirms her Muslim identity elsewhere. At her university campus, for example, she goes out of her way to educate people about Islam by organizing seminars and engaging in discussions about Muslim issues with her fellow medical students. While Zora feels safe to express her reactive ethnicity at her university campus, she does not feel the same way at airports and border crossings.

My interviewees' experiences illustrate how reactive identity formation is fluid and can manifest differently depending on the social location. Young Canadian Muslims are less likely to reveal their reactive identities when they encounter state security, particularly at airports and border crossings, because these are sites where their civil liberties and legal rights as Canadian citizens are most at risk, as illustrated in the previous chapter. This, in turn, makes them feel more marginalized and may reinforce their reactive identity formation.

Challenges Faced by Young Canadian Muslims

Yuval-Davis (2011) says that when political agents challenge hegemonic political powers, they also "struggle both for the promotion of their specific projects in the construction of their collectivity and its boundaries and, at the same time, use these ideologies and projects in order to promote their own power positions within and outside the collectivity" (20). Therefore, it is not surprising that when young Canadian Muslims in this study affirm their Muslim identity, creating reactive identities and growing closer to their Muslim community, they do not necessarily agree with that community on all issues. Instead, they begin to challenge certain practices of the older generation, some of which are advocated by their peers. Practices that frustrate them include segregation in Muslim communities, interpretations of Islam, fear of terrorism, gender discrimination, and how to present Islam.

Segregation in Muslim communities is a major issue. Many of the interviewees do not endorse how some older generations have split themselves into different branches of Islam such as Shia or Sunni Muslims. For example, when asked what Muslim sect they belong to, many interviewees refuse to answer; Aneesha and Haleema express the following sentiments:

ANEESHA: I like to define myself just as a Muslim, and I don't think I like to define myself another way. And I think that's another thing the youth are doing. Like, I've always been the type that didn't like to say I was Sunni, but now I'm seeing a lot of the youth go that route. Because when you

start saying you're Sunni or Shia, or this or that, then you're just causing
yourself to be put into a certain type of group as opposed to a community. Like, if you're a Muslim, then you're a Muslim, and that's it. You can
have different perspectives as a Muslim, but you still have to respect the
other side, and that's one problem within the community, I find.

HALEEMA: A lot of people don't like differentiating, just because of the
Prophet Mohammed. He always taught that the community should be
one. And because there's a lot of sects now, a lot of people just don't like
the idea of, "Well, I'm Sunni" or "I'm Shia."

Sunni Muslims make up the majority (85 per cent) of Muslims around
the world, while significant populations of Shia Muslims are found in
Iran and Iraq (Nimer 2002). They share fundamental Islamic beliefs
and articles of faith, and it has been argued that the division into Sunni
and Shia is because of political reasons, not theological ones (Nimer
2002). This may be one reason why interviewees are so opposed to
categorization.

However, on occasion, these practices of segregation are followed
by younger generations, and the young Muslims I interviewed may
find themselves butting heads with their peers. Leela, who is Ismaili (a
branch of Shia Muslim), expresses her frustration when she sees fellow
Ismailis forming cliques at university:

You see it everywhere, at Waterloo especially, because there's so many of
them. They [Ismailis] all just come together, and literally they ignore other
people, and they don't try and make friends with other Muslims. And to
me, it's stupid, they're doing it for the wrong reason. Like, I don't know
why they can't make friends with other people, just because they're not
Ismaili. You shouldn't be like that. But it happens a lot. That's why I don't
associate with a lot of Ismailis at U of T, because it bothers me.

Interesting, while Leela believes that Ismaili Muslims spend too much
time in their own cliques, other Ismailis talk about feeling marginalized and shunned by other Muslim communities. Sanya, who is Ismaili
Muslim, says:

I mean I feel I'm more part of the Ismaili community, I guess. Just because
I guess over the years, I felt somewhat we are separate from the Muslim
community as a whole. Like, I myself would identify as, yes, being part of
the Muslim community, but then sort of this subsect of it. And when I talk

to friends, who are say Sunni Muslim, a lot of them don't consider Ismailis to be Muslim. I definitely find that upsetting, especially when I try to do align myself with other Muslims. There's always this kind of like, "Oh, you guys aren't really the same" kind of thing.

I witnessed some of this inter-sect tension when I was recruiting interviewees. When I told one interviewee, who was trying to find me more potential interviewees, that I had interviewed a few Ismaili Muslims, she said that Ismaili Muslims are not really Muslims and implied that I should not be interviewing them.

But this lack of recognition made Sanya want to participate in the project. She was happy I had contacted the Ismaili Students Association because she believes they are often left out. Sanya also argues that young Ismailis make efforts to build better relationships with other Muslim student organizations:

I don't know about the communities as a whole, but I feel like my experience has been that they do things separately. But I know within our community, and we have an Ismaili Students Association here, like, on every campus at every university, and we try to do more things with the Muslim Students Association. Like breaking of the fast at Ramadan, or whatever, like [we] try to do more events because we do want to build bridges, and we don't want to have this conflict.

In short, segregation within the Muslim community is largely linked to the various branches of Islam. Many of my interviewees deplore these differences and seek to effect change, even though their efforts are not always successful. As mentioned earlier, many of the interviewees do not like it when earlier generations follow what they believe are cultural forms of Islam such as Bangladeshi Islam; instead, they advocate a revivalist form of Islam which they believe involves following the "pure tenants" of Islam. A discussion of revivalist Islam appears in the next chapter.

Another area of contention is related to how Islam should be interpreted. Some interviewees worry that certain Muslims are practising a "backward" interpretation of Islam. Salman says:

What I notice is that a lot of Muslims, um, they get so into it, then they somehow categorize themselves as fundamentalists. They try to live in the past, but as modernists, I don't think that you can do that. You can't live in a society, act religiously ... you can't breathe down people's necks and say, "Oh you're wrong because this is how it was done, you know, a thousand years ago."

Although many interviewees have a strong attachment to their religion, they can be critical of it when they do not like the way it is practised.

A few question how Muslims who have not been born or raised in Canada interpret Islam. Aneesha says:

> There are also those that just happened to come here a year after 9/11, and they have very different views. They feel that Islam is this, this and that, and that's it. They don't think Islam can have different perspectives on different issues. And that's where I think the differences lay between Canadian-born and non-Canadian-born. Like a Canadian-born will see Islam as being very encompassing, like, it will allow different perspectives. Where others that aren't Canadian-born, they seem to lack that aspect. It gets confusing, because the Canadian-born, they already have an open mind; they already know that this is how Christianity works, this is our duties, and they're surrounded by it. They wanna learn about Islam on their own terms, so that's one big thing about being Canadian: to learn on your own terms. But with non-Canadians, they're taught Islam in a very skewed way. So when they come here, they either stick with their skewed message, or they realize that it's very biased, and they go ahead, and they decide to figure things out for themselves.

Aneesha's comments suggest that some young Muslims who have been born or raised in Canada may feel their understanding of Islam is superior to those from other parts of the world. Ironically, although many young Muslims are critical of older generations for not being broad minded and inclusive of others, some young Canadian Muslims question the practices of immigrant Muslims.

Some of the interviewees also worry about misguided young Muslims who support terrorism. Amineh and Aamir express these concerns:

> AMINEH: Some young Muslims go about in the right ways, and some of them in all of the wrong ways. I think when one wants to seek knowledge, there are not a lot of people that can give them good and fair information, a lot of people. And then you go into the Muslim environment, and you are depending on [the fact that] that there are some good sheikhs, but there is one that is bad news, he made an anti-Semitic comment – I don't like him – people like him, they are the producers

of the extremists that can eventually lead to [terrorism]. I think that the Muslim community needs to shut them down because they are doing a disservice to everyone. He does not respect women, and his views are all twisted.

AAMIR: A few people in my class – you would think they are medical students, and that they would not be ignorant, but when things happen against the U.S., such as bombings, you can see that they are happy. I am disgusted by that ...They feel that since all of the discrimination that has happened – they feel that they have to fight back. But it's just going to get worse and worse. People are just going to be fighting and fighting. I am worried about that.

The possibility that due to a lack of proper guidance, some young Canadian Muslims may be misled into supporting terrorism is a pressing concern for most of the interviewees.

Gender discrimination in Muslim communities is another contentious issue, especially among the women, as evidenced by Aneesha's comments:

In my community, at least, they feel that if you wear the scarf, you're, like, a pure innocent girl and can do no wrong, and this and that, which isn't true. The standard is the girl that wears the hijab, and the person that doesn't is, like, below them, and I think that's wrong too. Because in Islam, there's no compulsion in religion, like, you can't be forced to wear the scarf. You can't be forced to do anything. And in the Pakistani community, girls will be forced to wear the scarf just to make their parents happy or something. And what's the point of doing that? When the girl leaves her house, she's just going to want to take it off. And I think that's the main issue that the Pakistani community has. They don't recognize that if you force your kids to do it, you are pushing them further away from Islam.

Aneesha brings up a controversial issue. Muslim communities have been increasingly portrayed in the media as oppressive to women. This is very upsetting for most of the interviewees, as the prevalence of gender inequality in Muslim communities has been grossly exaggerated (Ahmed 1992; Hoodfar 1993; Khan 1998; Abu-Lughod 2002; Razack 2004; Haddad 2007; Meetoo and Mirza 2007). In fact, gender inequalities can be found across all cultures and religions and are not restricted to Muslim communities.

Aneesha is particularly concerned that the hijab may be used to symbolize the purity of Muslim communities, and as a result, some girls may be pressured into wearing it. This use of the hijab echoes Hoodfar's (1993) sentiments about the veil. Hoodfar writes that women have used the veil as a way to free themselves from patriarchy, but in some instances, it is used as a mechanism to control Muslim women's lives. As noted previously, some of my interviewees use the hijab to express their political agency; they seek to become ambassadors while protecting their religion. But it is their decision and theirs alone.

While the hijab may be forced on women in some instances, I did not encounter this among my interviewees. However, Yen Espiritu (2003) argues that immigrant groups often use gender as a vehicle to assert cultural superiority over dominant groups. In her research on Filipino Americans, she shows how some Filipino communities utilize the virtue of their immigrant daughters to turn the negative ascription they experience as immigrants into an affirmation of higher morality. A similar phenomenon may be occurring in a few Muslim communities where the hijab becomes a way to symbolize the purity of Muslim women. This may be intended to show the higher morality of Muslim societies in comparison to Western ones, but it could result in inequalities for Muslim women. How young Canadian Muslim women deal with gender inequalities in a social climate where they are stigmatized and racialized for these inequalities is an issue for future research.

Amineh worries about equality when she expresses concern about female students having access to important positions in Muslim Student Associations (MSA):

> Our MSA is very liberal compared to other MSAs. We were the first MSA in BC to elect a women president. Before that you just had a lot of closed-minded people, and after that, we had three other women presidents. UBC and UVIC have still not had a women president. UVIC does not even allow women on their board. We have tried to talk to them. People come from abroad, and they come with their own cultural ideas, and they come and try to build an Egypt and a Pakistan here in Canada, and you know that does not work.

Clearly, gender discrimination may exist in organizations led by Muslim youth. Echoing back to my earlier comments on religious divisions, Amineh's comments allude to the tension between Canadian Muslims and immigrant Muslims. In some instances, young immigrant Muslims may try to reproduce their home country's gender hierarchy. However, it is also possible that Canadian Muslims may be shifting the blame for the gender inequality that exists in many student organizations to Muslims who are new to Canada.

A major challenge is how to present Islam and Muslim communities to other Canadians in the post-9/11 era. My interviewees are divided on this. Some interviewees believe Muslim communities often do not do enough to align themselves with the rest of Canadian society. For instance, Bushra and Barkat say:

BUSHRA: I think we almost put labels on ourselves, [so] that we segregate ourselves from the [Canadian] community, but I didn't feel the community segregated us, like, they didn't place us in a different category.

BARKAT: I just think Muslims have done a really bad job of actually connecting themselves to Canadian society, so they have isolated themselves. They haven't necessarily embraced others to come into the community. Others just kind of leave them alone, and do leave them alone. We'll just stay on our own side, then it'll be okay.

Another generational divide between older and younger Muslims is how much to integrate into Canadian society. Some young Canadian Muslims may seek more integration than their elders.

While some interviewees feel more needs to be done to integrate into Canadian society, others worry about making too many changes to their religious practices. For instance, Amineh says:

I think Muslims have become more apologetic and start changing things. All I am saying, that after 9/11, a lot of people started looking at religion and being, like, this is not fair to women and that we should change this. So we start changing things, and some changes are needed, but some of the ways people are going about changing things is in the wrong way. But I do not think they can really not pick and choose, and there is a [method to] the way things are [done], too. I think people just want it to seem like a very modern and equal religion, so they are being apologetic, but what are you being apologetic for? Judaism and Christianity have the same thing. Just because it is under the microscope, it does not mean that you have to go out and change everything.

In brief, young Canadian Muslims face complex issues when they begin to build closer ties with their Muslim communities. Some do not like certain practices within their own communities and want to alter them. Others don't want their communities to make too many changes to their religion just to appease those who have become critical in the post-9/11 era. As a result, when young Canadian Muslims become actively involved in their religion and Muslim communities, they often come into conflict with one another and with older generations.

Conclusion

The heightened emphasis on Muslim identity in response to increased and multifaceted discrimination in the post-9/11 era shows the importance of theorizing the formation of Muslim identity. Perhaps surprisingly, given the interest in Muslims and Islam, this has not yet been considered. This work begins to fill the gap in the literature. To this end, I accept and extend the existing work on reactive ethnicity, applying my term "reactive identity formation" to the social process of affirming identity in response to discrimination. Identity is not merely a feature of ethnicity; other important social attributes such as gender, class, religion, and age play a role in identity formation (Settles 2006). People may develop reactive identities when any one of these dimensions is challenged. My research shows that religious identity can become reactive when it is challenged.

Many of the young Muslims in this study demonstrate reactive identity formation, affirming their Muslim identity in a variety of ways. Some reassert their Islamic faith; others participate more in their Muslim communities, educate others about Islam, become ambassadors of Islam, reflect on what it means to be Muslim, highlight their Muslim identity in public, or became politically active. Their experiences reveal three key points. First, the young Muslims in this study affirm their identity to cope with the discrimination they face; this accords with the arguments of reactive ethnicity theorists. Second, with the increased societal interest in Islam, my interviewees have strengthened their Muslim identity by learning more about the religion and becoming more appreciative of it. Finally, resistance against the negative images of Islam can play an important role in reactive identity formation, something that reactive ethnicity theory does not consider. The experiences of the interviewees show that multiple factors can lead to the formation of reactive identities.

My research extends previous work on reactive ethnicity by documenting that reactive identity formation involves interplay between social forces and individual agency. Many of the young Muslims in this study affirm their Muslim identity to counter discrimination and increased interest in Islam post-9/11. Both personal and political motivations play a part in their decisions as well, making reactive identity formation a complex social process, involving both societal and self-ascription. Furthermore, the fact that multiple factors contribute to the reactive identity formation of the young Muslims in this study helps to explain why the majority experience it and may also explain why a similar phenomenon is occurring in the U.S. and the U.K.

Reactive identity formation can also be seen functioning as a "form of representation" (Hall 1990, 1991) or as a "narrative" (Yuval-Davis 2011). Through reactive identities, my interviewees resist the racialization of Islam by articulating a positive Muslim identity. However, like the black identity politics described by Hall, these reactive identities involve limitations, contradictions, and challenges. For one, when trying to represent the image of the "good Muslim," reactive identities can work not only to challenge hegemonic powers but also to gain approval from dominant Canadian society. Furthermore, as much as my interviewees may want to express their reactive identities, they do not feel safe doing so in certain contexts. When they face security procedures at airports and border crossings, where they feel most at risk of being stripped of their rights, they choose to conceal or downplay their Muslim identity, reminding us of the powerful ability of the state to discipline identities. Finally, when young Canadian Muslims develop reactive identities and become more involved in their religion and in their communities, they face challenges; they come into conflict with one another and with older generations on important issues, complicating their experience of reactive identity formation. An issue that especially divides younger and older generations is cultural affiliation, a topic discussed in the next chapter.

5 Choosing Religion over Culture: How Canadian Muslims Make Sense of Cultural Affiliations Post-911 Era

Introduction

Nashida speaks of a weak attachment to her Pakistani identity:

> I don't even believe in culture as much, I mean I could be Canadian, my parents could be Pakistani, I could marry someone – I'm not married, but I could marry someone Egyptian. What am I? I'm still Muslim, I'm still Canadian. I've never visited Pakistan in my life, I have never gone anywhere outside of North America, I don't even know if I'm Pakistani, you know.

As the previous chapter shows, through "reactive identity formation" many of my interviewees have intensified their religious identity as a way of dealing with the post-9/11 era. In this chapter, I explore what this affirmation of Muslim religious identity means for their cultural affiliations, their connections to the national origins of their parents, or for those not born in Canada. Does the importance they now place on religious identity coincide with a weak cultural one? How do cultural affiliations function for a group of young Canadian Muslims who hold on strongly to their Muslim identity in the post-9/11 era? For example, how do they make sense of being Egyptian, Indian, Pakistani, and Saudi Arabian in such a climate? In addition, has the emergence of reactive Muslim identities led to a collective Muslim identity that transcends traditional cultural boundaries?

Many young Canadian Muslims in this study do not maintain a close connection to their cultural affiliations in the post-9/11 era. Moreover, most push for a revivalist form of Islam, which involves separating what they believe to be cultural practices of the religion and returning to perceived "basic" tenants of Islam. Furthermore, this quest for revivalist Islam helps create a sense of collective identity among Muslims from diverse cultural backgrounds – though this collective identity is often contradictory and fragmented.

Collective Identities and Diaspora

The concept of diaspora is a good starting point for understanding collectivities that span geographical boundaries (Kelly 1998). While the diaspora literature can shed light on the emergence of a collective Muslim identity among diverse communities, the notion of diaspora is difficult to define and has been conceptualized in numerous ways by different academics. Steven Vertovec (2003) mentions that "diaspora" is often used today to describe practically any population considered "deterritorialized" or "transnational." Faiza Hirji (2010) concedes that there is no universally recognized definition of what a diaspora is, and it is perhaps best understand in what it is not: "It is not a nation in the same structured way as a legal polity, but it does contain elements of nationalist feeling. It is not necessarily a community of exiles, but exile may be a part of diasporaic experiences" (35). James Clifford (1994) lists the following main features of diaspora: "a history of dispersal, myths/ memories of the homeland, alienation in the host country, a desire for an eventual return, ongoing support for the homeland and a collective identity importantly defined by this relationship" (305). Meanwhile, for Stuart Hall (1990), diaspora involves ever-changing representations, allowing an "imaginary coherence" for a set of malleable identities; diasporan identities produce and reproduce themselves through transformation and difference.

While there is a lack of consensus about what actually constitutes a diaspora, there is some agreement in the literature that a lack of acceptance in the nation state can result in a heightened sense of belonging to a diaspora collective. For instance, Hirji (2010) says that immigrants who feel alienated from the nation state in which they reside may feel a renewed sense of loyalty to their homeland. In describing the black diaspora, Hall (1990) mentions that marginalization helps to create a sense of a larger community. Clifford (1994) asserts that diaspora cultures are, to varying degrees, created as a response to regimes of political dominance and economic inequality. Similarly, Paul Gilroy (2000) writes that "slavery, genocide, and other nameable terrors have all figured in the constitution of diaspora and the reproduction of a diasporan consciousness" – a particular kind of awareness generated among transnational communities (124).

Resistance to domination, then, is essential to diaspora affiliations. Gilroy (1987) elaborates that diaspora identification often exists in resistance to the political forms and modes of modern citizenship. For example, in reference to the black diaspora in Britain, he articulates that diaspora culture functions as a defence against policing and other forms of racist violence and as a critique of capitalism. Similarly, Clifford (1994) notes that racialization and economic marginalization can lead to the emergence of new coalitions such as anti-racial alliances forming between Afro-Caribbeans and Africans.

Diasporic consciousness can also result in identification with world-wide cultural and political forces – it is about feeling global (Clifford 1994). Association with international historical forces such as Islam allows claims against oppressive national hegemony. James Clifford (1994) asserts that violent practices of displacement do not strip people of their ability to create political communities and cultures of resistance. Hence, the term diaspora is not simply just a reference to transnationalism and movement – it is also about political struggle:

> Diasporic communities with varying degrees of urgency negotiate and resist the social realities of poverty, violence, policing, and racism, and political and economic inequality. They articulate alternative public spheres, interpretive communities where critical alternatives can be expressed. (315)

To this, Faiza Hirji (2010) adds that diasporic communities are often a means to create identities outside the conventional borders of home and host countries.

A key element, then, of a diaspora community is a sense of not belonging. Haideh Moghissi and associates (2009) assert that in contrast to the warmth and emotional support of ethnic belonging, the diasporic experience is marked by feelings of "not belonging." They use this insight to conceptualize the Canadian Muslim population as a diaspora. Despite the diversity of Muslim communities in terms of nationality, culture, class, and religious practices, Moghissi and associates contend that the Canadian Muslim population can be seen as a diaspora due to their collective consciousness of holding a marginal position in Canadian society. The group consciousness of a racialized religious identity brings diverse Muslim communities together in an expressive sense and politicizes them.

Adding to the difficulty defining what actually constitutes a diaspora, there is confusion about whether second or third generations can be seen as part of a diaspora. In her study of second-generation South Asians in Canada, Hirji (2010) regards her interviewees as a part of the South Asian diaspora or, at the very least, a part of the diaspora consciousness. She writes that even though they may not all long for return, many are "conscious of some allegiance to other South Asians or to those who share their religious background. These links may assume superficial forms at times, but they do exist and do shape the lives of these individuals in meaningful and lasting ways" (41).

Jennifer Kelly (1998) considers second-generation African Canadians as part of the collective black diaspora. Her study of African Canadian high school students confirms a diasporic consciousness. Using Gilroy's (1987) concept of "dynamics of remembrance and commemoration"– a positioning that leads to a sense of consciousness not dependent upon a state for fulfilment – Kelly illustrates how dynamics of remembrance allow students to utilize their shared experiences of marginalization within a white-dominated society to articulate a discourse of "blackness" and "belonging" that crosses geographic borders. She finds that despite coming from different ancestral backgrounds such as the Caribbean, Kenya, and Ethiopia, many African Canadian youth form a collective identity based on shared knowledge of black history and contemporary experiences. Hence, although aspects of culture related to origins are significant to identity formation, so too are the collective identities connected with racialization.

Following in the footsteps of Kelly (1998) and Hirji (2010), I consider second-generation Muslim Canadians part of the Muslim diaspora. This conceptualization is important because belonging to a diaspora space plays a key role in the transformation of religious identities (Vertovec 2003). Steven Vertovec (2003) claims that the study of diaspora can yield insights into general patterns of religious transformation associated with migration. He notes that religious identities often mean more to individuals away from their homeland and in the diaspora. The religious institutions built, adapted, and remodelled by immigrant groups become a world unto themselves. As a result, what it means to be a Muslim in the U.K., for example, is much different than what it means to be a Muslim in Pakistan (Vertovec 2003). Similarly, Hirji (2010) claims that living in a diaspora can sometimes inspire a desire to connect more intimately with religious traditions; it also becomes a place where accepted traditions can be questioned.

According to Vertovec (2003), the central question for diaspora communities is how to adapt to new environments without surrendering group identity. He notes that the process of adaptation that occurs through the conditions of diaspora and transnationalism leads to a fundamental question: What is essential to religious tradition? The conscious separation of religion from culture is often part an attempt to answer this, as those in the diaspora seek to adapt by distinguishing what is essential in religion and what is not. Living in a diaspora results in members reflecting on what is most significant in their religious traditions, leading to a separation of what is considered "truly" religious (core elements of belief and practice) from what is cultural (things specific to a particular country or region) (Vertovec 2003).

Hirji (2010) notes that distinguishing between religion and culture is especially common among second-generation immigrants, as diaspora provides the possibility of an in-depth exploration and understanding of faith. She notes that unlike their parents, second-generation South Asian immigrants are not born and raised in societies where their religious practices are dominant and have deep historical roots. As a result, they are more likely to ask questions and make comparisons. Therefore, among the second-generation, religious traditions that remain are those whose meanings have been interrogated and whose significance are better understood.

Empirical studies confirm Hirji's assertions. For example, Kim Knott and Sajda Khokher (1993) find that second-generation South Asian Muslim women in the United States establish a firm distinction between culture and religion, which differs from how their parents practise Islam. They reject what they see as their parents' cultural traditions and embrace a more "holistic" Muslim identity. Camilla Gibb's (1998) study of Canadian Muslim immigrants from the Ethiopian city of Harar is similar. Although a cultural form of Islam is practised in Harar, this has disappeared in the Canadian Muslim diaspora, and Harari children are turning away from religious practices that they believe are based on culture. Gibb asserts that in a diaspora, culturally specific aspects of Islam are likely to disappear because they are not shared and reinforced by Muslims from other places.

Nazli Kibria (2008) calls the movement, among second-generation Muslim youth, of trying to "purify" Islam from supposedly inherited culture elements of earlier generations and returning to what is believed to be the "core" tenets of Islam as "revivalist Islam."[1] Revivalist Islam involves a search for a "pure" Islam, one that is focused on a strict return to the "true" tenets of Islam – the principal teachings of the Quran. A key assumption of revivalist Islam is that some aspects of Islam (associated with past religious practices) are fundamental to the religion. Kibria (2008) questions this and instead argues that the momentum of revivalist Islam is tied to the current political and social context of Muslims living in Western nations. In her study of second-generation Bangladeshi youth in the United Kingdom and the United States, Kibria finds revivalist Islam tied to four main factors. First, she sees the growth of revivalist Islam among Bangladeshi youth as a response to the growing importance of "Muslim" as a public identity for Muslims in Western societies. Second, revivalist Islam, Kibria says, is tied to a deep sense of alienation from the West, an alienation fuelled by the racialization of Muslim identities. Third, among Bangladeshi youth, the desire to seek independence and distinction from older generations is tied to the growth of revivalist Islam. Fourth, like Vertovec (2003) and Hirji (2010), Kibria ties revivalist Islam to the social and psychological dislocation of migration – living in a society where Islam is not a normative and institutionalized practice can lead to questioning what it means to be Muslim.

Drawing on Stuart Hall's (1991) work, I further argue in this chapter that revivalist Islam also functions as a way for young Canadian Muslims to develop a collective Muslim identity that transcends traditional ethnic boundaries. According to Hall, the process of building collective identities in response to racism and marginalization almost always involves a search for roots. It is very difficult for cultural politics to wage a fight against hegemonic powers without returning to the past, one that is "retold, reimagined, rediscovered, and reinvented" (52). Hall (1991) says,

> This is an enormous act of what I want to call imaginary political re-identification, re-territorialization and re-identification, without which a counter-politics could not have been constructed. I do not know an example of any group or category of the people of the margins, of the locals, who have been able to mobilize themselves, socially, culturally, economically, politically in the last twenty or twenty-five years who have not gone through some such series of moments in order to resist their exclusion, their marginalization. That is how and where the margins begin to speak. (52–3)

According to Hall (1990), the reimagining of the past by searching for common roots is a very powerful force in the politics of representation and has played a critical role in the post-colonial struggles. He elaborates,

> In post-colonial societies, the rediscovery of this identity is often the object of what Frantz Fanon once called a passionate research ... directed by the secret hope of discovering beyond the misery of today, beyond self-contempt, resignation and abjuration, some very beautiful and splendid era whose existence rehabilitates us both in regard to ourselves and in regard to others. (1990, 393)

As Hall (1990) points out, what is recovered in this search for roots is not something that was buried or hidden by colonialism but instead a re-telling of the past that enables the production of collective identities. He writes that this recovery and reimagination of the past "offers a way of imposing an imaginary coherence on the experience of dispersal and fragmentation which is a history of all enforced diasporas" (394). For example, in his analysis of how a collective "black identity" emerged, Hall argues that this was made possible through imagining and re-discovering Africa as the mother of different civilizations, which then allowed for the encompassing of a variety of different groups from places like Jamaica, East Africa, West Indies, and Trinidad under one umbrella.

A similar phenomenon is occurring among my interviewees. Among young Canadian Muslims, the call to return to "basic" principles of Islam (revivalist Islam) functions similarly to the processes of "returning to the past" and "searching for roots" described by Hall (1990). This reimagination, reinvention, and recovery of a "pure" Islam has enabled my interviewees to develop a collective Muslim identity despite cultural and ethnic differences. This paves the way for an identity of resistance that challenges the demonization of Islam in the Western world.

Feelings about Cultural Identity

I start with an analysis of how young Canadian Muslims have come to understand their cultural affiliations: their ties to the national origins of their parents, or for those not born in Canada, to their country of birth. I refer to these affiliations as cultural identities, because my interviewees see their cultural backgrounds as connected to their ancestral origins. I have chosen not to call them national identities, because my interviewees strongly maintain that their nationality is Canadian (an issue explored in chapter 6), while their cultural identity is different as it reflects their families' ancestry. For example, my interviewees born in Pakistan or whose parents were born in Pakistan commonly refer to their cultural background as "Pakistani." Similarly, those born in Egypt or whose parents were born in Egypt see "Egyptian" as their cultural identity. My use of the term cultural identity follows Hall's (1990) theoretical insights. Hall says cultural identities are often based on shared history and ancestry. They can reflect common historical experiences and shared cultural "codes," which can allow us to see ourselves as "one people" (Hall 1990, 223). But like everything that is historical, they undergo constant transformations and are constructed through memory, fantasy, and myth. He elaborates that "heritage is an imagined part of a system of representation that has real, political, cultural and economic consequences in the present but to which we have a pre-eminently narrative, partly fictive relationship" (Hall 1996, 13–15).

The vast majority of the interviewees do not feel closely connected to their cultural identities. They have a wide variety of ancestral backgrounds, coming from India, Pakistan, Fiji, the West Indies, Libya, Bangladesh, Egypt, Jamaica, Saudi Arabia, and Syria. However, many say their cultural backgrounds are not that important to them. For instance, when I asked Zaahir, a twenty-two-year-old man raised in Canada, what being Pakistani means to him, he replied, "Not much." Sakeena, a twenty-seven-year-old Canadian-born woman, also says her cultural identity "doesn't mean a whole lot." In fact, many do not indicate having close ties to their cultural identity. This is in sharp contrast to how they articulate what their religious identity means to them, a point which will be discussed later in this chapter.

The interviewees who indicated a connection to their cultural identity often associate it with social practices such as food, dress, and language rather than identity formation. Bushra and Maria mention the following:

BUSHRA: That is more of a cultural thing, so being East African, being East Indian is a cultural thing – it's my language, my dress, it's my food, it's how I interact with other members of the community. But being Muslim is actually what defines me.

MARIA: It's more, like, cultural – we have a particular food, a particular dress, particular cultural music. It's not so much as something that defines me, as something that I tend to do for relaxing to have fun and sort of come together with other people who are from my background.

These women do not use their cultural backgrounds as part of their identities. Instead, culture is important socially, and they revert to it when it may be beneficial.

In contrast, four interviewees feel that their cultural identity plays a key role in how they define themselves. Cultural background is not merely a social tool for them but a source of pride and a guide to how to live their lives. Ayush, a twenty-eight-year-old man born and raised in Pakistan, says,

Pakistani means someone who is humble, friendly, who welcome their friends, someone who just wants to be happy. If you go to Pakistan, that's how people from Pakistan are; it doesn't matter what kind of money they are making. They are happy, and right now, there is so much stuff going on over there, but life over there is still very normal. We try to enjoy life, to have a balanced life, and that's something I really take pride [in].

Similarly, Azhar, a twenty-seven-year-old man born and raised in Iran, indicates that being Iranian is the most important aspect of his identity. Some interviewees feel that their culture and Muslim identities are intertwined. For instance, when asked what being Indian means to him, Umar, a twenty-two-year-old man who was born in India and came to Canada four years ago, replies: "It means to me that I am from India, I grew up there, I have family there, my cultural background is Indian, and a lot of the teachings from my Indian background go hand in hand with my Muslim identity." Umar, Azhar, and Ayush may have strong cultural affiliations because they were not born and raised in Canada. Umar and Ayush came to Canada when they were eighteen, and Azhar had only been living in Canada for a year when I spoke to him.

Their experiences are backed up by academics who argue that Muslims born and raised in Muslim majority societies[2] often develop religious identities that are intertwined with their cultural identities (Cesari 2004; Duderija 2007). Jocelyne Cesari (2004) finds that Muslim immigrants born and raised in Muslim majority societies often develop religious identities that are closely linked to their cultural background. In other words, their Islamic identity is tied to the dominant cultural and social practices of their former countries. For example, among Pakistani immigrants, the understanding of being Muslim is often closely linked to their identity as Pakistani. Similarly, Margo Rooijack-ers (1994) finds that among first-generation Turkish immigrants in the Netherlands, Islam plays an important role in maintaining their Turkish identities. As a result, these particular interviewees may have stronger ties to their cultural identities than their Canadian-born or raised counterparts.

While first-generation immigrants often assume religious identities that reflect their culture, Jocelyne Cesari (2004) asserts that second-generation immigrants born or raised in the West have different experiences and do not necessarily reproduce the cultural-religious identities of their parents. Adis Duderija (2007) writes, "Islamic identity for many western born Muslims is based upon a conscious choice of religious identity reconstruction and not merely on the basis of reproduction of an inherited aspect, or their ethnic heritage or tradition" (146). Not surprisingly, then, most second-generation Canadian Muslims in my study give precedence to their Muslim identity over their cultural one. Maria and Radi say the following:

> MARIA: Yes, I think that being Muslim and Canadian is really important to me, so that really takes preceden[ce] over where my ancestors are from.
> RADI: I see myself as Muslim first, because it is what you believe, and that is the most important thing. So that's more important than my culture.

Hall (1990) reminds us that cultural identity is not a fixed essence, lying unchanged outside history and social forces. Instead, cultural identities are subject to the continuous play of history, culture, and power, and, as a result, they undergo constant transformations. Hall asserts that "far from being grounded in mere recovery of the past ... which when found will secure our sense of ourselves into eternity, identities are the names we give to the different ways we are positioned by, and position ourselves within the narratives of the past" and present (225). Therefore, the priority my interviewees place on religious identities over their cultural ones needs to be understood in relation to the social and political context of living in Western societies in the post-9/11 era.

Having Muslim Identity Highlighted in the Post-9/11 Era

Young Canadian Muslims may prioritize their religious identity because in the post-9/11 era, being Muslim is highlighted by those around them. In the eyes of dominant society, being Muslim has more meaning than other aspects of identity (Kibria 2008). Zeba says,

> No, I think I just grew out of it [Indian identity]. Well, to a degree maybe possibly because I became more Muslim [after 9/11], so I had to give up one to accommodate the other, because I guess that's the way it works, but yeah, possibly. In terms of my Indian identity and my faith, I identify with my faith completely more than my Indian heritage. Simply because I guess I'm [a] visible Muslim, and society has put it upon me to determine myself that way.

As mentioned earlier, Hall (1990) argues that cultural identity is never solely individual but includes a dynamic relationship between the self and others, which are influenced by social, political, and historical factors. He writes, "Cultural identities are the points of identification, which are made within the discourses of history and culture. Not an essence but a positioning" (226).

For Hall (1990), there is "always a politics of identity and a politics of position which has no absolute in an unproblematic, transcendental 'law of origin'" (226). As mentioned in chapter 4, many young Canadian Muslims in this study have affirmed their Muslim identity to cope with discrimination and reclaim Islam in the post-9/11 era. As a result, they may give little credence to cultural identity. These experiences are illustrative of how identities are socially situated, fluid, and impacted by external labelling, a sentiment backed by a number of scholars (Cornell 1988; Nagel 1986; Waters 1990).

Interestingly, the three interviewees who report close ties to their cultural identity, Umar, Ayush, and Azhar, are among the minority who do not report affirming their Muslim identity in the post-9/11 era. This suggests that since 9/11, affiliation with cultural backgrounds may function differently for those Muslims who do not intensify their Muslim identity than for those who do. But since the majority of my interviewees do not belong in this category, I cannot say this definitively. The issue requires more research.

On some occasions, young Muslims may want their cultural backgrounds to be recognized, but this may not happen. Haleema, who wears the hijab (and who is not "black" but has brown skin), describes such an experience:

> Most people don't even know [I'm Jamaican]. I've had cases where, people would say, "Oh no, you can't be Jamaican." A lot of times it's just they

say things, and they don't think that I understand what they're saying. Like, I remember I was in line for lunch at the cafeteria once with my friends, and this one guy, it was nothing anti-Islamic or anything like that, but he [was] speaking Patwa, which is a Jamaican dialect. And he had no idea that I could understand what he was saying. And a lot of times, these things happen, and they don't associate the two. But it's interesting to surprise other Jamaicans, and they're really surprised, they're just like, "But you're Muslim." It's really not a negative thing. They're more interested in me being Muslim than anything else. I do identify as being Jamaican, but 9/11 might have also acted as a precursor to me going closer to Islam [than my cultural identity].

When one is Muslim, other aspects of one's identity may be invisible to society in the post-9/11 era, a phenomenon paralleling black identity in the U.S. Mary Waters (1990) notes that "Americans have generally paid a great deal of attention to cultural differences within the white race, while treating black Americans as if they were both a racial and an ethnic group with no internal differences" (45). So, too, when one is perceived as Muslim, aspects of one's cultural identity may be erased, thereby impacting how one views his/her identity.

Living in a Diaspora Space and Pushing for Revivalist Islam

Living in a diaspora affects how young Canadian Muslims make sense of their cultural identities. Because my interviewees were born and raised in societies where their parent's culture is not the dominant one, they may not have inherited an understanding of what it means, for example, to be Pakistani. In fact, many interviewees say they do not understand "what their cultural identities are supposed to mean" and, hence, do not know how to adopt it in their lives. For instance, Amber, whose mother is half German and whose father is half Pakistani, says,

My culture has been water[ed] down. I am not Pakistani. I am not German. I think of myself first and foremost as a Muslim, and that means having a set of beliefs about the world and about how things should be, rather than traditional cultural practices that are often associated with the faith.

Living in a diaspora allows for self-reflection on religious practices; this is particularly the case for second-generation Muslims, as evidenced by

Sanya, who says, "Canadian-born Muslims want to learn about Islam on their own terms. We want to do our own research."

Second-generation Muslims born and raised in Western countries may have difficulty relating to the cultural forms of Islam practised by their parents, a finding echoed by a number of other studies (Gibb 1998; Knott and Khokher 1993; Kibria 2008). Because they are more likely to ask questions about religious practices and to make comparisons, many develop a disdain for what they see as cultural interpretations of Islam and push for a revivalist Islam (Cesari 2004; Duderija 2007). As mentioned earlier, revivalist Islam involves a rejection of what is perceived as cultural interpretations of Islam (as it is practiced by older generations) and a return to what are considered "basic" principles of Islam (Kibria 2008). This is occurring among many of my interviewees. Yazeed, who comes from an Egyptian and Sudani background, says,

> One of the unfortunate things that is happening in the community is that it is run by the people from the older generations, though it is starting to be infiltrated by young generations. But is still run [by] people from older generations, and they come with their own biases and ideas about how people from certain areas of the world behave, and how they expect them to behave to begin with. For example, my mom wants to stick to the culture simply because for my mom's generation they're all either ex-slaves or ex-colonials, so they have a certain mentality. But we have a different mentality. For them, culture is very important ... they have to stick to it to maintain it. For us, it more like certain parts of our culture are just designed by people, and if I don't want to stick to it, I shouldn't have to. And I think for this generation, the teachings of the Quran and of the prophet – those are the things that are more important to them; that's what they would classify as being a Muslim.

Yazeed's sentiments echo Kibria's (2008) findings on Bangladeshi youth in the U.S. and U.K. Kibria states that many young Muslims have rebelled against Bengali Islam – the style of Islam practised in Bangladesh – creating a generational divide. Bengali Islam practices are seen by the youth as contrary to "pure" Islam, violating the religion's core tenets and spirit (254). Kibria notes that the adherence to revivalist Islam is leading Bangladeshi youth to develop a weak attachment to their Bengali identity. Similarly, I believe that for many of my interviewees, the desire for revivalist Islam reflects their weak cultural affiliations.

Embracing revivalist Islam is complex, however. To begin, as described in chapter 4, many young Canadian Muslims have created reactive Muslim identities in the post-9/11 era to cope with discrimination and to resist the negative portrayal of Islam. This affirmation of Muslim identity does not mean they blindly begin following the religious practices of earlier generations. Instead, they question previous practices and seek out a Muslim identity that makes sense to them, as illustrated by Yazeed's comments. Revivalist Islam provides an opportunity for second-generation youth to assert their independence from the immigrant generation (Kibria 2008), and their move towards it is related to the desire to create a distinct Muslim identity.

Among young Muslim women, this distinct identity may involve resisting practices they find to be sexist. For instance, Aneesha says,

> In Canada you can practise your religion without it being influenced by other perspectives. Like if I was raised in Pakistan, I would be taught that in order to be a good Muslim girl I have to obey my parents and my husband and this and that. Whereas, because I am in Canada, I can read the Quran on my own and understand it and be like, "Wait a minute, it does not really say that." So in Canada as a Muslim, I can learn about being Muslim [at] my own pace, it can't be shoved down on my throat. And I can put the hijab on my own terms and not because someone put it on my head.

Aneesha's comments suggest that living in a diaspora and reflecting on religious practices can pave the way for young Canadian Muslim women to speak out against practices they find oppressive to women. Ironically, little attention is paid to how Muslim women can use Islam to substantiate their rights. Mainstream society remains fixated on how Islam oppresses women.

Kibria (2008) asserts that revivalist Islam is particularly appealing to second-generation youth, because under hostile conditions, it offers a well-defined set of rules on how to conduct one's life and to create a sense of positive difference from dominant society. Revivalist Islam emphasizes the significance of Islamic thought in all aspects of life (Kibria 2008), and many interviewees mention this. For example, Zaahir and Rubina say:

> ZAAHIR: I guess it [Islam] is just a way of life that I apply to all aspects. I try to apply it to everything I do, pretty much. Like the way I look at it

is that there are guidelines for everything, so like, coming to school, or when I start working, it tells me what my religious responsibilities are, and how I can fulfil those responsibilities.

RUBINA: It [Islam] means a lot to me. It is part of my identity, and it is a large part of who I am. I think being Muslim shapes my personality, shapes my dreams. It also changes a lot of my values, the way I look at things, the way I want to live my live.

Islam also may give Canadian Muslims answers to some of life's more difficult questions. Samir says,

There are a lot of questions that people ask, like, you know, "Where do I come from? Where am I gonna go? What's the purpose of life?" Things like these. I thought Islam was able to answer those questions for me in a satisfactory manner. And that's what sort of gives me content, because you can't really get rid of physical suffering, but you can get rid of emotional suffering. You can understand how things work.

In this way, revivalist Islam can provide a sense of support and self-esteem, and it can offer instructions on how to conduct one's life.

In describing the emergence of the Muslim diaspora in the Western world, Riva Kastoryano (2006) notes that Islam is becoming the main element in how people act and react. They feel they are part of a community whose elements are based on Islamic practices, Islamic moral values, and social utility. Some interviewees say Islam gives them tools to bond with others. Haleema and Zeba say:

HALEEMA: So I find a lot of the times I just identify better with Muslims. Because culture can only take you that far, I find, whereas if you're in a religion like Islam where so many things are laid out, and you live your life by it, it's easier to get along with other people. Not necessarily get along, but if you're going to be hanging out with them 24/7. For example, I have a Muslim friend here, so we can go for the ritual washing before [we] pray together. It's just more things we can do together. Or, we don't have to worry about food, because we both eat the same food.

ZEBA: I am Indian but have friends from so many backgrounds such as Africa, Pakistan, Egypt. We are all Muslim with the same principles. Faith in my perspective holds a larger group of people together than culture. Faith allows you to unite with people that may not have the same culture as you, but the belief in one religion unites us all.

Jocelyne Cesari (2004) points out that religion may provide a sense of belonging for youth when other social institutions have failed. In the Canadian case, following specific rituals and rules, such as praying five times a day, may make it easier for young Canadian Muslims to associate with other young Muslims and form a collective bond.

The sense of belonging to a Muslim diaspora can be particularly helpful when Muslims are trying to cope with the challenges of living in a society where they are the minority and their religious identities are met with hostility. As mentioned earlier, a diaspora consciousness is often noted in reactions to feelings of displacement (Gilroy 1987; Clifford 1994; Hirji 2010). The turn towards revivalist Islam needs to be understood in similar terms. Since second-generation Muslims have higher expectations of equitable treatment from dominant society than previous generations, discrimination can result in a sharp reaction (Kibria 2008). Revivalist Islam may give a powerful sense of membership in a global community that transcends citizenship, cultural boundaries, and nationality. Similarly, Clifford (1994) argues, by allowing for association with world historical forces such as Islam, a diaspora consciousness challenges Western hegemony.

Therefore, the move towards revivalist Islam is a form of resistance among young Canadian Muslims. While dominant society may impose the label of "Muslim," young Canadian Muslims show agency by questioning and redefining what it means to be Muslim. In doing so, they create what Homi Bhabha (2004) calls hybrid identities. Bhabha describes hybridity as the process colonial powers undertake to translate the identity of the colonized (the other) within a singular framework; they ultimately fail and produce something familiar but different (Mythen 2012). For Bhabha (2004), the interweaving of the colonizer and the colonized results in the production of a new hybrid identity, which challenges the authenticity of any essentialist cultural identity. As hybrid identities evolve, they open up fresh political perspectives and challenge hegemonic ideologies (a more thorough discussion of hybrid identities and how they relate to being Muslim and Canadian is provided in chapter 6).

I see the movement towards revivalist Islam as allowing young Canadian Muslims to create a distinct way of being Muslim. In other words, when they express reactive identities as a result of being labelled Muslim in the post-9/11 era, they create their own definitions of what it means to be Muslim. They do not conform to how previous generations practised Islam. Rather, a revivalist Islam allows them to feel they belong in the larger Muslim diaspora collective. This feeling becomes a powerful tool of resistance, as described below in the next section. As Hall (1990) argues, it is difficult to build collective identities that can fight against hegemonic powers without some "rediscovery of the past" (393). By pushing for a return to the perceived "basic principles" of Islam, revivalist Islam plays a vital role in young Canadian Muslims' development of a collective Muslim identity that transcends traditional cultural and ethnic boundaries.

Creating a Collective Muslim Identity

Haj Yazdiha (2010) points out that hybridity can allow individuals to come together in a powerful solidary. For Yazdiha, hybridity has the ability to empower marginalized collectives by providing a means of reimagining an interconnected collective. Using these insights, I consider the hybrid identities of my interviewees as helping young Canadian Muslims from diverse cultural backgrounds to form a collective Muslim identity.

To start, it is important to note that a few interviewees feel Islam has always brought people together from different cultural backgrounds. Haleema and Samir say:

> HALEEMA: Oh definitely, and not just with 9/11. And that's one of the things that I really, really love about Islam, is that it's always, if you look at the history of Islam, it always has crossed cultural boundaries. Like the message of Islam was always ... there's no disputing the fact that it was always sent as a universal religion and taught as such. There's time when you just sit around, and you look at your friends, and you just see so many different hues and skin tones. It's really cool.
>
> SAMIR: Yeah, I think the Muslim community, for the most part, does cross cultural boundaries. I mean, the mosque that I grew up going to – there's people there that are Iranian, there's Indians, there's Pakistanis, there's Iraqis, there's Egyptians. There's no differentiation. I think it existed before as well. I think it got stronger in general in the community coming together. The community was already one, and they got closer after 9/11.

Some interviewees say Islam is inclusive of many different cultural backgrounds and feel this has strengthened since 9/11.

While some do not see segregation occurring in their communities, others feel that significant cultural divisions have lessened since 9/11. Zeba and Dawoud comment:

ZEBA: After 9/11, I think because all Muslims were vilified, it allowed Muslims to unite together, regardless of race, religion, because they're limited, they're a small population. So you have to rely on the resources you have, and you can't afford to be picky at this point. Pre-9/11, Muslims were not as united, because you could be picky, because everybody had their ethnic little mosques or masjids and stuff. But now, because the force was so much larger to combat it, they had to unite together.

DAWOUD: In the Canadian society, I think Muslims have always organized themselves along cultural lines. So you have predominantly Arab mosques, predominantly Pakistani mosques, predominantly Turkish, predominantly Bosnian. After 9/11, there was more of an effort between these cultural mosques to come out with a common vision of Islam and to present a common vision to the Muslim community. And because of that, what you started seeing is – whereas before someone who lived in this part of the city where the closest mosque was a Pakistani mosque, but because he was a Turkish guy, he would travel for twenty-five minutes to go the Turkish mosque, [he] started coming more to what was considered a Pakistani mosque.

Moghissi and associates (2009) note that Canadian Muslims come from diverse backgrounds such as Asia, the Arab World, Iran, Afghanistan, Africa, Latin America, and East and Southeast Asia. According to these authors, this diversity can result in the Muslim population in Canada being more fragmented than their European counterparts, as evidenced in mosques created along cultural lines.

However, Kastoryano (2006) says even if Islam appears to be fragmented, it represents a unifying force among Muslim immigrants where collective interests are concerned. In the Canadian context, having the common goal of defending their religion post-9/11 may provide an incentive for different Muslim communities to come together. Moghissi and associates (2009) point to an overarching collective identity emerging among Muslims that separates each Muslim community from its specific origins. Being marginalized and stigmatized for their Muslim identity links groups with distinct political histories and cultures. The incentive to come together may also be tied to the fact that individual Muslim communities in Canada, such as the Pakistani Muslim community, may not be large enough to fight the pervasive anti-Muslim sentiment.

Hall (1990) reminds us that collective identities and experiences are not givens, but they are constructed historically, culturally, and politically. According to Vijay Agnew (2007), identification with a collective identity requires three factors:

> First, there needs to be an availability of terms in public discourse that can pick out bearers of the terms by their ascriptive criteria; for example, man, woman, white, or black. Usually a consensus exists around these terms that are organized around a set of stereotypes (which may be true or false) ... Second, there needs to be an internalization of those identities or labels and a conception of oneself as a woman, man, white, or black in ways that "make a difference" and shape one's feelings and actions. Third, identification with a collective identity refers to a pattern of behaviour that is profoundly shaped (even in a sense produced) by histories of sexism, homophobia, racism, and ethnic hatred. (6)

These factors certainly played a role in the fading of cultural boundaries and the emerging of a collective identity among young Canadian Muslims. Bushra mentions,

> I think that 9/11, kind of from an outsider's perspective, grouped all different Muslims into one big clunk, and it made me almost realize, well, we may be different, but there still are a lot of similarities. So it was positive in that sense. It didn't make you discriminate more or less against Muslims from different backgrounds and made us realize we have common goals.

While the process of labelling may homogenize Muslims from different backgrounds into one group, Muslims may use this ascribed identity to form an identity of resistance. Through the collective identity, they work to deflect aggression directed to Muslim communities.

This move to establishing a collective Muslim identity is especially prevalent among young Canadian Muslims. Aneesha says,

> In the Muslim Students Association, there's a bit of everyone. Like, there's Somalis, Ethiopians, Saudis, like, [a] different mixture who are all doing the same thing. Like, we wanna make Islam accessible to Muslims on campus. And I find that that is the biggest thing that the youth are doing. They're getting together with a common goal, which is to unify Islam, but then adults aren't doing that as much. So hopefully, within my generation, we're already making strides. Like, we have this conference every December, you

might have heard of it, "Reviving the Islamic Spirit." Thousands of Muslims come to it, and it's run by a very diverse group of people. It's not all Pakistanis that run it, or all Somalis, or all Trinidadians. Like, it's a mixture of people. They do it according to your qualifications as opposed to your race. I think that's finally getting into the heads of the youth, but the adults are still behind. I don't see that change in the adults. I think Islam crosses cultural boundaries with the youth, but not with the adults. This is where I get confused, because I don't like to be within my community, because the way they practise the religion isn't Islam. They practise pseudo-Islam – it's, like, Islam and Pakistani culture combined, so I don't think that's religion at all.

Through revivalist Islam, young Muslims advocate for a collective identity that transcends cultural boundaries. Universities may provide an ideal setting for the blending of these boundaries. The conference mentioned by Aneesha, "Reviving the Islamic Spirit," is inclusive of many different cultural groups.

As mentioned earlier, older Muslims may be more reluctant to cross cultural boundaries, because they may still be attached to the cultural practices of their native countries. Young Muslims born and raised in Canada may not feel the same affiliations and hence may be more willing to form a collective Muslim identity by embracing revivalist Islam. Ultimately, this collective Muslim identity may allow them to connect with people with similar experiences of social exclusion who also object to how Islam has been demonized. For example, Sanya says,

A lot of us want to be pluralistic. We don't want to focus on cultural separations anymore. We feel we need to come together and do something about how the media was just totally destroying the image of Muslims. We want the outside society, as a whole, to see Muslims in a more positive light.

Forming a collective Muslim identity becomes a powerful tool of resistance that can be used to challenge global structures of domination.

Dibyesh Anand (2009) cautions that we should keep in mind the voices of the dominant groups within collective diasporan identities, as well as those of the silenced. Avtar Brah (1996) adds that all diasporas are differentiated, heterogonous, contested spaces, even as they are implicated in the construction of the common "we." Similarly, Hall (1990) recalls that in the movement to form a collective positive black identity, a tremendous amount of diversity and inequalities were suppressed. Furthermore, Hirji (2010) reminds us that resistance involves a delicate balancing act and is often filled with contradictions: "Resistance is complicated and laden with ambiguities for those who must live in a society while juggling competing demands for national, ethnic, and religious authenticity" (17). Therefore, although a collective Muslim identity may be emerging in Canada this does not mean all cultural tensions have been alleviated in Muslim communities. For example, Barkat says:

> I think that for a while, Muslim identity was strengthened. But I think that 9/11 happened so long ago, like, seven years, I think that they kind of fell back to the way they were. I think there was, for a little while after 9/11, more of a brotherhood and a sisterhood between Muslims. But there is quite a bit of racism in the Muslim community, which is funny because we sit here and complain about white Canada not accepting us, so we don't accept the other people within our culture. Arabs don't like Indians, Indians think that Arabs are arrogant, and nobody likes black people.

It is possible that once the motivation for coming together fades, the camaraderie may begin to disappear. As Barkat's comments reveal, racism is not limited to dominant groups; in fact, groups facing discrimination may display racial prejudices towards other groups. It may be difficult to remove these prejudices, even when efforts are made to bridge the gaps between groups. Furthermore, there may be some degree of internalized racial oppression among Muslim communities, what Hall (1986) defines as "the subjection of the victims of racism to the mystifications of the very racist ideology which imprison and define them" (26). He notes that internalized racism is one of the most common consequences of racism.

In their studies of second-generation South Asians, both Hirji (2010) and Amita Handa (2003) find that even among those individuals who work hard to challenge hegemonic practices, there is a level of internalized oppression. Hirji (2010) says it is difficult for marginalized groups to continuously engage in resistance when they face the pressure of managing multiple identities. Handa (2003) finds both the desire to resist pressures of assimilation and the temptation to blend in with mainstream Canadian society and downplay differences. In her study, second-generation South Asian women often attempt to blend in by distancing themselves from new South Asian immigrants, labelling new immigrants as FOBS (fresh off the boat) and criticizing them for not doing enough to assimilate.

In like fashion, some Canadian Muslims may be distancing themselves from Arab Muslims. For example, Amineh and Rubina say the following:

AMINEH: Quite honestly there are a lot of Muslims that do not like Arabs. They feel that Arabs are the ones that created all of this oppression. We are probably the most hated, even amongst Muslims. Not only are we hated from the fellow world, but even other Muslims do not like us, because they feel like we are the reason for all of this extremism and 9/11. They feel that we are the ones that started all of this ... After 9/11, there are a lot of Muslims that have been like, "this is all Arabs' fault" kind of thing. "They are the ones that are the terrorists and the bombers, and we are the ones that are paying the price for this whole thing." But the fact of the matter is that we are the ones that are in the Middle East, we are the ones with the oil, you know, and we are the ones that basically after World War I have been oppressed and colonized.

RUBINA: I am very proud of being Egyptian. Actually, being Egyptian kind of neutralizes the fact that I am a Muslim. Because when you say you are from Egypt, it neutralizes that you are Muslim. If you know about the history of the country, you know it is different than being Arab.

Since a lot of negative attention has been given to the Middle East in the post-9/11 era, some young Canadian Muslims may try to distance themselves from Arab Muslims. A few, like Rubina, may even highlight their cultural identity in order to create this distance. By doing so, they engage in "defensive othering," a form of internalized racism. Defensive othering refers to the "identity work engaged by the subordinate in an attempt to become part of the dominant group or to distance themselves from the stereotypes associated with the subordinate group" (Pyke 2010). In other words, it is a strategy of distancing oneself from negative stereotypes by suggesting these stereotypes are true – just not for oneself (Pyke 2010).

In the case of Canadian Muslims, by attributing the negative stereotypes often associated with all Muslims to Arab Muslims, a few young Muslims may try to create a positive identity of themselves as "good" Muslims at the expense of Arab Muslims. However, Karen D. Pyke (2010) rightly points out that when individuals engage in defensive othering, they end up reinforcing and supporting the very ideologies that oppress them. Therefore, by diverting attention to Arabs as extremists, a few young Canadian Muslims may actually be validating the argument that Islam produces fanatical individuals. However, it is important to point out that I did not find anti-Arab sentiment among the vast majority of my interviewees; most advocate for a collective Muslim identity rather than a shunning of Arab Muslims.

Conclusion

I began this chapter with the goal of learning how young Canadian Muslims are making sense of their cultural affiliations in the post-9/11 era. I find that most of my interviewees do not recall a close connection to their cultural backgrounds and prioritize their religious identities instead. Having a spotlight imposed on them after 9/11 affects how they make sense of their identities, revealing the role of social ascription on identity formation. Living in a diaspora also plays a role in how young Canadian Muslims negotiate their cultural affiliations. Because they were born and raised in Canada, many young Muslims find it difficult to relate to their parents' cultural practices. Instead, they begin to reflect on what is essential to the practice of Islam, leading to a desire to separate cultural practices from religion. The result is the espousal of a revivalist form of Islam, which involves a rejection of what they see as cultural interpretations of Islam and a return to what they perceive as being "basic" principles of Islam.

More than a simple desire to follow the basic teaching of the Quran, the move towards revivalist Islam is also fuelled by the current social and political environment. Revivalist Islam allows my interviewees to create distinct identities as Muslims at a time when they face the imposition of external labels. It also allows them to seek independence from earlier generations. It may present an opportunity for young Muslim women to speak out against practices they feel are sexist, and it gives young Canadian Muslims a romantic sense of belonging to a global Muslim community in a time of turmoil. Finally, this "rediscovery" and "reimagination" of Islam builds a collective bond between young Muslims from different cultural and ethnic backgrounds: they use the resulting collective identity to resist the demonization of Islam. Admittedly, however, this collective identity can be contradictory and ambiguous, and some fall prey to internalized racism.

It is often assumed that the move towards revivalist Islam can lead to second-generation Muslims becoming disloyal to Western societies. But Kibria's (2008) study on Bangladeshi Muslims reveals it does not necessarily mean hostility towards the West. In a similar vein, Clifford

(1994) asserts that although diaspora cultures may have separatist moments, they are not always separatist. He notes that the history of Jewish diaspora communities reveals selective accommodation with the political, cultural, commercial, and everyday life forms of "host societies." Clifford also cites the example of the black diaspora cultures in Britain, which he argues are concerned with different ways "to be 'British' – ways to stay and be different, to be British and something else complexly related to Africa and the Americans, to shared histories of enslavement, racist subordination, cultural survival, hybridization, resistance, and political rebellion" (312).

Even though my interviewees are pushing for a revivalist Islam and call for a diasporic collective Muslim identity, this does not mean they are becoming disloyal or expressing a weakened Canadian identity. How they manage to be both Muslim and Canadian in the post-9/11 era is explored in the next chapter.

6 "I Am Canadian": Reshaping Canadian Identity in the Post-9/11 Era

Introduction

Alisha voices the complexity of being Canadian for young Muslims in the post-9/11 era in the following protest:

> You know, I've embraced everything that people say is Canadian, and yet I'm not accepted as being Canadian, and this is my home, you know? This is what I call home, and yet people don't accept me here. It's weird. It's your home, and people don't accept you in your own home?

While they recognize themselves as Canadian, young Canadian Muslims are often treated as illegitimate members of Western nations. As pointed out previously, in reacting to these exclusions, many have affirmed their Muslim identities and developed a collective Muslim identity that transcends traditional cultural boundaries. Alejandro Portes and Rubén G. Rumbaut (2001) argue that when individuals develop reactive identities as a result of facing discrimination, they also develop a weakened national identity. As predicted by Portes and Rumbaut, many young Canadian Muslims have affirmed their Muslim identity after 9/11. But does having a stronger sense of Muslim identity alter their attachment to Canada, as predicted by reactive ethnicity theory? Do Canadian Muslims feel less attached to their Canadian identity? Or do they hold onto it, regardless of how others perceive them? Such considerations represent the next piece of the puzzle.

Exploring how Canadian Muslims make sense of their Canadian identities is particularly pertinent considering how Muslim identities are imagined in Western nations. As mentioned in chapter 1, a "clash of civilization" framework (Huntington 1993, 2004) has increasingly been used to understand the post-9/11 world. This framework divides the world ideologically into two spheres and considers the cultural and religious differences between Islam and the West to be at odds (Razack 2004). While the West is perceived as liberal, modern, and democratic, the Muslim world is imagined to be dangerous, barbaric, and premodern. Muslims are then considered outside the realm of Western civilization and labelled as disloyal members of Western societies.

The civilization framework was popularized by Samuel Huntington (1993) in a famous essay on the clash of civilizations. In it, he argues that for the past fourteen centuries, the relationship between Islam and Christianity has been characterized by intense rivalry and varying degrees of war. He argues that as long as Islam remains Islam and the West remains the West, the relationship between the two will be defined by conflict. According to Huntington, Muslims do not value Western cultures and consider Western secularism to be immoral. In more recent work on American Muslims, Huntington (2004) argues that because of the differences between Muslim and American cultures, Muslims are slow to assimilate compared to other post-1965 groups. He labels Muslim minorities as being "indigestible" by non-Muslim societies and concludes that the desire of Muslims to maintain the purity of their faith and religious practices has led them to conflict with non-Muslims.

The civilizations framework is widely disseminated by the media and is part of the moral exclusion process (Sirin and Fine 2008). The notion that Muslims living in Western nations have difficulty reconciling the two cultures has been spread with great fanfare by journalists and scholars on television and other forms of media. It is rationalized that if Muslims fail to reconcile the differences between the two clashing civilizations, they should be morally excluded from mainstream society (Sirin and Fine 2008).

In the Canadian context, this clash of civilizations framework is conflated with the presumed fragile nature of Canadian identity. Historically, Canadian national identity has been conceptualized as an insecure and weak entity requiring constant protection from racial others (Mackey 1999). It is often assumed that racial others, with their disloyalty, fragmentation, and unrecognizable demands, challenge the historically constituted authority of "real" Canadians. In recent times, the changing racial and ethnic composition of the population in Canada has led to heightened controversy over the definition and meaning of being Canadian, including a concern over the possible weakening of national boundaries (Handa 2003). It is feared that if immigrant populations alter the fabric of a Canadian identity based on white Anglo norms, they threaten the very definition of Canadian national identity. In the post-9/11 context, Muslims fill the archetype of the dangerous foreigner, a common figure in Canadian history (Zine 2012).

Contrary to popular rhetoric, I find that despite the undermining of their Canadian citizenship, which includes not being recognized as Canadians by others, most of my interviewees retain a strong sense of Canadian identity. Thus, it seems that in the Canadian context, facing discrimination does not necessarily lead to a weakened national identity. Nor do my interviewees recall difficulties reconciling their Muslim and Canadian identities, as predicted by the civilization framework.

My interviewees' continued attachment to Canada is complex and tied to multiple factors. First, the discourse of democratic racism helps to explain why they continue to see Canada in a positive light despite the multifaceted discrimination they face. Second, they use the symbolism of multiculturalism to resist discrimination; in doing so, they attempt to reshape what it means to be Canadian. Third, by maintaining a dual Muslim and Canadian identity, they have developed hybrid identities, which work to create alternative definitions of Canadian identity.

Feelings about Canadian Identity

Peter Nyers (2006) argues that since 9/11, the citizenship by birthright of Muslim individuals born in the U.S. has been perceived as accidental and is used to undermine their rights. Many of my interviewees feel that something similar is happening in Canada. Maria and Barkat mention:

> MARIA: When people look at me, nobody assumes that I was born in Kitchener [Ontario]. Even though I don't have an accent, it doesn't matter. Even my sisters, my friends, nobody assumes that we are born here. Even if we are born here – we are accidentally Canadian-born. People just assume that you were not born here.
>
> BARKAT: I'm a hyphenated Canadian, but I'm still Canadian. I am hyphenated by other people because I was not born here and because I am a Pakistani. My sister was born here, but they still see her as a hyphenated Canadian because she's not white. I think it's very difficult for non-whites to be considered Canadian.

Because Canadian identity has historically been based on whiteness (Thobani 2007; Boyko 1998), being born in Canada has a different meaning for members of minority groups, such as Muslim communities, than for white members of the population.

How does the lack of recognition as Canadian impact young Muslims' sense of being Canadian? Although a minority of interviewees, thirteen out of fifty (26 per cent), recall feeling less attachment to their Canadian identities in the post-9/11 era, the majority do not. Twenty-seven (54 per cent) feel it continues to be strong, while ten (20 per cent) have developed an even better sense of being Canadian. Many (37 of 50) do not report a weakened sense of national identity, which is in sharp contrast to the predictions of Portes and Rumbaut (2001).

Two interviewees citing less attachment to Canada since 9/11 era say the following:

AMBER: It [9/11] made me realize where I would fit into the society, and that I would always be an outsider. I would never be fully Canadian. My faith would always distinguish me; my political beliefs will always make me disagree with the government, so yeah, it made me re-evaluate my identity. It made me feel less at home.

YAZEED: 9/11 made everyone stop and think about it, and it made me set my priorities. Am I a Muslim person, or am I a Canadian person? And it strengthened [more] towards a Muslim than as a Canadian.

External forces can play an important role in how Muslim Canadians view their Canadian identity in the post-9/11 era. Thus, Amber and Yazeed internalize the meanings imposed on them by society and no longer have a strong sense of attachment to Canada.

Although individuals from similar backgrounds can have varying responses to marginalization, the majority of my interviewees feel strongly connected to their Canadian identity since 9/11. For instance, when I asked Aalia, a twenty-one-year-old woman, if the post-9/11 era has changed how she sees herself as Canadian, she responded, "Not at all." Aneesha adds:

The aftermath of 9/11 did not change how I saw myself as a Canadian. I think it changed how I saw myself as a Muslim [by affirming my Muslim identity], but not as Canadian. I've always seen myself as a Canadian. Like, I've been [in] the Canadian public school system since I was in kindergarten … Like, I don't like to keep myself within a certain area. I like to help out in different ways. I'm Canadian – that didn't really change after 9/11, but it changed my Muslim views.

In short, not getting recognition as being Canadian and facing discrimination does not necessarily result in a weakened national identity. My findings contradict those of Portes and Rumbaut (2001). Their study finds that second-generation American immigrants who have been victims of discrimination are less likely to see themselves as American than are second-generation youth who have not. However, as Aneesha's comments indicate, although my interviewees have developed a stronger Muslim identity, as shown in chapter 4, this does not mean they no longer see themselves as Canadians or that their loyalty to Canada has diminished. My research shows quite the reverse – that reactive identity formation does not necessarily result in a weakened national identity.

Interestingly, ten (20 per cent) of the interviewees have developed a stronger Canadian identity in the post-9/11 era. Dawoud and Asima comment:

DAWOUD: I think it has brought me closer to Canada. I developed, I think, a real appreciation for Canada in the way Canada responded to what happened. The Canadian decision not to directly take part in the war, first on Afghanistan, then on Iraq, and a much more measured approach, especially within the Liberal government. I would say that was something that impressed me quite a bit and brought me closer to Canada. I started to think at that time – I didn't realize it at the time, but if I look back now, it was around that time that I started seeing Canada as my home.

ASIMA: I think I became the happiest person in the world to be a Canadian. I mean, we did not enter the war. We did not support America. We are a country of peace, and to be associated with a country like that it is amazing. The kind of treatment you get by having Canadian citizenship is amazing. Just the whole thing Canada stands for I was proud of. I was extremely proud to be Canadian and was proud of the way we handled the whole situation.

Political and international policies can affect how Muslims make sense of their Canadian identity. While Amber no longer "feels at home" because she is upset with Canadian policies, others have a stronger sense of being Canadian because they are happy with the government's foreign policies.

Overall, most interviewees indicate that they still strongly identify as Canadian in the post-9/11 era. For most, not being recognized as Canadian and the discrimination they face has not weakened their perception of being Canadian, and a few have even strengthened their Canadian identity. This is an interesting phenomenon, considering many feel their Canadian citizenship is undermined through acts of discrimination. What are the possible explanations for this?

Democratic Racism

Frances Henry and Carol Tator (2006) argue that racism in Canadian society is justified through a discourse of democratic racism: because Canadian society is a liberal society that follows principles of individualism, tolerance, and freedom of expression, it can't be racist. Everyone has equal opportunity to succeed, and success is determined by individual merit. Racism is either something from the past or is perpetuated by socially deviant people. According to Henry and Tator, democratic racism allows for the coexistence of egalitarian values (i.e., fairness and equality) and non-egalitarian values (i.e., negative feelings and behaviours towards people of colour).

Among my interviewees, the discourse of democratic racism plays an important role in their attachment to Canada. They frequently discuss the rights and privileges that come with being Canadian. Bushra and Yaman explain:

> BUSHRA: I think with an international perspective, being Canadian has its advantages. And also I think, compared to living in other parts of the world, we have freedom of expression, freedom of assembly, freedom of speech, and different things that I guess I take for granted that other people can't. And also gender equality.
> YAMAN: I like the opportunities that we have in terms of education, and there are a lot of career opportunities for growth. I like health care and education in Canada. There are so many positives that you can mention. I guess another one is opportunity. One thing I really recognize, and for what I am really thankful, is that I think I would not be the same person if I didn't grow up in Canada.

Some hold onto the liberal principles advocated by democratic racism, but Henry and Tator (2006) caution that "liberalism is full of paradoxes and contradictions and assumes different meanings, depending on one's social location and angle of vision" (30). Although freedom of speech and access to social institutions is promised by liberalism, not all groups have equal access, as Canadian Muslims' experiences of exclusion demonstrate.

Nonetheless, I find that my interviewees utilize the discourse of democratic racism to continue seeing Canada in a positive light. Moreover, they feel Canada is more tolerant than other parts of the Western world of Muslim communities. Abbas, a twenty-year-old man who was born in Dubai and immigrated to Canada when he was eleven, and Fareeda say the following:

> ABBAS: I see myself as a Muslim Canadian first. I don't really think it [9/11] changed how I saw myself as a Canadian because out of three major countries, the U.S. and England, I think Canada has been the least anti-Muslim country. So I don't think it changed how I see myself as a Canadian.
>
> FAREEDA: I think in Canada, they view Islam better than they do in other places. Like Denmark, for example. [There] is such a large Islamic community here, and the Muslim community [is] actually quite active, I've heard, in Toronto and in Calgary and in Ottawa. So I don't think they view Islam as this barbaric, terrorist movement. I think it is better here than it is, for example, in the U.S.

Since the 1970s, Canada has used the discourse of multiculturalism to represent itself as a nation that is egalitarian, tolerant, and innocent of racism. From my findings, it appears that some young Canadian Muslims have bought into this image. Therefore, the hostility directed at Muslims globally in the post-9/11 era leads them to cling to the country they perceive as the least anti-Muslim. Although they are not necessarily happy with how Canadian Muslims have been treated in Canada, they feel the alternatives would be worse.

Multiculturalism plays an important role in the perpetuation of democratic racism. Henry and Tator (2006) say it is often believed that if everyone adopted the tenets of multiculturalism (i.e., tolerance, accommodation, harmony, and diversity), racism would disappear. Accordingly, my interviewees use the discourse of multiculturalism to continue to view Canada as an equalitarian society, despite hardships and exclusions. Sanya says the following about multiculturalism:

> I'm very happy to be Canadian. I think it's really a great society, and that it's multicultural. A lot of people from different backgrounds live here and

are tolerant of each other. I know its cliché, but I'm proud to be Canadian, because I just think that, you know, this country is more culturally toler-ant than any other country in the world. Even though you're part of a visible minority group, you're still Canadian. You're still embraced into the Canadian culture. So you feel like everybody can be Canadian. I feel like it's sort of very welcoming, and that we try to respect and appreciate all cultures.

Simply stated, young Canadian Muslims' belief in multiculturalism guides their vision of Canada, which includes seeing Canada as a land of opportunity and equality.

Some interviewees also believe that multiculturalism alleviates rac-ism and has directly benefited Muslim communities:

YAMAN: I think multiculturalism has helped a lot of communities in
    Canada, Muslim communities and others. I think it has helped me,
    because without Toronto pushing for that in a lot different areas, I think
    it is possible that I would have been discriminated against more so. Yes, I
    think it has helped a lot.
JALEEMA: I think because of multiculturalism, Muslims have been able to
    live here and be pretty open and pretty comfortable with the way they
    live, so I think it has made it easier to live in Canada.

Admittedly, a few interviewees have reservations; for example, Salim believes that "multiculturalism ignores systematic racism." The major-ity think quite highly of multiculturalism, however, despite their recent marginalization. How are we to make sense of this? Rebecca L. Malhi and Susan D. Boon (2007) argue that the discourses of democratic rac-ism used by dominant groups to dismiss racism are also used by mem-bers of racialized minority groups to deny the racism they encounter. Their study finds that second-generation South Asian Canadian women frequently exploit the discourse of democratic racism, including the idea that Canada is multicultural, to deny and rationalize incidents of racism. Similarly, Amita Handa (2003) finds that South Asian women believe Canadian schools and society are multicultural, thus prevent-ing them from seeing discriminatory acts as racist. My own findings vary somewhat. My interviewees vocalize and recognize incidents of racism; they are very articulate about the multifaceted discrimination they experience, as illustrated in the previous chapters. Nonetheless, they use the ideas associated with democratic racism to continuously perceive Canada as an egalitarian nation, despite their increasing marginalization.

Malhi and Boon (2007) note that by using the discourse of democratic racism, racialized minority groups legitimatize systems of domination. Democratic racism takes on a political dimension: if racism is denied, there is no need to change the status quo. Sherene Razack (2002) argues that if we continue to believe that we live in a tolerant and pluralist society, the fiction of equality can be maintained so we do not have to accept responsibility for racism.

Redefining Canadian Identity

The notion that Canada is a multicultural and tolerant society is transmitted to young Canadian Muslims in discourses of democratic racism, which are embedded in our education system, the law, media, and official rhetoric about inclusion. However, adherence to democratic racism provides only a partial explanation of why my interviewees are still strongly attached to Canada. I find my interviewees' support of multiculturalism complex, and they use multiculturalism to form an identity of resistance.

As mentioned earlier, multiculturalism in Canada functions both as an ideology and as a set of practices (Fleras 2009). For one thing, it creates an ideal image of how Canadians should live and interact in a pluralistic society; this includes valuing diversity and being tolerant, respectful, and non-discriminatory of others (Fleras 2009). Raymond Breton (1986) notes that the ideology of multiculturalism makes "symbolic statements of considerable importance" to immigrant communities (28). Echoing Breton, Patricia K. Wood and Liette Gilbert (2005) contend that multiculturalism offers "ethnic communities an instrument with which to work in their negotiation of Canadian politics and justice. They recognize the power of such a tool and thereby render it symbolic" (682). Similarly, Matt James (2012) mentions that historically, ethnocultural minorities have relied on multicultural policies to fight for their rights, such as advocating for strengthening hate crime and employment equity legislation. For example, the National Association of Japanese Canadians used the discourse of multiculturalism to call for a redressing of Japanese Canadian internment during the Second World War.

Although there is a deep contradiction between what multiculturalism promises and what it delivers (as discussed in chapter 2), I find that multiculturalism is a powerful symbol for my interviewees; they use its ideology to ground their identities as Canadians at a time where they face numerous exclusions. Umar uses multiculturalism to define what it means to be Canadian: "It's very simple. What it means to me is to identify yourself belonging to a mosaic of cultures, societies, backgrounds, religions – being somebody who is tolerant open to live in a multicultural society – so that to me is being Canadian."

Jennifer Kelly (1998) argues that our conception of Canadian identity and the meanings we attach to it affect our views of what is and what is not Canadian. Those who equate Canadian identity with Whiteness often believe that turbans worn by some members of the Royal Canadian Mounted Police (RCMP), for example, challenge the symbolic representation of what it means to be Canadian. But I find that those who use multiculturalism to define Canadian identity conceptualize the discrimination they face as anti-Canadian. This is seen in Umar's harassment at the hands of fellow university students:

> They pushed me and called me "terrorist" and told me to "go home," so I got a little upset about that because I am in a university that teaches tolerance, acceptance, living in a multicultural Canadian society, and the behaviour they had toward me was the opposite of what that the university and society teaches.

As Umar's experience shows, minority groups facing discrimination use multiculturalism to separate out individual acts of discrimination. In this context, they exploit the discourse of multiculturalism to safeguard their Canadian citizenship, even though it has been challenged.

These findings do not call for a celebration of multiculturalism. Rather, they show us that racialized groups can exploit the discourse of multiculturalism to advance their political views and to form an identity of resistance. Zeba, for example, is able to speak out against discrimination:

> I don't like it [discrimination]. I mean, I am Canadian. Like, I'm Canadian. I [was] born here and raised here. Just because I'm not a certain skin colour does not necessarily mean I'm not Canadian. Yeah, it's very upsetting. I'm probably a lot more Canadian than other supposed Canadians are. And I think in that I'm more a part of Canadian society. I take an active role in Canadian society. I participate a lot, while other people don't. Like, I become all rigid and tight inside. I'm member of society as [much as]

anybody else – I've never been treated in such a fashion. So it's very upsetting, very emotional – tears and crying, of course. We are supposed to be multicultural. Just because they look like they're Canadian, they look like a stereotypical Canadian, and they look white does not mean they are Canadian.

Using the discourse of multiculturalism, young Canadian Muslims like Zeba redefine Canadian identity and challenge the traditional notion that one has to be white to be Canadian.

The interviewees directly challenge the assertion that they do not in belong in Canada, as Amineh and Sakeena convey:

> AMINEH: I had this one [white] woman physically bump into me and elbow me at a mall in Vancouver, and she kept on looking back at me and giving me a dirty look, and then she came back to me and said in a different accent, "You are lucky to be here. You should go back to your country," you know, and I was like, "Who are you to give me a dirty look you and say you should not be here?" She even had an accent, and I was, like, "I was born here, and I have probably been here longer than you have, lady," and then she just walked away.
>
> SAKEENA: I think now my favourite question is being asked, "Where are you from?" I'll answer, and I'll immediately say, "Where are you from?" Because the reality of it is that everybody's an immigrant.

Similarly, Alisha (a twenty-six-year-old hijab-wearing Pakistani Canadian) recalls countering a white woman's comment that "in Canada we are not supposed to wear those things" with the retort "well in Canada we are not supposed to discriminate either."

Overall, my interviewees have developed strategies to respond to those who question their Canadian nationality. By speaking out against assumptions (that deny their Canadian identity), and by turning questions back onto the questioners, they challenge the entitlement of white Canadians and refuse to accept the dominant conceptions imposed onto them by others. In doing so, they challenge the sense of governmental belonging expressed by white Canadians. As mentioned earlier, governmental belonging (Hage 1998, 46) encompasses the belief that one has a right over the nation and a right to decide who should belong and not belong. Ghassan Hage (1998) argues that individuals in dominant positions often display their rights to governmental belonging in their everyday interactions with others. But my research shows that racialized minority groups can actively work to challenge governmental belonging in their attempts to reshape what it means to be Canadian.

Hybrid Identities

Attempts at resistance also involve refuting the notion that being Muslim somehow interferes with the ability to be Canadian. Zeba and Barkat say the following:

> ZEBA: They ask me, "So do you feel you're Muslim or do you feel you're more Canadian?" I've had people ask me, like professors and stuff ask me, "Am I more Canadian or Muslim?" And they think you can't be both, that somehow you have to pick one. And I think that's ridiculous to think that, especially in a multicultural society to be asking something like that. I don't think there is a tension between the two. I think outsiders feel there's a tension, but I don't personally feel that there is a tension.
> BARKAT: I don't think I am outside of being Canadian. I love being a Muslim in Canada. I think in terms of bigger issues is the fact that we are allowed to build mosques here and that women are allowed to wear the hijab. I think that is the most important part. I don't think I am outside of being Canadian. And I think that is one of the great things about Canada. My Canadian-ness and Muslim-ness can coexist and I am entitled to that.

Contrary to popular rhetoric, most of the interviewees do not feel that it is difficult to be both Canadian and Muslim. In fact, when I asked them, the answer was overwhelmingly "no." Umar says, "No, it's very simple actually, and I know a lot of people who find it very simple. I don't see a divide between the two [being Canadian and being Muslim]." These sentiments go directly against the clash of civilizations framework. My interviewees do not have problems reconciling their Canadian and Muslim identities. Instead, they have figured out a way to maintain a dual Muslim and Canadian identity. Similar studies on British and American Muslims have also discovered the creation of dual identity (Sirin and Fine 2008; Kibria 2008).

Homi Bhabha's (1990, 2004) work on hybridity helps explain dual identities. Hybridity is the process by which new identities emerge from interweaving elements of the colonizer and the colonized: the mixing of ideas and practices produces new cultural forms that disrupt binary positions and challenge the validity of essentialist cultural identities. Building on Bhabha's work, Gabe Mythen (2012) writes,

"Despite the intentions of the dominant group, encounters that arise out of the diaspora change the dynamic between the ex-colonizer and the ex-colonized and disrupt the notions of 'us' and 'them'" (394). Faiza Hirji (2010) argues that hybridity is "a tool for resistance, a way of over-coming a sense of isolation or marginalization while fighting against dominant cultures" (55).

Hybrid identities emerge in what Homi Bhabha (1990) calls the third space, an ambivalent space between colliding cultures that "gives rise to something different, something new and unrecognizable, a new area of negotiation of meaning and representation" (211). Identities are con-stantly formed and re-formed in this in-between space. By providing room for other positions to emerge, the third space challenges essen-tialist thinking and binary structures of power and knowledge (Bhabha 1990; Mythen 2012). Through its capacity to dissolve binary identities and to articulate new meanings, the third space enables cultural shifts and the material transformation in power (Bhabha 1990).

I have found my interviewees to be developing hybrid identities in the third space whereby they maintain a both a Canadian and a Muslim identity. In this way, they challenge the hegemonic beliefs that to be Canadian, one must be white, and that Muslim identities are irreconcil-able with Western ones.

The process of hybridity involves rearticulating not only what it means to be Canadian but also what it means to be Muslim. As described in chapter 5, rather than following the earlier practices of Islam, young Canadian Muslims are adopting a revivalist Islam – they are rejecting cultural interpretations of Islam and returning to "basic" tenets. These findings substantiate Handa's (2003) study, in which second-generation South Asian women in Canada negotiate the contradictions of being both Canadian and South Asian by articulating a third position of subjectivity that is neither traditionally Canadian nor South Asian but which speaks to the fluidity of categories. Thus, they work to unsettle and resist mainstream definitions of being both South Asian and Cana-dian. Similarly, my interviewees are developing a unique way of being both Canadian and Muslim.

Although Homi Bhabha (1990) conceptualizes the third space as challenging hegemonic systems of power, his work has been criticized for overlooking the strength of colonial power and the role of violence in securing hegemonic practices (Mythen 2012). For example, Floya Anthias (2001) says the concept of hybridity overlooks the alienation, exclusion, and violence that occurs with cultural encounters. This leads her to conclude that a "view of hybridized diasporas which neglect the power dimensions of social relations falls into the same cultural-ist essentialist traps as earlier notions of ethnicity" (637). As predicted by Bhabha (1990), the third space allows my interviewees to challenge hegemonic practices by forming identities of resistance.

But even though it is possible to locate their identities in the third space, this "third space itself is subject to configurations of power and bound socially prescribed norms" (Mythen 2012, 409). This can be seen in the interviewees' experiences. Regardless of how Canadian they feel, certain norms and practices are beyond their reach. Yazeed and Anee-sha say:

> YAZEED: I am Canadian and everything, except there is stuff that I can't get involved in. I am Canadian, but I do not drink. I am Canadian, but I don't like hockey. I definitely feel like I belong in Canada, but I do recog-nize that I am different.
>
> ANEESHA: Right now I am at Queen's University and the majority of out-ings revolve around drinking and clubbing. And there are even events where you can have a beer with the professor. And that is where a lot of students socialize with profs, but I just can't do that. I don't like to be around alcohol, so why would I put myself in an environment like that. So there are times where being Muslim does not help to be Canadian.

Similarly, Sanya mentions that although she feels as if she is a part of Canada, she feels like an outsider when "people constantly talk about Christmas and Christian holidays, and it's just kind of assumed that you celebrate these traditions or whatever." In other words, the third space has limitations. Although my interviewees strongly hold on to their identities as Canadians, this self-identification is not enough to challenge the dominance of white Canadian culture.

Furthermore, although many proudly declare that they are Cana-dian, the interviewees feel they have to prove their "Canadian-ness" to others:

> BARKAT: [After 9/11] we recognized that we're Canadian, and we are not going anywhere else. We're not going back to South Africa, or India, or Saudi, or whatever. This is where we're going to live, and this is where we are going to die. So if we're here for the long run, then we need to be, "Yeah Canada!" And being Canadian was something that we thought about, and that we need to make sure that we tell the rest of Canada:

"We're Canadian, so don't necessarily treat us differently" ... So yeah, I think we just realize that we need to embrace it, and make it so others will embrace us as well.

DAWOUD: We had moved in [to] the neighbourhood that we were in, about eight years before 9/11. But we still did not know our neighbours very well. After 9/11, we started having barbeques and inviting our neighbours to join us to show that, yes, we are Muslim, we're visible Muslims, but we're not horrible people they should be scared of, and we are Canadian. I made a very concentrated effort to make sure that I'm involved in Canadian society.

Faiza Hirji (2010) states that the process of hybridity is more complex than either resistance or assimilation. Even for individuals who have lived in Canada for many years, certain ambiguities may cloud their identity, even if they can state proudly that they are Canadian. As my interviewees make clear, practices of resistance often involve ambiguities and challenges, such as trying to prove one's "Canadian-ness" to others by gaining national capital through attempts to prove their safety.

Conclusion

This chapter explored how young Canadian Muslims negotiate their identity as Canadians in the post-9/11 era. In brief, despite not being recognized as Canadian by others, the vast majority cling to their Canadian identity, and a few have even strengthened it. My research suggests that facing discrimination does not necessarily result in a weakened national identity, in contrast to what Portes and Rambaut (2001) say in their work on reactive ethnicity. My findings also refute the clash of civilizations framework, in which Muslim and Western identities are irreconcilable.

In short, while young Canadian Muslims have affirmed their Muslim identities in reaction to discrimination and have attempted to develop a collective Muslim identity, this has not meant their loss of attachment to Canada. Not surprisingly, this attachment is complex and tied to multiple factors. First, my interviewees seem to be adhering to the discourses of democratic racism, which is deeply embedded in Canadian society. They uphold the notion that Canada is an equalitarian, liberal, and tolerant nation, despite the exclusions they face.

Second, my interviewees use multiculturalism to form an identity of resistance. Many conceptualize being Canadian as being multicultural;

this includes respecting cultural diversity and being respectful of others. Using this definition of multiculturalism, they understand the discrimination they face as an anti-Canadian sentiment, since such acts do not correspond with multiculturalism – a core Canadian value, in their view. They use the ideology of multiculturalism to reshape what Canadian identity can look like and what it means to be Canadian.

Third, my interviewees have developed hybrid identities whereby they have found a unique way of being both Canadian and Muslim. These hybrid identities present alternative ways of being Canadian, and they challenge hegemonic ideals, particularly the notion that one cannot be both Canadian and Muslim at the same time. However, as powerful as these hybrid identities are, they do not prohibit my interviewees from facing challenges when they express their Canadian-ness.

7 Conclusion

I began this book by describing how instances of racism in my early childhood made me question my Canadian identity. In my examination of how young Canadian Muslims experienced national belonging and exclusion in the three to seven years following 9/11, I found that racial discourses continue to thrive. In this book, I foreground their centrality in everyday experiences, state surveillance practices, and nation state projects. I also show the profound impact of racial discourses on young Canadian Muslims as they make sense of their religious, cultural, and Canadian identities.

To fully understand the continued salience of racial boundaries in Canada, it is important to return to the formation of nation states. Benedict Anderson (1991) argues all nations are imagined communities, "because members of even the smallest nations will never get to know most of their fellow members, meet them, or even hear of them, yet in the minds of each lives the image of their communion" (5). Further, nations are imagined as horizontal comradeships, despite deep inequalities and differences, making it possible for people to tie themselves to nation states and even sacrifice their lives for them. In a similar vein, Stuart Hall (1996) says we should understand national cultures as discursive devices, representing differences as either unity or identity. Like Anderson, Hall believes that nations are systems of cultural representations where people are not only legal citizens of a nation but participants in the idea of the nation as represented in its national culture. For Hall (1996), "a nation is a symbolic community and it is this which accounts for its power to generate a sense of identity and allegiance" (612).

Taking these insights a step further, Nira Yuval-Davis (2011) argues that nation states sustain themselves by engaging in what she call acts of active and situated imagination. Imagined communities, she says,

> do not come into existence just because of the inability of people to meet all the other members of their nation. On the contrary, this "dirty business of boundary maintenance" that underlines the politics of belonging is all about potentially meeting other people and deciding whether they stand inside or outside the imaginary boundary line of the nation and/or other communities of belonging, whether they are "us" or "them." (20)

Canada has historically imagined itself as a "white" nation, by making racial exclusions part of its nationalist project. In fact, the emergence of the Canadian nation state has been tied to what Sunera Thobani (2007) calls the "exaltation" of the white Canadian and the exclusion of the other: "It is this exclusion of the 'Other' that renders the nation possible and coherent and should this exclusion ever be transcended, the nation itself would cease to exist" (20).

Nation building though imagining and controlling the other has always been a part of Canada's political culture. Historically, the other was Aboriginal; today, it is also increasingly Muslim. The racialization of Islam allows the Canadian nation state to distinguish "real" Canadian citizens from "flawed" or "accidental" citizens, resulting in the exaltation of the white national Canadian subject. By conflating issues of security and patriarchy with religion, Islam becomes a structuring principle in defining Canadian national identity. The securitization of Muslims as dangerous others paves a way for "real" Canadians to come together and solidify their Canadian identity in their efforts to protect Canadian "values" and the "security" of the nation. Conveniently, this also allows for the facade of a unified Canada, despite the deeply entrenched inequalities that exist in Canadian society.

Hall's (1986, 1990, 1991, 1992, 1996) grammar of race provides important insights on how racial discourses play an important role in creating this dichotomy between Islam and the West. The grammar of race includes the naturalization of differences, the evacuation of history, and fixed relations of power.

In the Canadian context, Muslims' religious and cultural practices are often seen as too different to integrate with mainstream culture, implying that they cannot be assimilated. In the larger context, Muslim communities are imagined to be patriarchal, barbaric, and uncivilized, while Western ones are egalitarian, liberal, and modern. As a result, both identities are considered static and homogenous and destined to clash. The conflict between Muslim societies and Western societies is seen primarily as a result of cultural differences, not historical and political forces. Consequently, 9/11 and other terrorist events are perceived as attacks against the Western way of life, a notion legitimatized through the clash of civilizations framework. The historical, political, social, and economic factors that led to 9/11 and other terrorist activities are denied or minimized.

The labelling of Muslim cultures as inferior to Western ones reinforces Western hegemony. As in colonialism, there is an ideological division of the world, where the assumed inferiority of the Muslim other legitimizes the power of Western nations. In his post-colonial analysis, Homi Bhabha (2004) argues that rigid distinctions between the colonizer and the colonized have always been difficult to maintain. As a result, he argues that the West is often troubled by its "doubles" in the East. If the East is seen as similar to the West, how can the latter continue to explain its own identity? If Western civilization is seen as akin to other civilizations, how can it project itself as unique and superior? Accordingly, Western narratives create boundaries between the West and other civilizations (Bhabha 2004).

In effect, Islam functions as a fictional ideological label with no direct correspondence with the enormously varied life that happens within the Islamic world. According to Edward Said (1997), this label of "Islam" indiscriminately condemns the Islamic world and creates a rigorous binary between it and the Western world. Western nations have played a combative role in stigmatizing and heaping abuses on an abstraction called "Islam" to stir up anger and fear in North America and Europe. Said states that labels such as "Islam" and "West" have two distinct functions. First, they perform an identifying function, allowing us to distinguish between different entities ("them" and "us"). He notes that few people have a comprehensive understanding of all aspects of Western traditions or of the intricacies of Islamic jurisprudence. But this does not prevent people from confidently characterizing Islam and the West. Second, they produce complex meanings, wherein to speak of Islam in the West is to speak of a negative thing. Note that it is Islam versus the West, not Islam versus Christianity. The assumption is that the West has well surpassed the stage of Christianity and is now modern, while the Muslim world is not (Said 1997).

Ultimately, Islam is reduced to a small number of unchanging negative characteristics. It is seen as totalistic, with no separation between church and state or between religion and everyday life, in contrast to the liberal, equalitarian, secular, and modern West (Said 1997). These simplistic generalizations help push Islamic people into the role of the dangerous other.

Gender plays a crucial role in negative representation of Islam. The representation of Muslim women as victims of patriarchal and oppressive cultures justifies imperialistic behaviour and makes it easier to cast Muslim communities as other. The liberalisms that may exist in Islam are ignored, and, as a result, Muslim communities are assigned essentialist identities that can never measure up to the standards of Western civilizations (Bhabha 2004).

This polarization of cultures is simplistic and dangerous. If we continue to see cultures as stable and discrete identities, we risk the divisions between cultures becoming antagonistic (Bhabha 2004). If we know exactly where our identity ends and the rest of the world begins, it is easy to define the latter as other, different, inferior, or threatening and to eliminate any sort of equal dialogue (Bhabha 2004).

My research shows the consequences of seeing cultures in such binary terms. With the threat of the Muslim other playing a central role in the imagination of the Canadian nation, the dynamics of race relations and identity formation in Canada have changed. The experiences of young Canadian Muslims in my study raise important questions about the contemporary meanings of multiculturalism, Canadian citizenship, and national belonging.

In recent years, Canada has used the discourse of multiculturalism to project itself as a nation that has moved beyond being a white settler nation to a nation which values all citizens equally. The experiences of Canadian Muslims suggest this is just a story (to paraphrase B. Anderson 1991). In reality, Canada is dominated by white Canadian culture, which is willing to tolerate racial others as long as they do not challenge the hegemony of the dominant community. As my research illustrates, white privilege is rampant in Canada, and white Canadians feel they have the right to decide who belongs and who does not. They banish Muslims from public spaces, ridicule them for their religious practices, and ask them to leave the country. Sarah Ahmed (2000) argues that multiculturalism differentiates between those whose appearance of difference can be claimed by the nation and those who are the "stranger's stranger" – whose difference may be dangerous to the well-being of even the most heterogeneous of nations. Since Islam is now imagined as the biggest threat facing Western nations, Muslim cultures and religious practices are no longer welcomed in Canada, clearly evidenced by my interviewees' experiences.

Furthermore, because Muslim cultures are considered incompatible with Western ones, Canadian Muslims' exclusion from mainstream society and the political landscape is justified: they are unworthy of legal or human rights. This allows states of exceptions to emerge, giving the Canadian nation state a license to infringe on the legal citizenship of Canadian Muslims. This, in turn, alters the meaning of Canadian citizenship: it now functions to create divisions between "insiders" and "outsiders" rather than serving an equalizing and emancipatory purpose. The citizenship of Canadian Muslims is perceived as flawed and irregular; they are treated as second-class citizens, and they lose important legal protections. Canadian citizenship becomes a tool by which perceived outsiders are controlled and punished by the state.

The structuring of citizenship through security plays a vital role in the dismantling of Canadian citizenship. Historically, the state's claim to provide its occupants with security has been crucial in its ability to claim ownership of its citizens. Risks and insecurity, hence, affect "the meaning of citizenship, the ways state govern, and the way states govern themselves" (Nyers 2004, 205). However, framing the political in relation to security is problematic, because "any appeal to security must also include a reference to the fears that engender this call for reassurance ... such acts encourage fear, foster apprehension, and feed off nervousness in the population" (Nyers 2004, 205). Therefore, to bring security to the forefront of political debates and calculations has "profound implications for what it means to be a political subject ... as the citizen that needs to be secured is not the same as the secured citizen" (Neyer 2004, 205). Similarly, Zedner (2010) says the assertion of the state's duty to provide security for "legitimate" citizens provides a justification for security measures that work to create a category of "suspect citizens," a status that renders them potential threats even though they have done nothing wrong: "If there is a right to security – that right is extended only to those who can legitimately call upon the state to protect their interests, leaving a marginalized and often a vulnerable population beyond the pale of protection" (Zedner 2010, 394).

Since 9/11, there has been a securitization of citizenship in Canada, with security discourses used to define "legitimate" and "illegitimate" Canadian citizens. This securitization has been justified through a highly racialized discourse, which conceives Muslim identity as a threat to national security. This coupling of Islam with terrorism to justify new security configurations has disrupted the relationship between the Canadian state and Canadian Muslims. Deemed as security threats, Muslims living in Canada are now cast as suspect; since their presence is a threat to the nation, Canadian Muslims have become securitized citizens, as opposed to Canadian citizens.

This dismantling of Canadian Muslims' citizenship reveals the racist foundations of Canadian citizenship and the political processes by which Canadian citizenship emerged. Citizenship has historically functioned as a divisive and imperialistic practice, with Western political thought envisioning some groups (read, white) as being advanced and civilized enough to be worthy of it, and others as not worthy (Hindess 2004). According to Thobani (2007), Canadian citizenship has been based on the institution of white supremacy, with the clear intention to produce racial divisions and allow for the creation of a myth of a homogenous nation, despite the existence of heterogeneity. My research reveals that because race continues to underpin Canadian national identity, with the racialization of Islam particularly serving to solidify it, young Canadian Muslims have lost not only legal protections, but they have also been deemed as "outsiders" within the nation.

Because the image of the Muslim terrorist is now used to imagine the superiority of the Canadian nation and to securitize citizenship, the way that claims to national belonging are deployed has been impacted. Exalted national Canadian subjects now express *governmental belonging* (the belief that they have rights over the nation) in efforts to protect Canada from terrorism and from "inferior" culture practices. White Canadians feel justified in infringing on young Canadian Muslims' rights to public transportation, religious freedom, and employment equity. This is particularly dangerous for Muslim women, who are most vulnerable to the hate crimes directed at Muslim communities.

Cast as threats and as enemies to the nation, young Canadians Muslims are left trying to accumulate what Ghassan Hage (1998) calls *national capital*. To be seen as legitimate Canadian citizens, they try to prove they are "safe" Muslims, which takes various forms depending on the context. In their everyday lives, they try to be model representatives of their religion. When faced with state surveillance, they conceal or manage their Muslim identity.

However, my interviewees' responses are complex. In the long run, the disciplining of Muslim identities results in the development of reactive identities through politics of representation. Many affirm their Muslim identity through what I call "reactive identity formation," whereby they resist the racialization of Islam and reclaim their religion. They also attempt to develop a collective Muslim identity that transcends traditional cultural boundaries by advocating revivalist Islam, which involves a rediscovery of the "past" on their part.

Interestingly, even though young Canadian Muslims face charges that they are not really Canadian, most work hard to retain their Canadian identity, thereby reshaping what it means to be Canadian. Being Canadian is so important for most of my interviewees that they regularly draw on the symbolism of multiculturalism and develop hybrid identities, even though they are increasingly treated as less than full citizens in their interactions with fellow Canadians and the state.

My research highlights the importance of viewing cultures as hybrid and constantly evolving rather than static and distinct identities. Bhabha (2004) says cultures are always a matter of becoming. They are not permanent but are rather in constant flux and transformation. My interviewees provide good examples of this. They are redefining their identities as Muslims, as members of different cultural groups, and as Canadians, based on the contemporary context and on how others define them. Through these transformations, they are developing unique ways to be both Muslim and Canadian, challenging hegemonic ideals as they do so.

Appendix: The Interviewees

1. Aaeesha: A twenty-four-year-old woman who immigrated to Canada at the age of five and comes from a Pakistani background.
2. Aalia: A hijab-wearing, twenty-one-year-old woman who immigrated to Canada at the age of thirteen from Egypt.
3. Aamir: A twenty-three-year-old man who was born in Canada and comes from an Indian-East African background.
4. Aatifa: A hijab-wearing, twenty-four-year-old woman who was born in Saudi Arabia and immigrated to Canada at the age of thirteen.
5. Abbas: A twenty-year-old man who immigrated to Canada at the age of eleven from Dubai.
6. Abdual: A thirty-one-year-old man who came to Canada a year ago as an international student from Egypt.
7. Ali: A nineteen-year-old man who immigrated to Canada from Bangladesh two years ago.
8. Alisha: A hijab-wearing, twenty-six-year-old woman who immigrated to Canada at the age of twenty from Pakistan.
9. Amber: A twenty-four-year-old woman born in Canada to a Pakistani father and a German mother.
10. Amineh: A hijab-wearing, twenty-three-year-old woman born in Canada to a Libyan family.
11. Aneesha: A hijab-wearing, twenty-year-old woman that was born in Pakistan and came to Canada as a young child.
12. Asima: A twenty-three-year-old woman who was born in Canada and comes from an Indian-East African background.
13. Atiya: A hijab-wearing, thirty-one-year-old woman who was born in Canada and comes from an Indian-Fijian background.

14. Ayush: A twenty-eight-year-old man who immigrated to Canada at the age of eighteen from Pakistan.
15. Azhar: A twenty-seven-year-old man who came to Canada one year ago from Iran.
16. Baher: A twenty-year-old man who was born in Canada and comes from an Indian background.
17. Barkat: A thirty-year-old man who came to Canada as a young child from South Africa.
18. Bushra: An eighteen-year-old Muslim woman who was born in Canada and comes from an Indian and East African background.
19. Dawoud: A twenty-five-year-old who was born in Saudi Arabia and came to Canada as a young child.
20. Fahad: A twenty-eight-year-old man who immigrated to Canada from Syria at the age of fourteen.
21. Falak: A twenty-one-year-old woman who immigrated to Canada five years ago and comes from an Indian-East African background.
22. Farah: A twenty-year-old woman who was born in Canada and comes from an Indian and East African background.
23. Fareeda: A nineteen-year-old woman who immigrated to Canada at the age of ten from Saudi Arabia.
24. Fardeen: A twenty-six-year-old man who immigrated to Canada three years ago from Egypt.
25. Haleema: A hijab-wearing, nineteen-year-old woman who immigrated to Canada at the age of eight from Jamaica.
26. Jaleema: A twenty-five-year-old woman who was born in Canada and comes from a Pakistani background.
27. Kareena: A hijab-wearing twenty-one-year-old woman who was born in Canada and comes from a Bangladeshi background.
28. Leela: A twenty-year-old Muslim woman who was born in Canada and comes from an Indian-East African background.
29. Mohammed: A nineteen-year-old man who was born in Canada and comes from a Bangladeshi background.
30. Maria: A hijab-wearing, twenty-four-year-old woman who was born in Canada and comes from a Tanzanian background.
31. Mumtaz: A twenty-two-year-old woman who was born in Saudi Arabia and came to Canada when she was ten.
32. Nashida: A hijab-wearing, twenty-three-year-old woman who was born in Canada to a Pakistani background.
33. Radi: A twenty-five-year-old man who was born in Canada to a Pakistani family.

34. Ragheb: A twenty-six-year-old man who was born in Egypt and came to Canada when he was a young child.
35. Rashid: A twenty-two-year-old man who came to Canada at the age of fourteen and comes from an Indian background.
36. Rubina: A hijab-wearing, twenty-six-year-old woman who came to Canada as a young child from Egypt.
37. Sakeena: A twenty-seven-year-old woman who was born in Canada to a Pakistani immigrant family.
38. Salim: A nineteen-year-old man who came to Canada a year ago from Egypt.
39. Salman: A twenty-four-year-old man who came to a Canada a few years ago from Bangladesh.
40. Samir: A twenty-three-year-old woman who came to Canada as a young child from India.
41. Sanya: A twenty-five-year-old woman born in Canada to an Indian-East African family.
42. Saud: A twenty-two-year-old man born in Canada to a Pakistani family.
43. Umar: A twenty-two-year-old man who was born in India and came to Canada four years ago.
44. Yaman: A twenty-five-year-old man who was born in Canada and come from an Indian background.
45. Yazeed: A twenty-one-year-old man who was born in the Sudan and came to Canada when he was twelve years old.
46. Zaahir: A twenty-two-year-old man who came to Canada when he was four from Saudi Arabia.
47. Zamil: A twenty-nine-year-old man who has been living in Canada for one year and comes from a West Indies background.
48. Zeba: A hijab-wearing, twenty-two-year-old woman who was born in Canada and comes from an Indian background.
49. Zeshaan: A nineteen-year-old man who came to Canada one year ago from Pakistan.
50. Zora: A twenty-two-year-old woman who was born in Bangladesh and came to Canada when she was eight.

Notes

1 Introduction

1 Roughly 52,590 Muslims resided in Vancouver, 254,110 in Toronto, and 100,185 in Montreal.
2 Contrary to popular rhetoric, Islam is not a monolithic religion. There are over seventy-two sects within the religion. Apart from the major division between the majority Sunnis and the minority Shias, there are major subsects and divisions within each sect (Moghissi, Rahnema, and Goodman 2009; Watt 1998).
3 Aihwa Ong (2004) provides an example of this by describing how citizenship can evolve over time: while early Chinese immigrants to the U.S. were subject to the process of negroization, in the current age of globalized capitalism, they hold important economic and intellectual capital; they have now attained the status of ideal American citizens.

2 The Loss of National Belonging: Experiences of Young Canadian Muslims Post-9/11

1 Ismaili is a branch of Shia Islam. Shia Islam is the second largest denomination of Islam, after Sunni Islam.
2 Co-op work terms are summer work periods arranged by universities for students.

3 States of Exception: Canadian Young Muslims' Experiences of Security and Surveillance

1 Section 4.7 of the Aeronautics Act authorizes screening officers to search persons and their belongings both before boarding an aircraft and on board the aircraft. This act does not specify conditions under which searches can be conducted, other than to say that a search must be authorized. A search is considered authorized if it is carried out by a screening officer during the screening of persons and goods (Choudhry & Roach 2003).
2 This does not mean that the interviewees and their family or friends had experienced only eighty-one incidents at airports and border crossings. In the interviews, interviewees would often remark that they had experienced many problems, and then would describe a few incidents to me. Although the interviewees described a total of eighty-one incidents, in reality, they had experienced even more.
3 For instance, nineteen-year-old Ali mentioned that his uncle is now in jail in the United States because of 9/11. He says his uncle was arrested on suspicion of financing Al-Qaeda. Ali says the government closed down his business, and he lost his house. His uncle is now in jail for two years, although Ali says he has no links whatsoever to Al-Qaeda. He says his uncle got convicted without a trial because of the Patriot Act. Other incidents in the States are described by Salman, who is twenty-four years old. He discussed how his apartment was searched and how he was extensively questioned by the Immigration and Naturalization Service right after 9/11 because he was an international student. He recalled that this also happened to a lot of his friends who also were international students. He also conveyed that one of his friends who was from Saudi Arabia was detained and sent to a detention centre far away in some desert. His family had to pay $30,000 to get him out and he was later deported back to Saudi Arabia. Salman beleves that this happened to his friend because he was a part-time student and that now his friend refuses to come back to North America, even to Canada.

4 "Our Faith Was Also Hijacked by Those People": Reclaiming Muslim Identity in a Post-9/11 era

1 This chapter was previously published as "'Our Faith Was also Hijacked by Those People': Reclaiming Muslim Identity in the Post-9/11 Era," *Journal of Ethnic and Migration Studies*, 37 (3) (2011): 425– 41.

5 Choosing Religion over Culture: How Canadian Muslims Make Sense of Their Cultural Affiliations in the Post-911 Era

1 While Kibria (2008) refers to this phenomenon as revivalist Islam, other scholars use the term "global Islam" to describe this move towards following the basic principles of Islam and the rejection of cultural interpretations of Islam. Some scholars are reluctant to use term revivalist Islam because they feel it may have connotations related to fundamentalism in Islam. However, since Kibria does not use this term in this manner, I still use it.
2 While India may not necessarily be a Muslim majority society, Islam is one of the major religions followed in the country.

References

Abu-Laban, B. 1983. "The Canadian Muslim Community: The Need for a New Survival Strategy." In *The Muslim Community in North America*, edited by E. Waugh, B. Abu-Laban, and R. Qureshi, 75–89. Edmonton: University of Alberta Press.

Abu-Lughod, L. 2002. "Do Muslim Women Really Need Saving? Anthropological Reflections on Cultural Relativism and Its Others." *American Anthropologist* 104 (3): 783–90. http://dx.doi.org/10.1525/aa.2002.104.3.783.

Agamben, G. 2005. *The State of Exception*. Chicago: University of Chicago Press. http://dx.doi.org/10.1215/9780822386735-013.

Agnew, V. 2007. *Interrogating Race and Racism*. Toronto: University of Toronto Press. http://dx.doi.org/10.3138/9781442685444.

Ahmad, F. 2006. "British Muslims Perceptions and Opinions on News Coverage of September 11." *Journal of Ethnic and Migration Studies* 32 (6): 961–82. http://dx.doi.org/10.1080/13691830600761479.

Ahmad, M. 2002. "Homeland Insecurities: Racial Violence the Day after September 11." *Social Text* 20 (3): 101–15. http://dx.doi.org/10.1215/01642472-20-3_72-101.

Ahmed, L. 1992. *Women and Gender in Islam: Historical Roots of a Modern Debate*. New Haven, CT: Yale University Press.

Ahmed, S. 2000. *Strange Encounters: Embodied Others in Postcolonialty*. London: Routledge.

Aiken, S. 2007. "From Slavery to Expulsion: Racism, Canadian Immigration Law and the Unfilled Promise of Modern Constitutionalism." In *Interrogating Race and Racism*, edited by V. Agnew, 112–34. Toronto: University of Toronto Press. http://dx.doi.org/10.3138/9781442685444-004.

Akram, S., and K. Johnson. 2002. "Race, Civil Rights, and Immigration Law after September 11, 2001: The Targeting of Arabs and Muslims." *Annual Survey of American Law* 58 (3): 295–355.

Alba, R., and V. Nee. 2003. *Remaking the American Mainstream: Assimilation and the New Immigration*. Cambridge, MA: Harvard University Press. http://dx.doi.org/10.4159/9780674020115.

Alexander, C. 2000. *The Asian Gang: Ethnicity, Identity and Masculinity*. New York: Berg Publishers.

Alexander, C. 2004. "Imagining the Asian Gang: Ethnicity, Masculinity, and Youth after the Riots." *Critical Social Policy* 24 (4): 526–49. http://dx.doi.org/10.1177/0261018304046675.

Aly, A., and L. Green. 2010. "Fear, Anxiety and the State of Terror." *Studies in Conflict and Terrorism* 33 (3): 268–81. http://dx.doi.org/10.1080/10576100903555796.

Anand, D. 2009. "Diasporic Subjectivity as an Ethical Position." *South Asian Diaspora* 1 (2): 103–11. http://dx.doi.org/10.1080/19438190903109412.

Anderson, B. 1991. *Imagined National Communities*. London: Verso.

Anderson, K.J. 1991. *Vancouver's Chinatown: Racial Discourse in Canada, 1875–1980*. Montreal: McGill-Queen's University Press.

Anthias, F. 2001. "New Hybridities, Old Concepts: The Limits of Culture." *Ethnic and Racial Studies* 24 (4): 619–64. http://dx.doi.org/10.1080/01419870120049815.

Anthias, F., and N. Yuval-Davis. 1992. *Racialized Boundaries: Race, Nation, Gender, Color, and Class and the Anti-Racist Struggle*. London: Routledge.

Appiah, K.A. 2005. *The Ethics of Identity*. Princeton, NJ: Princeton University Press.

Arat-Koc, S. 2005. "The Disciplinary Boundaries of Canadian Identity After September 11: Civilization Identity, Multiculturalism, and the Challenge of Anti-Imperialist Feminism." *Social Justice* 32 (4): 32–49.

Arendt, H. 1951. *The Origins of Totalitarianism*. Orlando, FL: Harvest Books.

Bahdi, R. 2003. "No Exit: Racial Profiling and Canada's War against Terrorism." *Osgoode Hall Law Journal* 41 (2/3): 293–317.

Bannerji, H. 2000. *The Dark Side of the Nation: Essays on Multiculturalism, Nationalism and Gender*. Toronto: Canadian Scholars Press.

Banting, K., and W. Kymlicka. 2010. "Canadian Multiculturalism: Global Anxieties and Local Debates." *British Journal of Canadian Studies* 23: 43–71.

Beck, H., J. Reitz, and N. Weiner. 2002. "Addressing Systematic Racial Discrimination in Employment: The Health Canada Case and Implications of Legislative Change." *Canadian Public Policy* 28 (3): 373–94. http://dx.doi. org/10.2307/3552228.

Benhabib, S. 2003. *The Claims of Culture.* Princeton, NJ: Princeton University Press.

Beyer, P. 2005. "Religious Identity and Educational Attainment among Recent Immigrants to Canada: Gender, Age and 2nd Generation." *Journal of International Migration and Integration* 6 (2): 177–99. http://dx.doi.org/10.1007/s12134-005-1009-2.

Bhabha, F. 2003. "Tracking 'Terrorists' or Solidifying Stereotypes? Canada's Antiterrorism Act in Light of the Charter's Equality Guarantees." *Windsor Review of Legal and Social Issues* 16: 95–136.

Bhabha, H.K. 1990. *Nation and Narration.* New York: Routledge.

Bhabha, H.K. 2004. *The Location of Culture.* London: Routledge.

Bhandar, D. 2008. "Resistance, Detainment, Asylum: The Onto-Political Limits of Border Crossing in North America." In *War, Citizenship, Territory,* edited by D. Cowen and E. Gilbert, 281–302. New York: Routledge.

Black, D. 2014. "Immigration Experts Say Bill C-24 Discriminatory and Weakens Citizenship." *TheStar.com,* 27 June. https://www.thestar.com/news/immigration/2014/06/27/immigration_experts_say_bill_c24_discriminatory_and_weakens_citizenship.html .

Blackwood, L., N. Hopkins, and S. Reicher. 2012. "I Know Who I Am, but Who Do They Think I Am? Muslims Perspectives on Encounters with Airport Authorities." *Ethnic and Racial Studies* 36 (6): 1090–108. http://dx.doi.org/10.1080/01419870.2011.645845.

Boyko, J. 1998. *Last Steps to Freedom: The Evolution of Canadian Racism.* Ottawa: Canadian Council of the Arts.

Brah, A. 1996. *Cartographies of Diaspora: Contesting Identities.* New York: Routledge.

Breton, R. 1986. "Multiculturalism and Canadian Nation-Building." In *The Politics of Gender, Ethnicity and Language in Canada,* edited by A. Cairns and C. Williams, 27–66. Toronto: University of Toronto Press.

Byng, M. 2008. "Complex Inequalities: The Case of Muslim Americans after 9/11." *American Behavioral Scientist* 51 (5): 659–74. http://dx.doi.org/10.1177/0002764207307746.

Cainkar, L. 2005. "Violence Unveiled." *Contexts* 4 (4): 67. http://dx.doi.org/10.1525/ctx.2005.4.4.67.

Calliste, A., and G. Dei. 2000. *Anti-Racist Feminism.* Halifax: Fernwood Publishing.

Canadian Council on American Islamic Relations (CAIR-CANADA). 2004. "Today's Media: Covering Islam and Canadian Muslims." *Submission to Standing Committee on Transport and Communications*. Ottawa: CAIR-CANADA.

Canadian Race Relations Foundation (CRRF). 2000. *Unequal Access: A Canadian Profile of Racial Differences in Education, Employment and Income*. Toronto: CRRF.

Cardozo, A., and R. Pendakur. 2008. "Canada's Visible Minority Population: 1967–2017." MBC Working Paper 08-05, Centre of Excellence for Research on Immigration and Diversity. Simon Fraser, BC: Metropolis British Columbia.

Casanova, J. 1994. *Public Religions in the Modern World*. Chicago: University of Chicago Press.

Cesari, J. 2004. "Islam in the West: Modernity and Globalization Revised." In *Globalization and the Muslim World: Culture, Religion, and Modernity*, edited by B. Schaebler and L. Stenberg, 80–93. Syracuse, NY: Syracuse University Press.

Chen, C. 2008. *Getting Saved in America: Taiwanese Immigration and Religious Experience*. Princeton, NJ: Princeton University Press. http://dx.doi.org/10.1515/9781400824175.

Chon, M., and D.E. Arzt. 2005. "Walking While Muslim." *Law and Contemporary Problems* 68: 215–54.

Choudhry, S. 2001. "Protecting Equality in the Face of Terror: Ethnic and Racial Profiling s. 15 of the Charter." In *The Security of Freedom: Essays on Canada's Anti-Terrorism Bill*, edited by R.J. Daniels, P. Macklem, and K. Roach, 367–79. Toronto: University of Toronto Press. http://dx.doi.org/10.3138/9781442682337-024.

Choudhry, S., and K. Roach. 2003. "Racial and Ethnic Profiling: Statutory Discretion, Constitutional Remedies, and Democratic Accountability." *Osgoode Hall Law Journal* 41 (1): 1–36.

Clifford, J. 1994. "Diasporas." *Cultural Anthropology* 9 (3): 302–38. http://dx.doi.org/10.1525/can.1994.9.3.02a00040.

Coleman, R., and M. McCahill. 2011. *Surveillance and Crime*. London: Sage.

Commission for Labour Cooperation. 2010. "A Guide to Employment Discrimination Laws in Canada." http://www.ohrc.on.ca/en/policy-discrimination-against-older-people-because-age/5-employment.

Connell, R. 1987. *Gender and Power*. Stanford, CA: Stanford University Press.

Connell, R. 1995. *Masculinities*. Cambridge: Polity Press.

Cornell, S. 1988. *The Return of the Native: American Indian Political Resurgence*. New York: Oxford University Press.

Cornell, S.E., and D. Hartmann. 2007. *Ethnicity and Race: Making Identities in a Changing World*. London: Pine Forge Press.

Creese, G. 2007. "From Africa to Canada: Bordered Spaces, Bordered Crossings and Imagined Communities." In *Interrogating Race and Racism*, edited by V. Agnew, 352–85. Toronto: University of Toronto Press. http://dx.doi.org/10.3138/9781442685444-014.

Creese, G., and E.N. Kambere. 2003. "What Colour Is Your English?" *Canadian Review of Sociology and Anthropology / Revue Canadienne de Sociologie et d'Anthropologie* 40 (5): 565–73. http://dx.doi.org/10.1111/j.1755-618X.2003. tb00005.x.

Dion, K.L., and K. Kawakami. 1996. "Ethnicity and Perceived Discrimination in Toronto: Another Look at the Personal/Group Discrimination and Discrepancy." *Canadian Journal of Behavioural Science* 28 (3): 203–13. http://dx.doi.org/10.1037/0008-400X.28.3.203.

Dossa, S. 2008. "Lethal Muslims: White-Trashing Islam and the Arabs." *Journal of Muslim Minority Affairs* 28 (2): 225–36. http://dx.doi.org/10.1080/ 13602000802303169.

Dua, E. 2000. "'The Hindu Woman's Question': Canadian Nation Building and the Social Construction of Gender for South Asian-Canadian Women." In *Anti-Racist Feminism*, edited by A.Calliste and M. Aguiar, 55–72. Halifax: Fernwood Publishing.

Dua, E., N. Razack, and J. Warner. 2005. "Race, Racism and Empire: Reflections on Canada." *Social Justice* 32 (4): 1–10.

Du Bois, W.E.B. 1903. *The Souls of Black Folk: Essays and Sketches*. Chicago: A.C. McClurg & Co.

Duderija, A. 2007. "Literature Review: Identity Construction in the Context of Being a Minority Immigrant Religion: The Case of Western-Born Muslims." *Immigrants & Minorities* 25 (2): 141–62. http://dx.doi. org/10.1080/02619280802018132.

Edney, D. 2012. "The Politics of Fear." In *Omar Khadr: Oh Canada*, edited by J. Williamson, 270–79. Montreal: McGill-Queen's University Press.

El-Halawany, H. 2003. "Highly Educated Egyptian Women's Responses to Gender Role Challenges in Post 9-11 America." PhD diss., University of Pittsburgh. *Dissertation Abstracts International* 64 (7): 2658-A.

Espiritu, Y.L. 2003. *Home Bound: Filipino American Lives across Cultures, Communities, and Countries*. Berkeley: University of California Press.

Esses, V.M., and R.C. Gardner. 1996. "Multiculturalism in Canada: Context and Current Status." *Canadian Journal of Behavioural Science* 28 (3): 145–52. http://dx.doi.org/10.1037/h0084934.

Esterberg, K. 2002. *Qualitative Methods in Social Research*. Boston: McGraw-Hill Press.

Fekete, L. 2004. "Anti-Muslim Racism and the European Security State." *Race & Class* 46 (1): 3–29. http://dx.doi.org/10.1177/0306396804045512.

Fleras, A. 2009. *The Politics of Multiculturalism: Multicultural Governance in Comparative Perspective*. Toronto: Palgrave Macmillan. http://dx.doi.org/10.1057/9780230100121.

Forcese, C. 2014. "A Tale of Two Citizenships: Citizenship Revocation for 'Traitors and Terrorists'." *Queen's Law Journal* 39 (2): 551–85.

Forcese, C., and K. Roach. 2015. "Why Can't Canada Get National Security Laws Right?" *Walrus*, 9 June. https://thewalrus.ca/why-cant-canada-get-national-security-law-right/.

Foucault, M. 1977. *Discipline and Punish: The Birth of the Prison*. New York: Vintage Books.

Foucault, M. 1980. *Power/Knowledge: Selected Interviews and Other Writings 1972–1977*. Edited by Colin Gordon. New York: Pantheon.

Fredickson, G.M. 2002. *Racism: A Short History*. Princeton, NJ: Princeton University Press.

Galabuzi, G. 2006. *Canada's Economic Apartheid*. Toronto: University of Toronto Press.

Gibb, C. 1998. "Religious Identification in Transnational Contexts: Becoming Muslim in Ethiopia and Canada." *Diaspora* 7 (2): 247–69. http://dx.doi.org/10.1353/dsp.1998.0020.

Gillespie, M. 2006. "Transnational Television Audiences after September 11." *Journal of Ethnic and Migration Studies* 32 (6): 903–21. http://dx.doi.org/10.1080/13691830600761511.

Gilroy, P. 1987. *There Ain't No Black in the Union Jack: The Cultural Politics of Race and Nation*. London: Hutchinson.

Gilroy, P. 1990. "One Nation under a Groove: The Politics of 'Race' and Racism in Britain." In *Anatomy of Racism*, edited by D. Goldberg, 263–82. Minneapolis: University of Minnesota Press.

Gilroy, P. 2000. *Against Race: Imagining Political Culture Beyond the Color Line*. Cambridge, MA: Harvard University Press.

Glavanis, P.M. 1998. "Political Islam within Europe: A Contribution to the Analytical Framework." *Innovation: The European Journal of Social Science Research* 11 (4): 391–409.

Goldberg, D. 2002. *The Racial State*. Malden, MA: Blackwell Publishers.

Grewal, I. 2003. "Transnational America: Race, Gender and Citizenship after 9/11." *Social Identities* 9 (4): 535–61. http://dx.doi.org/10.1080/1350463032000174669.

Gupta, M.D. 2004. "A View of 9/11 Justice from Below." *Peace Review* 16 (2): 141–8. http://dx.doi.org/10.1080/1040265042000237671.

Haddad, Y. 2007. "The Post-9/11 *Hijab* as Icon." *Sociology of Religion* 68 (3): 253–67. http://dx.doi.org/10.1093/socrel/68.3.253.

Hage, G. 1998. *White Nation: Fantasies of White Supremacy in a Multicultural Society.* North Melbourne: Pluto Press Australia.

Hall, S. 1986. "Gramsci Relevance for the Study of Race and Ethnicity." *Journal of Communication Inquiry* 10 (2): 5–27. http://dx.doi.org/10.1177/019685998601000202.

Hall, S. 1990. "Cultural Identity and Diaspora." In *Identity: Community, Culture, Difference*, edited by J. Rutherford, 222–37. London: Lawrence & Wishart.

Hall, S. 1991. "Old and New Identities, Old and New Ethnicities." In *Culture, Globalization and the World-System*, edited by A.D. King, 41–68. Basingstoke, UK: Macmillan.

Hall, S. 1992. "The New Ethnicities." In *Race, Culture and Difference*, edited by J. Donald and A. Rattansi, 441–9. London: Sage.

Hall, S. 1996. "The Question of Cultural Identity." In *Modernity: An Introduction to Modern Societies*, edited by Stuart Hall, David Held, Don Hubert, and Kenneth Thompson, 596–623. Oxford: Blackwell.

Hameed, Y., and B. Nagra. 2015. "Bill C-51 Will Worsen Racial Profiling of Muslim Canadians." *Ricochet*, 27 March. https://ricochet.media/en/364/bill-c-51-will-worsen-racial-profiling-of-muslim-canadians.

Handa, A. 2003. *Of Silk Saris and Mini-Skirts: South Asian Girls Walk the Tightrope of Culture.* Toronto: Women's Press.

Harb, Z., and E. Bessaiso. 2006. "British Arab Muslim Audiences and Television after September 11." *Journal of Ethnic and Migration Studies* 32 (6): 1063–76. http://dx.doi.org/10.1080/13691830600761529.

Helleiner, J. 2010. "Canadian Border Resident Experience of the 'Smartening' Border at Niagara." *Journal of Borderland Studies* 25 (3–4): 87–103. http://dx.doi.org/10.1080/08865655.2010.9695773.

Helleiner, J. 2012. "Whiteness and Narratives of a Racialized Canada/US Border at Niagara." *Canadian Journal of Sociology* 37 (2): 109–35.

Helly, D. 2004. "Are Muslims Discriminated against in Canada since September 2001?" *Canadian Ethnic Studies Journal* 36 (1): 24–48.

Henry, F., and E. Ginzberg. 1985. *Who Gets the Work? A Test of Racial Discrimination in Employment.* Toronto: Urban Alliance on Race Relations and the Social Planning Council of Metropolitan Toronto.

Henry, F., and C. Tator. 2006. *Racial Profiling in Canada Challenging the Myth of "A Few Bad Apples."* Toronto: University of Toronto Press.

Hiller, H. 2010. "Airports as Borderlands: American Preclearance and Transitional Spaces in Canada." *Journal of Borderland Studies* 25 (3–4): 19–30. http://dx.doi.org/10.1080/08865655.2010.9695769.

Hindess, B. 2004. "Citizenship for All." *Citizenship Studies* 8 (3): 305–15. http://dx.doi.org/10.1080/1362102042000257023.

Hirji, F. 2010. *Dreaming in Canadian: South Asian Youth, Bollywood and Belonging.* Vancouver: UBC Press.

Hoodfar, H. 1993. "The Veil in the Minds and on Our Heads: The Persistence of Colonial Images of Muslim Women." *Resources for Feminist Research* 22 (3/4): 5–18.

Holston, J. 1998. "Spaces of Insurgent Citizenship." In *Making the Invisible Visible: A Multicultural Planning History*, edited by Leonie Sanderock, 37–56. Berkeley: University of California Press.

Huntington, S.P. 1993. "The Clash of Civilizations?" *Foreign Affairs* 72 (3): 22–49. http://dx.doi.org/10.2307/20045621.

Huntington, S.P. 2004. *Who Are We? The Challenges to America's National Identity.* New York: Simon and Schuster.

Jackson, R. 2005. "Security, Democracy, and the Rhetoric of Counter-Terrorism." *Democracy and Security* 1 (2): 147–71. http://dx.doi.org/10.1080/17419160500322517.

Jain, H., and J. Lawler. 2004. "Visible Minorities under the Canadian Employment Equity Act, 1987–1999." *Relations Industrielles* 59 (3): 585–609. http://dx.doi.org/10.7202/010926ar.

James, M. 2012. "Neoliberal Heritage Redress." In *Reconciling Canada: Critical Perspectives on the Culture of Redress*, edited by J. Henderson and P. Wakeham, 31–46. Toronto: University of Toronto Press.

Jamil, U., and C. Rousseau. 2012. "Subject Positioning, Fear, and Insecurity in South Asian Muslim Communities in the War on Terror Context." *Canadian Review of Sociology* 49 (4): 370–88. http://dx.doi.org/10.1111/j.1755-618X.2012.01299.x.

Jiwani, Y. 2005. "The Great White North Encounters September 11: Race, Gender, and Nation in Canada's National Daily, 'The Globe and Mail.'" *Social Justice*, 32 (4): 50–68.

Jiwani, Y. 2010. "Doubling Discourses and the Veiled Other: Mediations of Race and Gender in Canadian Media." In *States of Race*, edited by Sherene Razack, Malinda Smith, and Sunera Thobani, 59–86. Toronto: Between the Lines.

Jiwani, Y. 2012. "Omar Khadr, the Carceral Net, and the Muslim Body." In *Omar Khadr: Oh Canada*, edited by J. Williamson, 376–89. Montreal: McGill-Queen's University Press.

Joppke, C. 2004. "The Retreat of Multiculturalism in the Liberal State: Theory and Policy." *British Journal of Sociology* 55 (2): 237–57. http://dx.doi.org/10.1111/j.1468-4446.2004.00017.x.

Kallen, E. 1982. "Multiculturalism: Ideology, Policy and Reality." *Journal of Canadian Studies / Revue d'Etudes Canadiennes* 17 (1): 51–63. http://dx.doi.org/10.3138/jcs.17.1.51.

Kashmeri, Z. 1991. *The Gulf Within: Canadian Arabs, Racism and the Gulf War.* Toronto: James Lorimer.

Kastoryano, R. 2006. "French Secularism and Islam: France's Headscarf Affair." In *Multiculturalism, Muslims and Citizenship*, edited by T. Modood, A. Triandafyllidou, and R. Zapata-Barrero, 57–70. London: Routledge.

Kelly, J. 1998. *Under the Gaze: Learning to Be Black in White Society.* Halifax: Fernwood Publishing.

Khalema, N., and J. Wannas-Jones. 2003. "Under the Prism of Suspicion: Minority Voices in Canada Post September 11." *Journal of Muslim Minority Affairs* 23 (1): 25–39. http://dx.doi.org/10.1080/13602000305928.

Khan, S. 1998. "Muslim Women: Negotiations in the Third Space." *Signs* 23 (2): 463–94. http://dx.doi.org/10.1086/495259.

Khan, S. 2012. "Politics over Principles: The Case of Omar Khadr." In *Omar Khadr: Oh Canada*, edited by J. Williamson, 51–66. Montreal: McGill-Queen's University Press.

Kibria, N. 2008. "The 'New Islam' and Bangladeshi Youth in Britain and the US." *Ethnic and Racial Studies* 31 (2): 243–66. http://dx.doi.org/10.1080/01419870701337593.

Klausen, J. 2005. *The Islamic Challenge: Politics and Religion in Western Europe.* London: Oxford University Press.

Knott, K., and S. Khokher. 1993. "Religious and Ethnic Identity among Young Muslim Women in Bradford." *New Community* 19: 593–610.

Kobayashi, A. 1993. "Multiculturalism: Representing a Canadian Institution." In *Place/Culture/Representation*, edited by J. Duncan and D. Ley, 205–31. London: Routledge.

Korteweg, A. 2008. "The Sharia Debate in Ontario: Gender, Islam, Representations of Muslim Women's Agency." *Gender & Society* 22 (4): 434–54. http://dx.doi.org/10.1177/0891243208319768.

Kundnani, A. 2002. "An Unholy Alliance? Racism, Religion and Communalism." *Race & Class* 44 (2): 71–80. http://dx.doi.org/10.1177/0306396802044002976.

Kymlicka, W. 1995. *Multicultural Citizenship: A Liberal Theory of Minority Rights.* London: Oxford University Press.

Labelle, M. 2004. "The Language of Race, Identity Options and Belonging in the Quebec Context." In *Social Inequalities in Comparative Perspective*, edited by Mary Waters and Fiona Devine, 39–64. New York: Blackwell. http://dx.doi.org/10.1002/9780470753576.ch3.

Lyon, D. 2006. "Airport Screening, Surveillance, and Social Sorting: Canadian Responses to 9/11 in Context." *Canadian Journal of Criminology and Criminal Justice* 48 (3): 397–411. http://dx.doi.org/10.3138/cjccj. 48.3.397.

Mackey, E. 1999. *The House of Difference: Cultural Politics and National Identity in Canada*. New York: Routledge.

Macklin, A. 2001. "Borderline Security." In *The Security of Freedom: Essays on Canada's Anti-Terrorism Bill*, edited by R.J. Daniels, P. Macklem, and K. Roach, 383–99. Toronto: University of Toronto Press. http://dx.doi.org/10.3138/9781442682337-025.

Macklin, A. 2007. "Who Is the Citizen's Other? Considering the Heft of Citizenship?" *Theoretical Inquiries in Law* 8 (2): 333–61. http://dx.doi.org/10.2202/1565-3404.1153.

Macklin, A. 2014. "Citizenship Revocation, the Privilege to Have Rights and the Production of the Alien." *Queen's Law Journal* 40 (1): 1–54.

Mahmood, S. 2005. *Politics of Piety: The Islamic Revival and the Feminist Subject*. Princeton, NJ: Princeton University Press.

Malhi, R.L., and S.D. Boon. 2007. "Discourses of 'Democratic Racism' in the Talk of South Asian Women." *Canadian Ethnic Studies* 39 (3): 125–49. http://dx.doi.org/10.1353/ces.0.0026.

Mannheim, K. 1952. "The Sociological Problem of Generations." In *Karl Mannheim: Essays on the Sociology of Knowledge*, edited by Paul Kecskemeti, 276–320. London: Routledge.

McDonald, J. 2007. "Citizenship, Illegality, and Sanctuary." In *Interrogating Race and Racism*, edited by V. Agnew, 112–34. Toronto: University of Toronto Press. http://dx.doi.org/10.3138/9781442685444-005.

Meetoo, V., and H. Mirza. 2007. "There is Nothing Honourable about Honour Killings: Gender Violence and the Limits of Multiculturalism." *Women's Studies International Forum* 30 (3): 187–200. http://dx.doi.org/10.1016/j.wsif.2007.03.001.

Miles, R. 1989. *Racism*. New York: Routledge.

Moghissi, H., S. Rahnema, and M. Goodman. 2009. *Diaspora By Design: Muslims in Canada and Beyond*. Toronto: University of Toronto Press.

Morgan, E. 2001. "A Thousand and One Rights." In *The Security of Freedom: Essays on Canada's Anti-Terrorism Bill*, edited by R.J. Daniels, P. Macklem, and K. Roach, 405–11. Toronto: University of Toronto Press. http://dx.doi.org/10.3138/9781442682337-026.

Muller, B. 2004. "(Dis)Qualified Bodies: Securitization, Citizenship and 'Identity Management.'" *Citizenship Studies* 8 (3): 279–94. http://dx.doi.org/10.1080/1362102042000257005.

Murphy, C. 2007. "Securitizing Canadian Policing: A New Policing Paradigm for the Post-9/11 Security State?" *Canadian Journal of Sociology* 32 (4): 449–75. http://dx.doi.org/10.2307/20460665.

Mythen, G. 2012. "Identities in the Third Space? Solidity, Elasticity, and Resilience amongst Young British Pakistani Muslims." *British Journal of Sociology* 63 (3): 393–411. http://dx.doi.org/10.1111/j.1468-4446.2012.01416.x.

Naber, N. 2006. "The Rules of Forced Engagement: Race, Gender and the Culture of Fear among Arab Immigrants in San Francisco Post 9/11." *Cultural Dynamics* 18 (3): 235–67. http://dx.doi.org/10.1177/0921374006071614.

Nagel, J. 1986. "The Political Construction of Ethnicity." In *Competitive Ethnic Relations*, edited by S. Olzak and J. Nagel, 93–112. New York: Academic Press.

Nakano Glenn, E. 2002. *Unequal Freedom: How Race and Gender Shaped American Citizenship and Labor*. Cambridge, MA: Harvard University Press.

Naples, N. 2003. *Feminism and Method: Ethnography, Discourse Analysis and Activist Research*. New York: Routledge.

Ng, Roxana. 1996. *The Politics of Community Services: Immigrant Women, Class and State*. Halifax: Fernwood Publishing.

Nimer, M. 2002. *The North American Muslim Resource Guide: Muslim Community Life in the United States and Canada*. New York: Routledge.

Nyers, P. 2004. "Introduction: What's Left of Citizenship?" *Citizenship Studies* 8 (3): 203–15. http://dx.doi.org/10.1080/1362102042000256961.

Nyers, P. 2006. "The Accidental Citizen: Acts of Sovereignty and (Un) Making Citizenship." *Economy and Society* 35 (1): 22–41. http://dx.doi.org/10.1080/03085140500465824.

Oikawa, M. 2002. "Cartographies of Violence: Women, Memory, and the Subjects of the Internment." In *Race, Space and the Law: Unmapping a White Settler Society*, edited by S. Razack, 71–98. Toronto: Between the Lines.

Omi, M., and H. Winant. 1994. *Racial Formation in the United States*. New York: Routledge.

Ong, A. 2004. "Latitudes of Citizenship: Membership, Meaning, and Multiculturalism." In *People Out of Place*, edited by Alison Brysk and Gershon Shafir, 53–70. New York: Taylor and Francis.

Oreopoulos, P. 2011. "Why Do Skilled Immigrants Struggle in the Labor Market? A Field Experiment with Thirteen Thousand Resumes." *American Economic Journal: Economic Policy* 3 (4): 148–71. http://dx.doi.org/10.1257/pol.3.4.148.

Parliament of Canada. 2012. "Proceedings of the Special Senate Committee on Anti-terrorism: Issue 2 – Evidence – Meeting of April 23, 2012." 23 April. Ottawa. http://www.parl.gc.ca/content/sen/committee/411/ANTR/02EV-49469-e.HTM.

Peek, L. 2003. "Reactions and Response: Muslim Students' Experiences on New York City Campuses Post 9/11." *Journal of Muslim Minority Affairs* 23 (2): 271–83. http://dx.doi.org/10.1080/1360200032000139910.

Peek, L. 2011. *Behind the Backlash: Muslim Americans after 9/11.* Philadelphia: Temple University Press.

Pendakur, K., and R. Pendakur. 2011. "Color by Numbers: Minority Earnings in Canada, 1995–2005." *Journal of International Migration and Integration,* 12 (3): 305–29.

Perry, B. 2010. "Policing Hate Crime in a Multicultural Society: Observations from Canada." *International Journal of Law, Crime and Justice* 38 (3): 120–40. http://dx.doi.org/10.1016/j.ijlcj.2010.10.004.

Portes, A., and R.G. Rumbaut. 1990. *Immigrant America: A Portrait.* Berkeley: University of California Press.

Portes, A., and R.G. Rumbaut. 2001. *Legacies: The Story of the Immigrant Second Generation.* New York: Russel Sage Foundation.

Portes, A., and R.G. Rumbaut. 2006. *Immigrant America: A Portrait.* 3rd ed. Berkeley: University of California Press.

Poynting, S., and B. Perry. 2007. "Climates of Hate: Media and State Inspired Victimisation of Muslims in Canada and Australia since 9/11." *Current Issues in Criminal Justice* 1 (2): 151–71.

Pratt, A., and S. Thompson. 2008. "Chivalry, 'Race' and Discretion at the Canadian Border." *British Journal of Criminology* 48 (5): 620–40. http://dx.doi.org/10.1093/bjc/azn048.

Pyke, K.D. 2010. "What is Internalized Racial Oppression and Why Don't We Study it? Acknowledging Racism's Hidden Injuries." *Sociological Perspectives* 53 (4): 551–72. http://dx.doi.org/10.1525/sop.2010.53.4.551.

Ramadan, T. 2010. "Good Muslim, Bad Muslim." *NewStatesmen,* 12 February. http://www.newstatesman.com/religion/2010/02/muslim-religious-moderation.

Razack, S. 1998. *Looking White People in the Eye: Gender, Race, and Culture in Courtrooms and Classrooms.* Toronto: University of Toronto Press.

Razack, S. 2002. *Race, Space and the Law: Unmapping a White Settler Society.* Toronto: Between the Lines.

Razack, S. 2004. "Imperilled Muslim Women, Dangerous Muslim Men and Civilized Europeans: Legal and Social Responses to Forced Marriages." *Feminist Legal Studies* 12 (2): 129–74. http://dx.doi.org/10.1023/B:FEST.0000043305.66172.92.

Razack, S. 2005. "Geopolitics, Culture, Clash, and Gender after September 11." *Social Justice* 32 (4): 11–21.

Razack, S. 2008. *Casting Out.* Toronto: University of Toronto Press.

Razack, S., M. Smith, and S. Thobani. 2010. *States of Race*. Toronto: Between the Lines.

Reitz, J.G., and R. Breton. 1994. *The Illusion of Difference: Realities of Ethnicity in Canada and the United States*. Toronto: C.D. Howe Institute.

Roach, K. 2002. "Canada's New Anti-Terrorist Law." *Singapore Journal of Legal Studies:* 122–48.

Rooijackers, M. 1994. "Ethnic Identity and Islam. The Results of an Empirical Study among Young Turkish Immigrants in the Netherlands." In *Belief and Unbelief: Psychological Perspectives*, edited by D. Hutsebaut and J. Corveleyn, 99–107. Amsterdam: Rodopi.

Roy, O. 2004. *Globalised Islam: The Search for a New Ummah*. London: Hurst and Company.

Said, E. 1979. *Orientalism*. New York: Vintage Books.

Said, E. 1981. *Covering Islam: How the Media and the Experts Determine How We See the Rest of the World*. New York: Pantheon Books.

Said, E. 1997. *Covering Islam: How the Media and the Experts Determine How We See the Rest of the World*. Rev. ed. New York: Vintage Books.

Salter, M. 2007. "Governmentalities of an Airport: Heterotopia and Confession." *International Political Sociology* 1 (1): 49–66. http://dx.doi.org/10.1111/j.1749-5687.2007.00004.x.

Samuel, J., and K.G. Basavarajappa. 2006. "The Visible Minority Population in Canada: A Review of Numbers, Growth and Labour Force Issues." *Canadian Studies in Population* 32 (2): 241–69.

Sassen, S. 2004. "The Repositioning of Citizenship." In *People out of Place*, edited by A. Brysk and G. Shafiir, 191–208. New York: Taylor and Francis.

Scharff, C. 2011. "Disarticulating Feminism: Individualization, Neoliberalism and the Othering of 'Muslim Women'." *European Journal of Women's Studies* 18 (2): 119–34. http://dx.doi.org/10.1177/1350506810394613.

Schildkraut, D. 2004. "Identity, Perceptions of Discrimination and Political Engagement: The Causes and Consequences of Reactive Identity among Latinos." Paper presented at the Annual Meeting of the American Political Science Association, Hilton Chicago and the Palmer House Hilton, Chicago, IL, 2 September.

Schrier, D., and F. Ip. 1991. *British Columbia's Changing Ethnic Mosaic*. Population Reports. Vancouver: Government of British Columbia. http://www2.gov.bc.ca/gov/content/data/statistics/people-population-community/population.

Settles, I. 2006. "Use of an Intersectional Framework to Understand Black Women's Radical and Gender Identities." *Sex Roles* 54 (9): 589–601. http://dx.doi.org/10.1007/s11199-006-9029-8.

Sharma, N. 2006. "White Nationalism, Illegality and Imperialism: Border Controls as Ideology." In *Gendering the War on Terror: War Stories and Camouflaged Politics*, edited by K. Hunt and K. Rygiel, 121–43. Aldershot, UK: Ashgate.

Simpson, Audra. 2008. "Subjects of Sovereignty: Indigeneity, the Revenue Rule, and Juridics of Failed Consent." *Transdisciplinary Conflict of Laws* 71 (3): 191–215.

Sirin, S., and M. Fine. 2008. *Muslim American Youth: Understanding Hyphenated Identities through Multiple Methods*. New York: New York University Press.

Smith, C. 2007. "Borders and Exclusions: Racial Profiling in the New World Order." In *Interrogating Race and Racism*, edited by V. Agnew, 352–85. Toronto: University of Toronto Press. http://dx.doi.org/10.3138/9781442685444-010.

Smith, D. 1987. *The Everyday World as Problematic: A Feminist Sociology*. Boston: Northeastern University.

Stasiulis, D., and A.B. Bakan. 1997. "Negotiating Citizenship: The Case of Foreign Domestic Workers in Canada." *Feminist Review* 57: 112–39. http://dx.doi.org/10.1080/014177897339687.

Statistics Canada. 2001. "Population by Religion, by Provinces and Territories." *2001 Census*. Ottawa: Statistics Canada. http://www.statscan.ca/.

Statistics Canada. 2002. *Ethnic Diversity Survey*. Ottawa: Statistics Canada. http://www23.statcan.gc.ca/imdb/p2SV.pl?Function=getSurvey&SDDS=4508.

Statistics Canada. 2006. "Population by Religion, by Provinces and Territories." Ottawa: Statistics Canada. http://www.statscan.ca/.

Stein, E. 2003. "Construction of an Enemy." *Monthly Review* 55 (3): 125–9.

Thaler, H.L. 2004. "The Rift in the Subject: A Late Global Modernist Dilemma." *Current Sociology* 52 (4): 615–31. http://dx.doi.org/10.1177/0011392104043494.

Thobani, S. 2004. "Exception and Rule: Profile of Exclusion." *Signs* 29 (2): 597–600. http://dx.doi.org/10.1086/378569.

Thobani, S. 2007. *Exalted Subjects: Studies in the Making of Race and Nation in Canada*. Toronto: University of Toronto Press.

Vertovec, S. 2003. "Diaspora, Transnationalism, and Islam: Sites of Changes and Modes of Research." In *Muslim Networks and Transnational Communities in and across Europe*, edited by S. Allievi and J. Nielson, 312–26. Boston: Brill.

Waters, M. 1990. *Ethnic Options: Choosing Identities in America*. Berkeley: University of California Press.

Watt, W. 1998. *The Formative Period of Islamic Thought*. Oxford: One World.

Williams, M.C. 2003. "Words, Images, Enemies: Securitization and International Politics." *International Studies Quarterly* 47 (4): 511–31. http://dx.doi.org/10.1046/j.0020-8833.2003.00277.x.

Williamson, J. 2012. "Introduction: The Story So Far." In *Omar Khadr: Oh Canada*, edited by J. Williamson, 3–48. Montreal: McGill-Queen's University Press.

Wise, T. 2008. *White Like Me*. Brooklyn: Soft Skull Press.

Wood, P.K., and L. Gilbert. 2005. "Multiculturalism in Canada: Accidental Discourse, Alternate Vision, Urban Practise." *International Journal of Urban and Regional Research* 29 (3): 679–91. http://dx.doi.org/10.1111/j.1468-2427.2005.00612.x.

Yazdiha, H. 2010. "Conceptualizing Hybridity: Deconstructing Boundaries through the Hybrid." *Formations* 1 (1): 31–8.

Young, I.M. 1998. "Polity and Group Difference: A Critique of the Ideal of Universal Citizenship." In *The Citizenship Debates*, edited by G. Shafir, 263–90. Minneapolis: University of Minnesota Press.

Young, I.M. 2003. "The Logic of Masculinist Protection: Reflections on the Current Security State." *Signs* 29 (1): 1–25. http://dx.doi.org/10.1086/375708.

Yousif, A. 1953. *Muslims in Canada: A Question of Identity*. New York: Legas.

Yuval-Davis, N. 1997. *Gender & Nation*. London: Sage.

Yuval-Davis, N. 2011. *The Politics of Belonging: Intersectional Contestations*. Los Angeles: Sage.

Zedner, L. 2010. "Security, the State, and the Citizen: The Changing Architecture of Crime Control." *New Criminal Law Review* 13 (2): 379–403. http://dx.doi.org/10.1525/nclr.2010.13.2.379.

Zine, J. 2012. "Stolen Youth: Lost Boys and Imperial Wars." In *Omar Khadr: Oh Canada*, edited by J. Williamson, 390–449. Montreal: McGill-Queen's University Press.

Index

Page numbers with (t) refer to tables.